HUMAN RESOURCE DEVELOPMENT

HUMAN RESOURCE DEVELOPMENT
Challenges and Opportunities

Edited by
Neelu Rohmetra
Professor
Department of Management Studies
University of Jammu, Jammu, J&K State
INDIA

ANMOL PUBLICATIONS PVT. LTD.
NEW DELHI - 110 002 (INDIA)

ANMOL PUBLICATIONS PVT. LTD.
4374/4B, Ansari Road, Daryaganj
New Delhi - 110 002
Ph.: 23261597, 23278000
Visit us at: www.anmolpublications.com

Human Resource Development: Challenges and Opportunities

First Published, 2005

ISBN 81-261-2326-5

PRINTED IN INDIA

Published by J.L. Kumar for Anmol Publications Pvt. Ltd., New Delhi - 110 002 and Printed at Mehra Offset Press, Delhi.

For My Parents

CONTENTS

FOREWORD

Human resources make the difference to societies and organisations. If two countries have roughly equal resources but different levels of development, the difference is accounted by its human resources. In a knowledge economy, scale and success are a function of the ability and attitude of people.

A macro view of human resource development is based on cradle to grave perspective based on the realisation that much of the development of the child takes base while she is still in the mother's womb and depends on mother's health. By the time corporates hire people, fundamental attitudes, beliefs and assumptions about life are already shaped during the socialization process in the earlier years. Therefore human resource development professionals have a big challenge in seeking to mould and integrate different personalities from divergent backgrounds and engineer a common culture and balance the interests of the individual with those of the organization.

In the context of global competition HR professionals need to focus not merely on cost cutting but also, more importantly on moving up the value chain in the global production systems and service and distribution networks and focus on value addition and value creation. The three key challenges of the function are to optimise the resource utilisation sub-serving in a balanced and integrated manner the interests of different stakeholders, innovation and building and maintenance of relationships with each of the key stakeholders.

Human resource development specialists would do well to realise that a third each of their function is getting automated, outsourced and going back to line managers. If HR is to be taken seriously personnel managers should give it away. If HR is to have the respect and acceptance of top management, HR should not compete for CEO's role; instead, HR should seek to become the coach for the CEO and the top management.

Neelu Rohmetra is an accomplished HR professional. The volume edited by her comprises 18 chapters contributed by nearly as many professionals from academic and practicing worlds, both from India and abroad. Each of the contributors is an expert on the subjects to which they contributed. This is evident from the richness of the content and its presentation. The coverage is a bit wider and diverse. As a result though it lacks depth, the sheer breadth of the coverage compensates to an extent and caters to a wider clientele and a general reader on the subject than merely the specialists. Yet, dominantly the focus is on micro level than the macro aspects. At the macro level, governments in developing countries like ours need to do lot more than what is being done currently in terms of making basic education and skills training (BEST) to all citizen. A notable weakness of our education system is that only 5 per cent of the people aged between 18-24 in India are currently having vocational skills training against about 95 per cent in South Korea. The skills gap is a crucial disadvantage for India to emerge a global player and leverage on the potential of the relatively younger workforce that India will continue to have over the next few decades.

The volume is useful in addressing some of the vital issues relating to international human resources, cross cultural management and training and development leveraging the potential of information technology. The papers deal not merely with HRD issues concerning managers and professionals, but also the workers. It deals with the challenges for HRD arising out of globalisation, technology and competition. Some of the chapters specifically take stock of the current status of the profession, competency requirements, emerging challenges and future roles and future of HRD itself.

I congratulate Neelu Rohmetra and the others who have contributed to this volume and feel that it will be found useful by not only HRD professionals but also by others who have an interest in HRD.

C S Venkata Ratnam
Professor, Institute of Management Technology,
Ghaziabad & Director,
GITAM Institute of Foreign Trade,
Visakhapatnam

PREFACE

Globalisation is the primary trend affecting organisations and thus Human Resource Development. Remarkable transformations are taking place on global scale, which have a direct impact on organisations and their people. Today's work environment is characterised by a shift away from predictable and deterministic patterns of work behaviour. The new management challenges can be condensed into a single profound question: 'Are we going to manage' or 'Are we going to get managed?'. In other words, will we allow ourselves to be swept aside by the vast changes consequent to globalisation, technological advancements and the information boom, or take advantage of these developments? The new context, in fact, presents new opportunities and challenges, and it is for managers to seize these opportunities by nurturing change in their organisations, and giving shape to it on their own terms and without duress.

The changing context, however, needs individuals who are dynamic, have significant diagnostic, analytical and problem solving capabilities, capacity for continuously learning new technologies, and can operate in an environment flooded with highly variable customer demands. In this regard, human resource development as a key to harnessing change through appropriate skills, attitude and competency development, besides promoting a learning culture, has never been so crucial as it is today, and its importance will keep growing prolifically in future as well. Also, with a shift in focus over to capital of intangible assets (customer satisfaction index, employee satisfaction, knowledge management, relationships, company's integrity, etc.), human resource development needs to take on the opportunity to reconsider its role in shaping local, national and global development with concern for human and environmental needs. Consequently, emerging trends and scenarios have placed new demands on human resource development. These trends provide us with insight into the challenges in the field. Failing to acknowledge these challenges will marginalise the contribution of human resource development within organisations.

This work entitled: " Human Resource Development in the Changing Context – Challenges and Opportunities" was conceived in this backdrop about a year back, and with the grace of God today stands completed with the valuable support and contribution of distinguished experts and professionals in the area. The volume is an effort in the direction of raising certain queries and concerns in the field, as a contribution towards enabling human resource development to become more accountable and integrated part of organisational life. The work is also directed at engaging in deeper meaningful debate to construct workable, effective and useful approaches, in an effort to strengthen the future of human resource development. It is hoped that this volume will serve to highlight a need for further paradigm exploration in the study of organisations and their management.

The analysis across the broad theme of the book (Chapter 1) is the outcome of my understanding about the discipline, which has developed over a period by virtue of my research across issues in the fields of Human Resource Development (HRD), Cross - Cultural Management, Change Management and Organisation Behaviour. The said initiatives in research received the support and guidance of several individuals both in formal and informal capacity, and thus, I owe the credit of completing this work to these individuals.

My understanding in the field of HRD started to develop and take shape under the guidance of Dr. K.K. Arora and Prof. J.R. Dhotra who worked as my supervisors for the doctoral research. The improved version of the research stands published as book under the title: "Human Resource Development in Commercial Banks in India", ASHGATE Publishing, Gower House, Aldershot, UK. I am grateful to both of them for their useful inputs and facilitation. I am also thankful to Prof. T.V. Rao, the pioneer of HRD movement in India for his valuable advice and guidance in the field as and when I required it. I am equally thankful to Prof. C.S. Venkataratnam for his specific help, insight and support in all my research initiatives in the field in general, and for doing the foreword for this volume in particular.

I also feel indebted to my family. My husband, Er. Sudhir K. Gupta, daughter Dhanak, and son Raghav deserve heart - felt thanks for their accommodation, encouragement and moral support all through. In particular, I would like to acknowledge the contribution of my parents in the building of my skills, attitude, competence and value base that has always worked well for me in fulfilling such initiatives successfully.

Special thanks are due to Sabine Manning, Coordinator of 'ehrd- network' of HRD professionals across globe for circulating the 'Call for Papers' among the members, time and again on my behalf. Thanks are also due to Anmol Publications Pvt. Ltd., New Delhi for having provided a platform whereby the book will reach wider audience. Above all, I will always remain grateful to all the authors of the papers in this volume. Their views, comments, arguments and enquiries have indeed made this work a useful piece of reference, in furthering the HRD thought and practice.

The book is a constellation of varied issues under the umbrella of the concern for managing human resources and their development. The papers in the volume provide an opportunity to the reader to comprehend human resource function in different national/cultural settings and across varied groups and organisational contexts. It is hoped that the book would prove useful to all categories of readers – academicians, educationists, professionals and practitioners interested in human resource areas, entrepreneurs, research scholars and students. May the DIVINE bless this endeavour!

Neelu Rohmetra
Professor, Department of Management Studies
University of Jammu, Jammu, J&K State, India.

ABOUT THE CONTRIBUTORS

Professor Geoff Chivers holds the Chair of Risk and Professional Development in the Business School at Loughborough University, UK. Professor Chivers has maintained a lifelong involvement with adult education and training, especially in the context of vocational and professional development. He has been heavily involved in the movement to establish human resource development as a field of teaching and research in higher education in UK and Europe.

Prof. J. R. Dhotra is currently Head in the Department of Management Studies, University of Jammu, India. His area of specialisation is Human Resource Management and Industrial Relations. Professor Dhotra is the author of many research articles, which have been published, in edited volumes and journals of repute.

Sandeep K. Krishnan and Amit Pande are Fellows in Programme in Management in Indian Institute of Management (IIM), Ahmedabad, India. Their research papers have been published in journals of national and international repute.

Dr. Paul Hill is a Senior Lecturer at Newcastle Business School, Northumbria University in the area of Organisation Behaviour and Human Resource Management. His current areas of interest are international human resource management and cross cultural issues. He is currently managing International Business Management Programmes at Northumbria University.

Dr. Xiao Jian Wu is lecturer in the area of management learning and organisational development at the Newcastle Business School, Northumbria University, England. Educated in China but received research training at universities in the UK, his research interest covers knowledge management and learning in organisational context, cross border knowledge transfer and comparative management study. Dr. Wu is a recipient of research grants from a number of international agencies including the British Council and National Foreign Experts Administration in China.

Dr. Jim Grieves is a Senior Lecturer at Scarborough Management Centre, University of Hull. He has also worked at Northumbria University as Head of Organisational Behaviour and Human Resource Management. He was previously Editor of "The Learning Organisation" and is currently on its Editorial Advisory Board. His recent research includes barriers to learning; issues of governance and practice in the public sector; and recruitment and selection practices in education.

Aquil Busrai is Director HR, Shell Malaysia and Managing Director, Shell People Services Asia Sdn Bhd. He is based in Kuala Lumpur, Malaysia. Mr Busrai has been actively involved with Management movement in India having been Executive Council Member of AIMA; Co-Chairman of Board of Governors, AIMA Distance Education; President of Delhi Management Association and Northern Region President of National HRD Network.

Dr. David Mankin is a Senior Lecturer in HRM at the Oxford Brookes University Business School. His areas of interest are Human Resource Development and Organisational Knowledge and Learning. He has worked in the public and private sectors in a variety of capacities including Total Quality Manager and, subsequently, Personnel Development Manager.

Professor Bhupen Srivastava has been involved in teaching, research and consultancy activities in India, U.S.A, Canada, Europe and Africa for over three decades. His assignments include Dean, IILM, New Delhi; Director, FORE School of Management, New Delhi; Professor, IIM Calcutta, IMI New Delhi, University of Northern Iowa, U.S.A; Specialist and Head, HRD, BHEL; Dy. Director, PECCE; Senior Fellow, National Labour Institute, New Delhi. He was Commonwealth Advisor and Principal Consultant Eastern and Southern African Management Institute, Arusha, Tanzania; Visiting Professor/Fellow; International Centre for Public Enterprises, Lublijana, Yugoslavia; McGill University, Montreal, Canada; and UNDP/ILO Fellow in Holland and U.K. Prof Srivastava has authored numerous books and articles.

Dr P S Yadapadithaya is Senior Reader, Department of PG Studies and Research in Commerce, Mangalore University, Karnataka, India. He did his post-doctoral research on "HRD policies and practices: A cross-national study of India and Britain" during 2001-02 at Nottingham Business School, UK under the Commonwealth Fellowship scheme. At present, he is working on a UGC major research project titled "An evaluation of trends and status of HRD practices in the Indian corporate sector"

Professor Jim Stewart is Professor of Human Resource Development, Department of Human Resource Management, Nottingham Business School, the Nottingham Trent University, Nottingham , UK. He is also Chair of the University Forum for HRD (UK and Europe).

Prof. T. V. Rao is Chairman TV Rao Learning Systems Pvt. Ltd., Ahmedabad, India. He is also the Chairman, Academic Council, Academy of Human Resource Development, Hyderabad and was the Founder President of the National HRD Network. Dr Rao has been Professor

Organisation Behaviour area at IIM-Ahmedabad, Larson and Toubro Professor of HRD at XLRI, Jamshedpur. He has also been the Visiting Research Associate at Harvard University. A pioneer of HRD movement in India Dr. Rao has authored, co-authored and co-edited several books in areas of HRD, Organisation Behaviour and Performance Management.

Raju Rao is Director and Soumya Dixit is Research Associate at T V Rao Learning systems Pvt. Ltd., Ahmedabad, India

Harsh Rai Puri is currently working as Sr. DGM at M/s BHEL Bhopal. He is a professional member of Indian Society for Applied Behavioural Science (ISABS) accredited to conduct Sensitivity or T-Group Training. He has vast experience in designing and conducting management development and organisation development programmes covering all levels of employees. His writings have been published in leading Indian publications like The Economic Times, Financial Express, Hindustan Times, ISABS Newsletter & Journal, ISTD Journal, and has presented various papers at national conventions and national seminars on the theme :"OD Approaches for Revamping of Regional Rural Banks" in the last 15 years.

Piyali Ghosh is a doctoral student under the Junior Research Fellowship Scheme of UGC at School of Management Studies, Motilal Nehru National Institute of Technology (Deemed University), Allahabad. She has authored over six research papers presented and published in several symposia and conferences.

Dr. Philip Wilding is a Senior Lecturer at Newcastle Business School, Northumbria University. He joined NBS following a career in human resource management from both an operational and consultancy role in a variety of business sectors. His main research interests are in strategic human resource management, barriers to organisational learning and the development of HRM to line managers.

Dr Janice McMillan is Principal Lecturer in Organisation and Public Services Management and Director PhD Programmes, Newcastle Business School. She specialises in public policy and management and has published widely on public service reform in the UK with particular reference to the civil service. She is Chair of the Political Studies Association Public Administration Specialist Group.

Dr. Robert Freund is an independent expert on Mass Customization and Personalization (MCP) and a distance-learning specialist. His concept is based on the combination of MCP and Gardner´s Multiple-Intelligence-Theory. He was speaker at eLearn China 2003 and at the Second World Congress on MCP 2003 in Munich. Dr. Freund is founding member of the International Institute of MCP and is involved in national and European projects on adult education.

Dr. Gabriele Laske is an Industrial Psychologist with experience in project management, organisational design, problem solving, curriculum development, and intercultural communication. He holds the Knowledge in the affairs of European community programs and projects. After many years of working as senior researcher at the Institute for Technology and Education (ITB), University of Bremen, he is presently working as manager and senior researcher at ICCR (Intercultural Comparison and Research - www.Iccresearch.com), an independent research and consulting company.

Dr. Daniele Flannery is an Associate Professor of Adult Education at The Pennsylvania State University, Harrisburg. Her primary research focus is in adult learning, particularly women's learning and issues of adult learning and culture.

She serves as a reviewer for the Human Resource Development Review and the Journal of Health Education and Behavior.

Elizabeth Coyle is an Assistant Professor in the Department of Education at Elizabethtown College in Elizabethtown, PA. She teaches courses in Child and Adolescent Psychology, Classroom Inclusion Practices and School Violence Prevention. She also provides training and consulting to businesses and schools on issues of violence prevention, anger management and team building. She has co-authored numerous articles and conference papers on female entrepreneurs' learning and violence prevention.

Dr. Irena Marinko .is the Director of College for Business Secretaries, a branch of Leila d.o.o., one of the first private employment agencies in Slovenia.

PROLEGOMENA

The volume is the result of the efforts of twenty-five professionals who have reflected wide range of issues, concerns and arguments in the field through their research papers and articles. These professionals are: Geoff Chivers, Loughborough University, UK, Amit Pande and Sandeep Krishanan, IIM Ahmedabad, India, Paul Hill, X-Jian Wu and Jim Grieves, Northumbria University, UK, Aquil Busrai, Director HR, Shell Malaysia, Malaysia, David P Mankin, Oxford Brookes University, Oxon, Bhupen Srivastava, IMI, New Delhi, T.V. Rao, Raju Rao and Soumya Dixit, TV Rao Learning Systems Pvt. Ltd., Ahmedabad, India, P.S. Yadapadithaya, Mangalore University, Karnataka, India and Jim Stewart, Nottingham University, UK, Harsh Rai Puri, BHEL, India, Piyali Ghosh, Motilal Nehru National Institute of Technology, Allahabad, India, Jim Grieves, University of Hull, Janice McMillan and Philip Wilding, Northumbria University, UK, Robert J. Freund, an independent expert, Germany, Gabriele Laske, ICCR, Daniele D. Flannery, The Pennsylvania State University, Harrisburg and Elizabeth Coyle, Elizabethtown College, Prof. J.R. Dhotra, University of Jammu, India, Irena Marinko, Slovenia and myself.

These academicians, professionals and practitioners have contributed to this volume in the form of eighteen research papers and articles, making it a volume with eighteen chapters. I have picked up the theme of the volume in the first Chapter wherein challenges confronting the field of HRD in the new context, have been presented in wider detail. These challenges range from the challenge of globalisation to the challenges in research and practice, besides those in relation to learning, strategic orientation, performance linkage, diversity and industrial relations. The objective has been to set the stage for further reading and insight through the issues and perspectives of human resource development.

In Chapter 2, Geoff Chivers has aptly attempted to highlight the need for developing the HRD professional for a challenging future. He argues that HRD professionals hold the development of other professionals, members and managers of the general work force in organisation in their hands, and thus it is essential that their development follows best practice and is imaginative and offers very wide ranging learning experiences. The author believes that the four key areas of professional competence viz; knowledge and understanding (especially in concepts), functional skills (occupation specific), personal or behavioural competence, and values and ethical competence (personal and professional), interact in complex ways during learning and during professional performance. However, will to improve performance and learning is crucial for continuing professional development. The author has also thrown some light on the changing role of HRD professional from the one that has been traditionally associated with delivery of training, to encompass 'learning and change agent'. Thus, the roles of HRD professionals are today very varied within work organisations. Hence, a 'one curriculum fits all' approach is not appropriate for developing a nation's HRD profession, and no HRD professional can 'rest on their laurels' in terms of believing that their existing professional competence will be sufficient to see them through their career.

Chapter 3, as authored by J.R. Dhotra reflects the main theme of the volume. The author asserts that HRD managers have a complex role to perform. The competitive advantage as understood in terms of providing unique features in product or service, offering the customer some advantages, has three important dimensions for HRD professionals to ponder over. These are: evolving need based HRD strategies, ensuring employee participation, and developing an enabling culture for planned change. These objectives call for holistic and integrated view of HRD with specific reference to organisational analysis, HRD strategy formulation and careful implementation.

Globalisation is providing opportunities for Indian firms to reach foreign markets. Globalisation also presents a new challenge to Indian firms – the challenge to develop competent managers who would be able to work in new environments efficiently and will act as a bridge between the parent company and its subsidiaries. The globalisation will also bring new employees to the Indian firms, with different origin, language and national culture adding to complexity. Organisations thus need to develop and train managers for expatriate assignments and to handle the cultural diversity. The task can be achieved by well-designed cross-cultural training programmes, which will hold employees in coping with stress and cultural shock while dealing with new culture. These are the concerns that have been explored by Amit Pande and Sandeep Krishnan in Chapter 4 of the volume. The authors have explained how people and practices differ across cultures. They have also attempted to define expatriate competencies and the objections of cross-cultural training. The context of cross-cultural training should incorporate dimensions related to both general orientation and specific skill development. The authors have also made efforts in identifying training methodology in cross-cultural training. In sum, the authors contend that a large degree of uncertainty, which an employee might face while moving to a foreign land and culture, can be reduced through organisational support in terms of cross-cultural training. This can save the huge costs that an organisation might face due to expatriate failure.

In Chapter 5, Paul Hill, X-Jian and Jim Grieves have attempted to present the relationship between cognitive/cultural elements and learning/application of management idea. The authors have developed the case of a small Chinese business firm, which seeks to address, in particular, the issue of acquisition of knowledge in relation to management of employee commitment and performance. The investigation focuses on the extent to which organisational commitment and performance as understood in the west, flow naturally across geographical boundaries comprising different political, cultural and ideological perspectives. The research paper is a case study of Kaihua Bio-product and Services Ltd. in China. The study highlights two distinctive culturally rooted issues relating to management learning and organisation development. First, special consideration attached to the requirements of family members in private business in China and second how individual staff are treated and valued in a cultural environment featuring collectivism like China.

In Chapter 6, Aquil Busrai in his superb style of presenting the issues has raised the query: Do smart people find it difficult to learn? The author advises that any organisation aspiring to succeed has to understand that though success in the ever-increasing competitive market place depends on learning, yet most people donot know how to learn. Most perplexing is the fact that well-educated, high-powered professionals who occupy key leadership positions may not be good at learning. Consequently, organisations make mistakes in their efforts to become a learning organisation. The author suggests that for organisations to become learning institutions, the managers need to critically examine their own behaviour and then change, as required. Organisations also need to come out of the assumption that getting people to learn is largely a function of motivation. Only concentrating on a motivating environment is a faulty strategy to create a learning organisation. Instead, organisations have to promote a climate where open feedback becomes an accepted norm; where questioning someone's reasoning is not seen as a sign of mistrust but a valuable opportunity to learn; where failures are not viewed as final condemnation but a step in having learnt something new out of the experience; and, where managers reason productively and not carry on a task based only on skill- sets they have learnt.

In Chapter 7, David P. Mankin questions whether nurturing social capital is the principal lever in developing HRD's contribution to organisational success. The paper argues that the future success of HRD lies in the ability of practitioners to develop strategies, policies, processes and practices that can nurture or cultivate social capital. The underlying premise of the paper is that it is a fallacy to believe that knowledge can be managed; or, at least managed effectively. Rather, it is the organisational context that has to be nurtured to stimulate learning, knowledge creation and knowledge sharing processes. This recognizes the role of informal processes, such as social networks and communities of practice, which elude formal structures and management interventions. The author cautions that developing social capital will be a difficult challenge for HRD practitioners who are more accustomed to focusing on the development of individuals. By focusing on social capital we are recognising the socially embedded nature of knowledge and learning process and the significant contribution that social relationships can offer an organisation. The chapter also offers some perspectives on how this might be achieved and the difficulties likely to be encountered.

In Chapter 8, Bhupen Srivastva has portrayed the emerging perspectives on training and employability within the larger context of human resource development. The author argues that in the changing scenario, organisations have to generate options to ensure their continuance and growth without sacrificing the goodwill of the people directly or indirectly, engaged in contributing to their existence as producers of wealth and providers of services. This calls for developing active adaptive and coping strategies to respond to the changes within and outside their boundaries. He supports that HRD effort must inextricably be linked with strategic thinking and organisation design and development efforts. The interrelationship among the three is interactive and dynamic characterised by directive correlation. The strategic HRD issues of concern to organisations relate to mutuality of influence, organisational membership, career systems, job security, reward systems, work system, training and retraining. The thrust areas for training and retraining include multi-skilling, team management, customer orientation, productivity and quality, entrepreneurship, empowerment, perspective building, and desirable value set.

In Chapter 9, P.S Yadapadithaya and Jim Steward have deliberated upon the transformative perspective of strategic human resource development. They support that HRD does not have any definitive form or definition, and instead takes diverse forms in different contexts and times. As such, strategic human resource development must take a transformative approach to allow for the flexibility in education, training, development and learning. Strategic HRD brings a transformative focus to the HRD and its holistic orchestration of learning within organisations. It is concerned with the management of employee learning for the long term, keeping in mind the explicit corporate and business strategies. It indeed refers to the development that arises from a clear vision about people's abilities and potential, and operates within the overall strategic framework of the business.

In Chapter 10, T.V. Rao, Raju Rao and Soumya Dixit have attempted to identify the effectiveness with which various leadership and managerial roles are performed by Indian CEOs. In a case study of leadership roles, styles, delegation and qualities of CEOs across 26 firms, the results suggest that the Indian CEOs perform transactional roles more effectively than the transformational roles. The effectively performed transactional roles relate to managing impressions on their seniors, and not with juniors and unions. These CEOs follow a developmental style, characterised by consultative and transformative empowerment. The chapter highlights how the development style of the Indian CEOs is oriented towards transformative empowerment of their subordinates, where the subordinates are encouraged to learn from their own experiences.

Harsh Rai Puri, in Chapter 11 provides insight into three dimensions: 'Integrating HRD with Applied Behavioural Science,' 'Challenge For HRD – When Dreams Die' and The EKLAVVA Syndrome'. The author advocates the need to align HRD to the REAL needs of the organisation, redefine its customers/clientele, constantly learn and adopt and harness support treating EACH individual as a resource. HRD has to be promoting 'shared values', multi-tasking abilities, and coaching and risk-taking abilities. The role of HRD has to be akin to that of the 'Genome' in living organism – the focus has to be on an ongoing process that moves through networking and, is a subtle interplay of competition and collaboration, creation and mutual adaptation. The author believes that there is a dreamer hidden in each one of us. Any process of change has to have two essential components: a dream for the future or "where/what we want to reach/achieve", and an introspective diagnosis of the "present" that embodies our history and values. If the dream dies, closely following in its path is the dreamer. The challenge to HRD lies in the fact that special endeavour is needed to keep the dreamer alive as a vital organisational resource. The author further emphasises empowerment of the individual – through various integrated value based approaches without personal prejudice – leading to an effective human network as the need of the hour.

In Chapter 12, Piyali Ghosh talks about the human resource component in IT industry in a bid to redefine strategic partnership. The author attempts to bring out the element of competitive advantage brought about by the strategic partnership of information technology and human resources. She believes that Indian economy, in its journey towards a developed nation, has experienced a significant paradigm shift in embracing the IT industry. The chapter points out the need for a strong, educated and trained manpower base comprising of professionals in IT industry, who can learn continuously and are also able to create intellectual assets from their experience. Human resource development thus finds a new challenge in adding business value to the organisation and in deriving synergistic benefits accruing from such a relatively young industry.

In Chapter 13, Neelu Rohmetra, asserts that, technological advancements have necessitated change in manpower composition and skills. The new knowledge economy has opened up a whole set of opportunities for emerging markets such as India. Accordingly, change is vivid in the service sector including banking services, where Indian banks are confronted with unprecedented challenges. The chapter portrays the case of the Jammu and Kashmir Bank Ltd. (JKB), in the State of Jammu and Kashmir, so as to understand the impact of computerisation on the employees' attitude, response and behaviour. The research seeks to present the transformative potential of information technology and highlights the perceptual response of the employees handling the computerised banking services. The work seeks to ascertain the current status of IT and its transformative efficacy, and goes on to establish the interface/linkage with human resource development climate in the bank. The study reports that computerisation in JKB is suffering because of inadequate system of training and development. Nevertheless, computerisation has enabled better access to information and more control over work. However, an unimpressive HRD climate and the current IT perspective have not been able to contribute towards each other. A good training and development could possibly boost up the technological environment or a good technological environment could facilitate development of human resources.

Organisational learning (OL) is a critical component of strategic human resource development (SHRD). Without OL it would not be possible to engage with the creative faculties of individuals, teams and organisations. Consequently, it would be pointless to engage with the drive to empower individuals in order to maximize their own potential and thereby the potential to develop the organisation from within. Jim Grieves, Janice McMillan and Philip Wilding in Chapter 14 have raised these concerns. The authors argue that organisational learning, as the underpinning process for strategic human resource development, has not yet reached a sufficient degree of maturity. Whilst organisations desire OL in order to achieve positive outcomes and eliminate negative outcomes in performance, it is equally clear that in order to create flexible employees and a learning culture capable of generating organisational effectiveness, SHRD needs to reassess the contribution of OL. The authors also suggest that managers should be capable of diagnosing organisational context not simply for learning capability but for organisational constraints that limit the actions of individuals and groups to learn effectively. In order to redress this problem they suggest that greater attention has to be paid on the social barriers to OL. Besides, the paper seeks to show that the more organised the individuals and their motives then the stronger are the rules governing their conduct.

Mass customisation and personalisation can help to overcome the efficiency paradox of developing and delivering education and that the customer is the major limiting factor at the final frontier of mass customisation in education market. This premise forms the basis of Chapter 15, authored by Robert J.Freund. The paper shows how to gain competitive advantages in education markets. Until now mass customisation have mainly been turned towards the product, whereas this paper argues that there might be a need for an increased focus on the fulfillment of customer needs. The author's proposed approach to mass customisation in education and training is based on the organisational strategy of mass customisation and personalisation.

Gabriele Laske in Chapter 16 presents an insight into structural and professional prerequisites for the development of future vocational identities of nurses in Estonia, Germany and France. The findings of the research presented in the paper reveal that nurses in all three countries already working in this profession for several years have developed strong vocational or professional identies, though the three health care systems offer different contextual conditions.

Daniele D. Flannery and Elizabeth Coyle in Chapter 17 on: 'Learning from a position of power: Female entrepreneurs in male-dominated business contexts' have attempted to develop understanding of how the position of power influenced the learning of female entrepreneurs operating their businesses in male dominated business arenas. Specifically the research investigated the combined influence of power and context on the learning of female entrepreneurs, the notion that positionality influences female entrepreneurs' creation of knowledge and how female entrepreneurs are both shaped by and shape their learning experiences through their acts of agency. The results of the study indicated that the intertwining of personal power, positions of power and the use of power within shifting gendered contexts impact the types of knowledge women entrepreneurs create.

Irena Marinko in Chapter 18 raises the issues of globalisation and ethics in business education in Slovenia. The study presents opinions of Slovenia politicians, scientists, economists and writers about Slovenian joining the European Union and globalisation and then analyses what Slovenian Business College teachers think about these processes and how they intend to prepare business students for their future work. Slovenian Business College teachers believe that the present model of capitalising will cause problems because of the social injustice. Accordingly, human resource development in a small transition country should try to find links between economic interests of globalisation and pro-national interests, and therefore, business students should be acquainted with the subjects and themes like team work, communication skills, better knowledge of foreign countries, listening skills, tolerance of foreigners, considering foreign ideas, increasing trust in a common future of all nations, feasibility in contacts with foreigners and a better knowledge of foreign languages. The national identity should be developed by acquainting students with the national economy and trade, examples of successful domestic entrepreneurs, achievements of nation and with intercultural education.

1

HUMAN RESOURCE DEVELOPMENT IN THE CHANGING CONTEXT: SOME INSIGHTS

*Dr. Neelu Rohmetra**

World is witnessing rapid process of economic and social change. Growing global interdependence, technological innovations, intense competition, increased capital mobility and rising expectations of consumers and workers are having far reaching and perceptible influences on the structure of economies. These compelling forces are prompting organisations to realign their systems and processes with the priorities and essentials of the changing contexts while recasting and remolding visions so as to cope and adapt to these transitions. Clearly, winning in the real world and free environment of today requires an evolved understanding of intrinsic risk and rewards that surround change and uncertainty (Bhamidipati and Makhijani, 2003). Accordingly, navigating extreme uncertainty in these turbulent times will require successful orchestering a mindset change amongst the organisational members and business partners that uncertainty is here to stay and their current patterns of working may not be adequate and appropriate to succeed. Besides, organisations are often tempted to predict the future by extrapolating past

* Professor, Department of Management Studies, University of Jammu, Jammu. Dr. Rohmetra can be reached at nrohmetra@yahoo.co.uk

trends. However, this is just a trap that needs to be avoided when the environment has changed fundamentally (Maira, 2003) triggering further uncertainty, competition and volatility. The changed business environ thus implies that human capital, creativity and innovation provide the basis for succeeding. It also suggests an awareness that change is invariably intertwined with human understanding, acceptance and implementation besides concerning with managing people's fears, anxieties, aspirations and motivations (Verma, 2000). Thus, the challenges of change and competition enforce the need for appreciating the role of human resource management and development in ensuring success. As Verma (2000) emphasises: "Human resource development has taken on the avalanche of changes comprising competition, technological changes, and challenges in its trail, opening the eyes of responsible people in organisations to HRD's vast potential to make meaningful and irrefutable contributions to mainstream activities." Focus on the increasing relevance of human resource development profiles and patterns and on working arrangements and attitudes (which are both productive and motivating) is also apparent when C.S. Venkataratnam (1999) opines: "Competitiveness of enterprises and the economy will become the means to social progress if attention is paid, both at macro and micro levels, to action in three areas: human resource development, labour market flexibility and labour standards." Hence, human resource development and creation of a highly skilled and flexible workforce are especially important in a global economy as these enable enterprises and nations to remain competitive (ILO, 1997).

Human resource development (HRD) as a field of study, research and practice is in the process of discovery and transformation. At present, the field is a mosaic of multiple perspectives, wherein the quest for the essence of HRD and how to deliver it is predominant. The discipline is emerging, dynamic and molded by the context, circumstances and cultures in which it occurs (Dilworth, 2003).

HRD in India has mainly been seen as synonymous with the training function. Traditionally, the other related activities that HRD has been usually carrying out are performance appraisal, job rotation and career planning. Again the focus of all these activities has been primarily on the executive development and very little attention was paid on the role HRD should be playing in promoting the development among the workers. In reality, HRD was seen and believed to be an isolated cell – unconnected with mainstream activities concerning higher productivity, better quality, cost effectiveness and the competitiveness of the organisation (Verma, 2000). Leonard Nadler in 1969 described HRD as a service of organise activities conducted within a specified time and designed to produce behavioural change. More specifically, Nadler conceptualized human resource development as referring to three activities, namely training, education and development. Pat McLagen in mid 1980s also viewed HRD as consisting of three components viz; training and development, organisation development (OD) and career development. Besides Nadler and McLagen there are a wide range of definitions, which have been propounded by various experts and practitioners in the area. The concept of human resource development is not an import to India. Human resource development is an Indian value concept having philosophical orientation. As Dr. T.V. Rao (1986) states: "Human resource development in the organisational context is the process by which the employees of an organisation are helped in a continuous planned way to: (i) acquire or sharpen capabilities required to perform various functions associated with their present and future expected roles; (ii) develop their general capabilities as individuals and discover their own inner potential for own and/or organisation development purposes; (iii) develop an organisational culture in which superior – subordinate relationships, teamwork and collaboration among sub-units are strong and contribute to the professional well-being, motivation and pride of employees."

Silveira (1988) comments; "HRD represents a new paradigm, a new world view or way of looking at the world around us. It involves long-term perspective, which visualises change through involvement and ownership of such change by the participants. The new paradigm takes a positive view of people and their potential and tries to foster a climate conducive to growth and development". According to Mirza S Saiyadain (1991), "HRD is a process undertaken to promote the intellectual, moral, psychological, cultural, social and economic development of the person so that he can contribute his best to the community and nation."

In the present times, human resource development is expanding in vision, orientation as well as scope, and the shift is visible towards its strategic profile. As Dilworth (2003) observes: "HRD is the creative design and commingling of strategies, structures, systems, technologies, and human beings in ways that promote both individual and organisational learning and builds and sustains organisational effectiveness." Focus on strategic change management, integration of learning processes, knowledge management, career development, team building, training technologies, productive and healthy work relations, HRD-IT interface, leadership development, intervention strategies and socio-technical fit, is implicit in this portrayal of HRD concerns. This current understanding of HRD is based on a growing realisation that developing a competitive workforce has become the key differentiator of success in the global market place. However, a juxtaposition of both retrospective and prospective views of HRD is required to determine the demands and influences that can be expected to shape HRD for the future. In view of the present complexities there is more than one past, and there is more than one future, depending on the context, reference, culture and domain in view. "The search toward future role of HRD involves total systems perspective: cutting across the entire supply chain, from employees/customers to senior corporate leaders, HRD scholars, HRD professionals and consultants, deliverers and developers of HRD services and all those who contribute or are affected by HRD"(Dilworth, 2003).

In this background, the current Chapter unfolds some of the major issues, concerns and challenges confronting the field of human resource development in the changing context. This Chapter sets the background for the present volume entitled: 'Human Resource Development in the Changing Context-Challenges and Opportunities'. These challenges and opportunities are discussed in the following paragraphs.

Strategic HRD

Human resource management is now seen as a key component of business strategy (Mankootam, 1996; Venkataratnam, 1996; Sodhi; 1993). Since staying in a competitive environment demands greater responsibility and innovative approaches, human resource function as a developmental tool is increasingly viewed as a vital component of corporate strategy, for ushering innovation, professionalism, flexibility and competitiveness into organisation systems as a whole. Since long, HR practices and the very existence of HR departments have been viewed as maintenance and routine activities (Chanda and Kabra, 2000). However, in the changing context organisations have realised that the one factor that can give them sustained advantage is their people.

Accordingly, as Chanda and Kabra (2000) contest: "Today the human resource function has a more strategic role. A changing business environment can influence the outcome of current operations, stakeholders and corporate strategy as a whole. The HR function plays an important role in viewing and integrating business opportunities, stimulating employees, developing employee strengths and creating corporate teams that share the company's vision and translate this concern into profit." Figure 1 exhibits the strategic human resource perspective. The HR – business process linkage supports the argument that people's capabilities need to be synonymous with business capabilities of an organisation. The people's requirements determine HR strategy, reflected through the management practices of the organisation. Consequently, while historically, businesses would account for human resource development activities as an expense, in the present context of change and competitiveness, human resource development is contemplated as an investment that can lead to future exponential benefits and returns. Thus, in the era of changes and complexities successful business is as much the outcome of the perceptive comprehension and strategic management of human resources as it is the appreciation and management of financial and physical variables. Implicit in the argument is the need to have a human resource development function and activities that flow from the organisational goals and mission. Where such goals and missions are not well articulated the HRD function should contribute toward the same. Where it is articulated well, efforts should be geared to design and use development systems to meet the various learning challenges, which requires emphasis on quality, efficiency, speed, productivity, skill development and customer delight. In this context, T.V. Rao, (1995) had long back argued: "HRD departments have to change their orientation to become more task-oriented without losing sight that people are their focus. In the past, some of the HRD departments focused only on people and since there were other mechanisms to ensure the achievement of business goals and no other function took care of the development

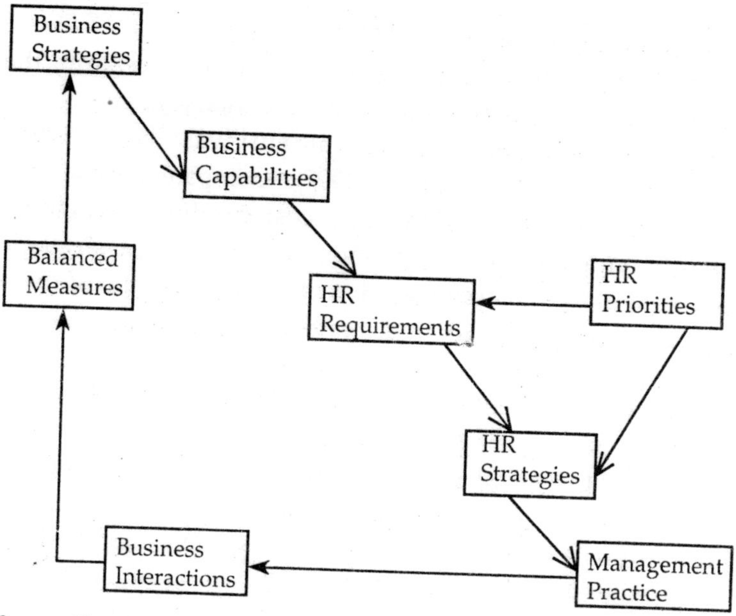

Source: Chanda, Ashok and Kabra, Shilpa (2000) '*Human Resource Strategy-Architecture for Change, Response Books, Sage Publications: New Delhi.*

Figure 1: Strategic Human Resource Perspectives

and motivation of people. With liberalisation the very existence of some of the organisations is threatened, and, therefore a time has come where HRD departments need to integrate their work with the business goals of the organisation. For this, the HRD staff would be required to focus their attention on the mission, vision and business goals of the organisation and may even lead organisations to refocus themselves. Productivity, quality, cost effectiveness market leadership, small group work, total employee involvement, continuous improvement etc. should become obsessions of the HRD staff. The HRD staff may need to acquire new competencies in this direction". Thus the concern with learning and unlearning initiatives is clearly apparent.

HRD and Organisation Learning

To add to the complexity, in the present scenario, the traditional sources of competitive advantage have become the pre-condition for mere corporate survival (Shukla, 1997). According to Mudhukar Shukla (1997): "Companies had always relied on factors like productivity, cost, product positioning, quality, innovation, speed and service to gain strategic advantage over competitors. In a given market, one of these factors set the standards, and created the basis of winning the competitive game..................Now, there is hardly any company which is not decreasing its costs, aiming at innovative offerings, trying to provide better service and quality, etc. What used to be strategic initiatives earlier have now become the norm – a pre-condition for corporate survival, instead of constituting a competitive edge." In this emerging paradigm knowledge and knowledge – based learning organisations have acquired critical relevance in our understanding of the nature of contemporary business. Thus, there is an increasing focus on the need to build a learning organisation which facilitates the learning of its members and continually transforms itself (Pedler, 1989); "where people continually expand their capacity to create the results they truly desire, where new patterns of thinking are nurtured, where collective aspiration is set free, and where people are continually learning how to learn together"(Senge, 1990). Further, a learning organisation is one that has embedded a continuous learning process and has an enhanced capacity to change or transform. This means that learning is a continuous, strategically used process – integrated with and running parallel to work – that yields changes in perceptions, thinking, behaviours, attitudes, values, beliefs, mental modes, systems, strategies, policies and procedures. Learning is sought by individuals and shared among employees at various levels, functions or units. As a result, learning is embedded in an organisation memory of past wisdom, current repertoire of beliefs and actions, and future thinking processes. Clearly, thus the task calls for developing an innovative HRD orientation that concentrates on leveraging learning potential and accelerates organisation learning deemed crucial for truly global organisation.

Further, organisations often expect that learning and knowledge creation will take place continuously for individuals and that they will share what they know in ways that promote learning in groups and throughout the organisation (Marsick and Watkins, 2003). It is also argued that learning must be captured and embedded in ongoing system, practices, and structures so that it can be shared and regularly used to intentionally improve change in knowledge performance. In order to accomplish so, human resource development in organisational context must proactively influence the direction, salience and pace of learning in work places. To play this role well, just focusing on what constitutes learning organisation is not enough; identifying ways to implement these abstract ideas across national as well as local cultures and in wide variety of organisations constitute the challenge for human resource professionals. In this regard, a model of change guided by organisational learning diagnostics (as developed by Gephart, Marsick, Van Buren and Spiro, 1996; Marsick and Watkins, 1999; Marsick and Watkins, 2003) that are used to assess gaps, guide interventions, and subsequently measure changes could prove useful for inculcating learning cultures.

Learning culture is a concept that reflects organisational behaviour from the perspective of learning and development. Practitioners in human resource development,so as to nurture a learning culture in their organisation, need to work on tools that can help diagnose the organisation's current learning behaviours and identify strategic steps to build a learning organisation. Besides, for the purpose of establishing the relationship of learning culture with other organisational variables, it is critical to have assessment instruments that are both valid and reliable in measuring this concept.

Elucidating further, human capital or the professional intellect of the organisation exists at four levels viz; cognitive knowledge or the basic mastery of the discipline, advanced skills or the ability to solve real world problems, systems understanding or the ability to solve complex problems, and, self-motivated creativity (Quinn, Anderson and Finkelstein, 1996). The responsibility for managing organisation's human capital resides with HRD professionals, who must fully appreciate the relationship between learning (individual, team and organisational) and performance. Individual, team and organisational learning and performance interact and affect one another (Figure 2). As Russ-Eft and others (1977) put it: "Individual learning directly affects and is affected by team and organisational learning, in addition to individual, team and organisational performance. Similarly, team learning directly affects and is affected by individual and organisational learning and by individual, team, and organisational performance. Finally, organisational learning directly affects and is affected by individual and team learning, in addition to individual, team and organisational performance." These effects however occur through feedback for organisational learning and performance as: "Individuals take action, which precipitates an organisational action, which in turn creates an environmental response. The environmental response reinforces or alters the individual's beliefs, which in turn influence the individual's actions."(Dixon, 1990). Further, all these relationships in learning and performance are influenced by internal and external environmental factors such as economic conditions, standards and regulations, management practices and attitudes. Besides, learning precedes performance initially, but performance can affect later learning. Further, while learning whether individual, team or organisational cannot be observed, performance is observable.

In the light of the above, the HRD professionals, practitioners and researchers need to understand the interdependency between learning and performance and accordingly undertake initiatives toward appropriate knowledge acquisition, its sharing and apt utilisation for organisational learning and thus in turn affect performance levels.

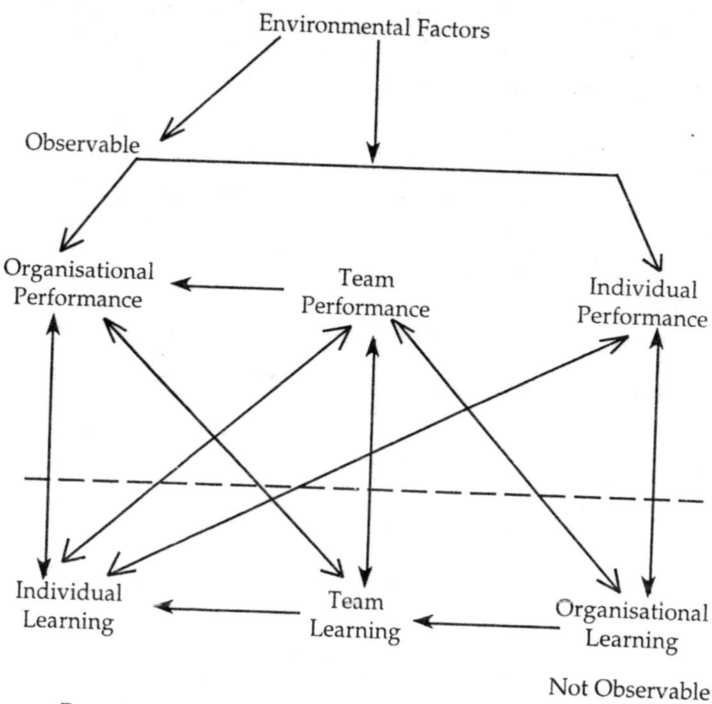

Source: Russ Eft, Darlene, Preskill, Hallie and Sleezer, Catherine (1997),*'Human Resource Development Review- Research and Implications'*, *Sage Publication: London.*

Figure 2: Expanded Model of Learning and Performance Feedback

In the context of organisational learning, HRD challenges include:

- The nature of managerial learning experiences,

- The sharing and integration of managerial learning within organisation,
- The institutionalisation of learning, and,
- The relationship between organisational learning and performance.

A study conducted by the National Research Council Committee for the Army Research Institute, USA and reported in Druckman and Swets (1988) provided a series of questions that HRD practitioners should answer before making decisions regarding proposed training and development system, so as to yield clarity about what the organisation needs in terms of learning and performance outcomes. These issues are:

- What changes (in learning, retention, reproduction and generalisation) will the method produce?
- What evidence exists to support claim for the method?
- What theories support the method or components of the method?
- Who will be able to use it?
- What are its implications for the organisation's operations?
- How does the method fit with the organisation's philosophy?
- What are the costs and benefits?

Thus, changing work place demands now challenge human resource developers to extend the scope of their practice from predominantly one of training individuals, to one of facilitating learning of individuals, teams and organisations. HRD professionals are uniquely positioned and thus can successfully play the role of learning specialists to facilitate organisational learning (Dixon, 1990) A practice based definition which captures such vision for the field of human resource development states: " Human resource development is the field of study and practice responsible for the fostering of a long-term, work related learning capacity at the individual, group and organisational levels. As such, it includes – but is not limited to – training, career development, and organisation development." The argument suggests the challenges confronting HRD professionals and facilitators in reference to their wider and enhanced share of roles and responsibilities in an effort to building learning organisation, which according to Argyris and Schon (1978) occurs when "members of the organisation act as learning agents for the organisation, responding to changes in the internal and external environments of the organisation by detecting and correcting errors in organisational theories-in-use, and embedding the results of their inquiry in private images and shared maps of organisation." In this backdrop, the human resource developers will be called on to (Watkins and Marsick, 1992):

- Break the training frame;
- Embed continuous learning strategies (learning groups, learning labs with self-learning materials available, on line learning resources, etc.);
- Teach people how to learn from experience, to think systematically;
- Conceptualise and plan individual development as long-term multi-career, and as preparatory for multiple organisational futures;
- Monitor and upgrade the overall knowledge/skill set of the whole organisation;
- Help people enact more participative, democratic work places and more autonomous environments;
- Leading the organisation's development toward a learning organisation and be able to measure its progress; and

- Craft policies, which make learning continuous, self-regulated and autonomously funded.

The task of building learning organisation that has an enhanced capacity to change or transform offers a challenging opportunity to human resource developers and professionals as it encompasses the potential to expand their role to include not only changing the threshold of skills in the organisation, but also to become partners in the transformation of the entire organisation. Thus, to conclude, "Learning organisation construct brings together the fields of training, career development and organisation development into a single vision of the role of human resource developer." (Watkins and Marsick, 1992).

Besides, HRD professionals play a critical role in determining overall team effectiveness by focusing on the methods and processes and overcoming problems associated with team performance. According to Orasanu and Salas (1993): "Teams make decisions in the context of a larger task, team members have specialised knowledge and skills relevant to the task or decision, and the task conditions under which teams operate include high work loads and time pressures." In this regard, HRD personnel need to share the responsibility of preparing team members to use effective team skills, develop lists of characteristics to differentiate high and low performance teams, and design team-building interventions to develop more successful teams (McClernon and Swarson, 1995).

HRD and Cross-Cultural Concerns of Diversity

Globalisation is the primary trend affecting organisations and thus HRD. The process of globalisation embraces many issues including crossing boundaries of space, time, geography, culture, and the like. The HRD implications of globalisation relate to the need for better understanding and integrating inter-cultural practices into global organisation. HRD must reflect about the effect of globalisation on all aspects of work and culture. Managing across cultures is one of the several potential areas of HRD practice requiring cultural sensitivity, especially when working internationally or with cross-cultural teams (Yorks and Sauquet, 2003). Team learning is pivotal to organisation learning. However, it is important to understand that the manner in which these learning behaviours manifest themselves are culture specific and vary across cultures. Thus, leading, working and facilitating learning across cultures and in multicultural teams represents one of the hardest challenges to HRD professionals. Consequently, when recognised and understanding cultural diversity is a pre-requisite towards achieving synergistic learning, characterised by the development of a collectively held and understood view (Kasl, Marsick and Dechant, 1997), HRD is expected to develop a cultural understanding among employees so as to help multicultural team leaders and members to create and support a learning environment.

As Bhandarker and Singh (2003) assert: "Cross-cultural encounters are ultimately creating a global culture. The shift to the new millennium is thus a quantum shift demanding a part of the global economy. With the business scenario turning into a 'Corporate Olympiad', Indian companies have to trim their size, get more focused and efficient in order to survive in the face of competition. The fundamental compulsions faced by organisations call for a transformation in the mindset and perspective and in the approach to business and people." Accordingly, the emerging inter-related phenomena pose challenges manifested in borderless world, diversity and knowledge power and culminating in 'Olympian' competition (Figure 3).

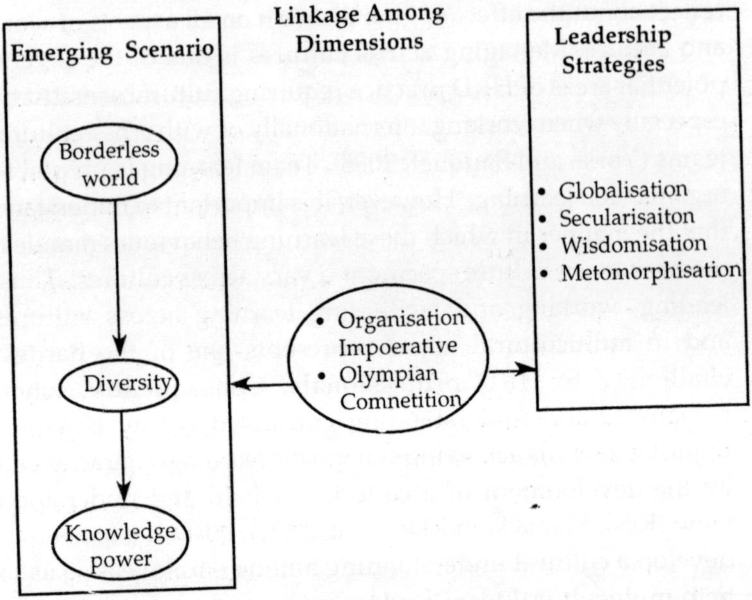

Source: Bhandarker, Asha and Singh, Pritam (2003) 'Leading to Win' Background Papers, AIMA 30th National Management Convention, September 15 – 17.

Figure 3: Underlying Linkage among the Parameters: Emerging Scenario

The emergence of a borderless world, increased diversity and knowledge power base have increased the level of competition and added on to the complexity of managing business environments. The borderlessness is evident in the manner the works get executed in different parts of the globe. For example, finance and insurance operate through global markets and world's major stock markets are all meshed together into one operating system. Today thousands of people work as partners with Intel without being direct employees. Interestingly and surprisingly organisations are competing as well collaborating simultaneously in different segments of the world economy and as such they are redefining their boundaries in a manner that they are effective competitors and collaborators in various markets (Bhandarkar and Singh, 2003).

The borderless world is creating a new class of people global in character, tastes, attitudes and outlook and accordingly, the organisations do confront in a big way the challenge and complexity of managing diverse work force across cultures in a borderless economy. Grappling with multi-gender and multi-ethnic work forces, multiple approaches to decision making and problem solving, different attitudes in respect to work, and the understanding about concept of time constitute some of the issues demanding attention while handling people from diverse socio-cultural backgrounds.

So as to cope accurately with these aforesaid challenges the organisations need to develop a global vision, a global perspective, and, a global mind frame that align themselves with the emerging imperatives. At the same time, the local orientations have to be blended and gel well with, without sacrificing global strengths, so as to ensure success across cultures. This understanding has to work as the key force driving change in HRD orientation, encompassing respect and acceptance of other cultural contexts.

HRD and Technology and Knowledge

Knowledge is the basis for competing effectively and clearly, therefore, those organisations that will assiduously pursue knowledge (and share it as well) will be victorious in the emerging scenario.

HRD must fulfill a key role in knowledge creation and management in organisations. HRD professionals need to strengthen their role in helping individuals, organisations and nations to acquire knowledge, absorb knowledge and communicate knowledge. Besides, effective use of technology is critical to HRD professionals. A valuable use of technology in the development of people suggests its ability to spread knowledge. Technology is a force that will continue to fundamentally shape organisations. Technology has affected the learning practices, such as e-learning and virtual offices. HRD would need to harness and explode the potential of technology, while also effectively integrating with the premises of well-defined learning theories.

HRD and Globalisation

According to Michael Marquardt and Nancy Berger (2003): "Globalisation is used to define a combination of factors – a single market place with growing free trade among nations; the increasing flow and sharing of information, connections or links of people around the world; the opportunity for organisations and people to shop around the world and not be constrained by national boundaries." Thus, a globalised world is one in which there is a free movement of ideas, people, values and systems across the globe. Marquardt and Berger (2003) consider seven areas as crucial for HRD in view of globalisation. They believe and assert that without deliberating on these critical variables/dimensions, HRD professionals will continue to remain on the periphery of creating and sustaining meaningful change for global, national and community development. These dimensions are:

1. HRD and economic growth – by significantly influencing the local and national economy through the development of workforce skills and intellectual capital. HRD can prove critically useful in building and maintaining the reservoir of skill base as a prerequisite to economic and social development.
2. HRD and political development – role of HRD in "the development of democracies, in creating clean and transparent governments, in propounding fair, non-discriminatory legal practices."

3. HRD and organisational learning – working as a strategic partner with other functions such as information technology and organisation development; reconsider the way human capital is led; and working through the organisations to facilitate shared knowledge and innovation.
4. HRD and education and vocational training – demonstrating the ability to creatively and cost – effectively support learning through mentoring, communications networks, cross-cultural team experiences, international apprenticeships, cross-boundary assignments, action-research and learning. The challenge lies in appropriately and effectively using methodologies and tools in a wider range of cultural/ social settings.
5. HRD and technology and knowledge – use of technology in the development of people for the purpose of facilitating knowledge generation and sharing.
6. HRD and global leadership development – reflects an opportunity to develop an understanding of and openness to global concepts across levels in organisation as a key to success. HRD can play a catalytic role in steering the entire organisation toward developing a global mind-set characterised by tolerance, curiosity, flexibility and ability to deal with ambiguity.
7. HRD and global environment – HRD needs to play a promotive role in ecological initiatives of the organisation for supporting a sustainable environment, which as a pro-bono ensures meaning-of-work opportunity for workers.

HRD and Industrial Relations and Worker Issues

The human side of technology caters to issues of employment, changing occupational profiles, education and training, working arrangements and managerial attitudes, industrial relations (IR) and trade union dynamics, communication and consultation. In the changing context, new forms of organisation with new forms of human resource policies are emerging (Hiers and Kuruvilla, 1997), with multi-skilling, flexibility, and involvement becoming popular. The variable of flexibility includes issues and concerns of non-conventional work arrangements, multiple tasks and skills and wage flexibility and new pay systems. Issues of ownership and control relate to unilateral human resource policies and new patterns of collective bargaining. Training and development is also receiving prime attention especially in banking, white goods and information technology sectors (Kuruvilla, 1999). Globalisation has leaded traditionally managed companies to professionalise their managerial staff, decentralize and restructure their business set ups, and most significantly, adopt professional human resource practices. Thus, any successful industrial relations and human rèsource systems must exhibit stability, flexibility (efficiency) and equity: 'stability' at structural and institutional level, 'flexibility' to adapt to changes in economic environment, a variable that is critical to organisational productivity and 'efficiency' and 'equity' as necessary to achieve a stable and flexible system that does not result in erosion of employees'/workers' rights. Emphasis on principle of equity is vivid when Kuruvilla, Katz and Turner (1995) argue: "While there are examples of stable and flexible systems without worker protection and rights (such as in Korea), their experience suggests that sustained repression of labour rights leads to periods of explosive conflict and destabilisation of IR. Not only is labour repression economically inefficient in terms of conflict and reduced standards of living for one section of the population, it is also incompatible with the increasingly industrialised status of South Asian countries which are also firmly committed to democracy."

Accordingly, Venkataratnam and Verma (1997) aptly portray the changing focus of HRD and IR in the following words: "With increasing competition due to international trade and deregulation among other factors, firms are faced with a growing demand for higher quality at moderate cost, innovation, service and specialisation. The dynamic nature of global markets requires that firms move up-market to higher value added products and be adaptive and flexible in their response to a changing market place. The workforce under these conditions would have to be more skilled and trained, involved with the production process and flexible and adaptable to shifting market conditions. To ensure such a workforce, firms will have to increase their investment in the following resource policy areas; training, employee involvement, sharing and flexible work organisation. Inevitably, these may also force change in work place governance. The role of unions may change, although it is difficult to predict these newer roles. In some cases, unions may play a bigger role, in other instances, union power may diminish reducing it to the status of a minor player in collective bargaining."

HRD and Change and HR Adjustment

Automation, managing transition and adjustment constitute prime concerns in organisations today. The key role for HRD in future would be enabling people overcome resistance to change and cope and integrate better with changing trends and scenarios.

It is important to understand uncertainty in the environment because it is a significant source of our inability to make predictions about the future. Although considering uncertainty does not allow predictions of the future, it does allow the formulation of plausible circumstances, any one or combination of which might evolve to become the future. Figure 4 depicts the critical uncertainties and their corresponding challenges to HRD, as conceived by Chermack, Lynham and Ruona (2003). The uncertainties identified are competition, globalisation, locus of control -organisations or individuals, next age and technological explosion.

Adjustment is adaptation to change in the environment. It is a process and not an event. The pressure to adjust comes from internal and external forces in a firm's environment. Human resource adjustment focuses on the issue of man-made human obsolescence, not biological (Venkataratnam, 1999). It relates to the obsolescence, which is caused, expedited and exacerbated by human failure. Technological progress is accelerating human obsolescence particularly in contexts where skills-development is not a life long pursuit. Other internal factors accounting for human resource obsolescence are improper/inadequate HR planning, wrong selection, recruitment and placement, inadequate training, improper motivation, inadequate reward system. Variables external to organisation constitute structural and product/process changes, rapid advances in technology, chronic sickness and corporate failures. Countering HR obsolescence calls for undertaking initiatives and steps, which ensure to bridge the gap between acquired and required skills on the one hand and combine worker flexibility with employment security on the other, besides addressing the concerns of multi-skilling, retraining and relocation.

Further, HRD initiatives have to seek socially responsible structuring/restructuring. At enterprise level, HRD in the changing context needs to focus on finding answers to the five below stated paradoxes (Starcher, 1999):

1. Are we moving away from HR practices, which provide more meaningful work and higher quality of work?
2. Will downsising adversely affect human and social capital?

3. If firms are not loyal to employees (internal customers) will they help create loyal external customer base?
4. Will downsising really have the desired impact on enterprise performance?
5. Do mergers and acquisitions fail because of failure to integrate people?

Critical Uncertainty	*Core challenge to the HRD* profession
1. Competition for the "expertise elite'	• What is HRD's role in recruiting or developing increasingly competent and expert workers?
2. Globalisation	• How will HRD balance boundaries of time, space, geography and culture, while maintaining its focus on developing work place expertise?
3. Locus of control—— organisations or individuals	• How will HRD strike a balance between ever demanding organisations and individuals?
4. Marketability of knowledge	• What is the role and responsibility of HRD in developing, sharing, transferring and protecting organisational knowledge?
5. Next age	• How can HRD assure that it is flexible enough as a discipline to respond effectively to the demands of a variety of "ages" and the priorities they will bring?
6. Technological explosion	• How will the role of HRD shift in the context of a highly automated, technologically demanding workplace?

Source: Chermack, Thomas J., Lynham, Susan A., and Ruona, Wendy E. (2003) 'Critical Uncertainties Confronting Human Resource Development', *Advances in Developing Human Resources*, Vol.5, No. 3, August.

Figure 4: Critical Uncertainties and their Corresponding Challenges to Human Resource Development

Challenge in Relation to Research, Practice and Profession

The challenge to HRD researchers is to anticipate what

research is needed and how it can contribute to HRD practice in coming years. In turn, the challenge to HRD practitioners is to focus on the future direction of their organisation, to operate as partners within the business to achieve those visions, to pay attention to emerging learning technologies and cutting-edge research and to be strategically proactive rather than reactive. A common challenge to HRD researchers and practitioners alike is to be more externally focused on the outcome-level problem. This is to move beyond and embrace that organisational problems are systemic and require systemic solutions, which requires that HRD practitioners have to work in problem -focused, solution-driven and multi-discipline teams within organisations.

HRD as a profession has not been able to strengthen its image. Although HRD as a field has made some progress, there is little evidence that these efforts have had an impact on the key factor of professionalisation. HRD faces a major challenge in this regard. HRD will fail to command a professional status in the organisations as long as HRD is seen as fad driven and those who are devoid of complete understanding of core HRD theory and practices occupy HRD jobs. To make it happen Bing and others (2003) assert: "Efforts to build professional recognition will require that HRD constructs a sound theory base, a sound education for HRD professionals with accompanying certification and continuing professional development, and ethical standards that are understood and applied by professionals and overseen by professional bodies. More important, as we promote awareness and recognition of HRD as a profession, we must keep our focus on values, ethics, the quality of practice, and set of competencies through which both research and practice can be undertaken and avoid investing energy in the building of bureaucratic process of credentialing and standardisation"

The foregoing arguments suggest that the emerging trends

and scenarios have placed new demands on HRD. These trends provide us with insight into the challenges in the field. Failing to acknowledge these challenges will marginalise the contribution of HRD within organisations. The objective behind raising above stated issues is to enable HRD to become more accountable and integrated part of organisational life, and to engage in deep meaningful debate to construct workable, effective and useful approaches to strengthen the future of HRD. HRD's sphere of interest and intended impact has been expanded. HRD today besides individual levels also encompasses team and organisational levels. The focus has also moved from performance of tasks to encompass the effectiveness of processes and systems. In this regard, linking learning and human process to performance constitute cardinal challenges to the field. Thus, Bing, Kehrhahn and Short (2003) assert: "HRD professionals must become skilled systems thinkers who can design and conduct measurement and analysis across the organisation and pinpoint the influences of HRD efforts on employee productivity and organisational performance linking past research results to current practice. HRD professionals must have the skills to identify valid measures of learning and growth, develop meaningful and accurate interpretations while being ever mindful of the myriad of intervening variables that can influence learning and performance curves in work settings." Clearly therefore, when learning and human development are inseparable phenomenon, learning methodologies have to be effectively used and integrated in a systematic manner in organisations, while HRD simultaneously must focus on creating cultures that are truly conducive to learning. The real task before HRD is to find new technologies that are efficient and effective and that deliver immediate, strategic and influential results. Though training continues to occupy an important concern in HRD literature, in view of the changing context, besides traditional concerns, HRD must look at wider horizons which include learning domains and HRD's strategic orientation that embrace a performance improvement mission. Evidently, HRD must make its relevancy, contribution and impact on organisational strategy and build a research and knowledge base that supports this. As Russ Vince (2003) comments: "In order to thrive, HRD may have to get more complicated. It is time to start thinking about HRD less as people development and more as an approach that supports the impact that people can have on organising. HRD can and should make a distinctive contribution to organising. It is an intervention within a political system; a practice of management and leadership..........HRD needs to construct itself critically and as an integral part of continuous learning and change. It has to take a lead in creating the designs and developments for future business-and this means a focus on how learning and change are avoided as well as planned, on the different forms and approaches to leadership required, and on consulting for organisation development. The focus of HRD is on action, on developing the capacity to act, on generating credibility through action and on influencing and working with others in situations loaded with emotion and politics." Hence, HRD is expected to create processes that reveal what people think, to empower collective voices and to mobilize participation in change. The role also demands dealing with the disappointment of undermined and unfulfilled expectations and the cynicism that can arise from them. In addition, HRD implies how an organisation has managed to become set in its ways, to organise opportunities for change that can challenge a tendency to resist change and to impinge and deliver processes that can underpin organisational development and transformation. HRD needs to be understood less as a set of skills and techniques, and more as inquiry into knowledge, fears, frustration, emotions, politics, and power relations that surround attempts to both promote and avoid learning and change (Vince, 2003). HRD needs to lead the idea that strategic learning can happen, that there are likely to be benefits from decentralisation and democracy, and that leadership is more about creating the conditions and enabling them to be put into place, than it is about trying to control a process once it has been set in motion.

To sum up, change has become the fact of business activity and thus HRD should take the opportunity to reconsider its role in shaping local, national and global development with concern for human and environmental needs. HRD is a pivotal process in organising for the future since its primary concern is strategic learning and change. HRD has the capacity to influence individuals, organisations, local and national governments, and global entities in building a more integrated global future that recognises international interconnectedness. HRD has implications for future ways of behaving, structuring and organising across organisations and organisational domains. HRD can be characterised as evolving practice that properly designed and implemented can work toward exploring possibilities of learning for the betterment of people, institutions and communities.

REFERENCES

Argyris, C. and Schon, D.A. (1978) *'Organisation Learning: A Theory of Action Perspective'*, Reading M.A.: Addison- Wesley.

Bhamidipati, Ravi and Makhijani, Rajer (2003) 'Changing Mindsets', Background Papers, AIMA 30th National Management Convention, September 15-17.

Bhandarker, Asha and Singh, Pritam (2003) 'Leading to Win', Background Papers, AIMA 30th National Management Convention, September 15-17.

Bing, John W., Kehrhahn, Marijka and Short, Darren C. (2003) 'Challenge to the Field of Human Resource Development', *Advances in Developing Human Resources,* Vol. 5, No. 3 August.

Chanda, Ashok and Kabra, Shilpa (2000) *'Human Resource Strategy-Architecture for Change,* Response Books, Sage Publications: New Delhi.

Charmack, Thomas J. Lynham, Susan A. and Ruona, Wendy E. (2003) 'Critical Uncertainties Confronting Human Resource Development' *Advances in Developing Human Resources*, Vol. 5, No. 3 August.

Dilworth, Lex (2003) ' Searching for the Future of HRD', *Advances in Developing Human Resources*, Vol.5, No. 3, August.

Dixon, Nancy M. (1990) 'Organisation Learning: A Review of Literature with Implications for HRD Professionals' *Human Resource Development Quarterly*, Vol. 3, No. 1.

Driskell, James E. and Salas, E. (1992) 'Collective Behaviour and Team Performance', *Human Factors*, Vol.34, No. 3.

Druckman, D. and Swets, J.A. (1988) (eds) *'Enhancing Human Performance: Issues, Theories and Techniques'* National Academy Press: Washington, DC.

Gephart, M.A., Marsick, V.J., Van Buren, M.E and Spiro, M.S (1996) 'Learning Organisations Come Alive', *Training and Development*, Vol. 50, No. 12.

Hiers, W. and Kuruvilla, S (1997) 'Globalisation and Industrial Relations in India' Paper for ILO Bangkok.

International Labour Organisation, (1997) ' ILO Enterprise Forum, Geneva 1996,' Summary of proceedings.

Kasl, E., Marsick, V.J. and Dechant, K (1997) 'Teams as Learners: A Research Based Model of Team Learning', *Journal of Applied Behavioural Science*, Vol. 33.

Kuruvilla, S. (1999) 'Impact of Globalisation on Economies and IR/HR Systems – Theory and Evidence' in Sivananthiran, A. and VenkataRatnam, C.S. (eds.) *Globalisation and Labour Management Relations in South Asia*, Indian Labour Organisation Publications.

Kuruvilla, S. Katz, H.S. and Turner, L. (1995) 'Workers in an Integrated World', Paper on World Bank Policy, World Bank, Washington.

Maira, Arun (2003), 'Setting the Course Amidst Turbulence', Background Papers, AIMA 30th National Management Convention, September 15 – 17.

Maira, Arun and Abraham, James (2003) 'Accelerating Organisational Learning' Background Papers, AIMA 30th National Management Convention, September 15 – 17.

Mamkootam, K. (1996) 'Globalisation, Restructuring and Industrial Relations in India', Paper presented at the Regional Meeting of the Asian Industrial Relations Association, Taipei, Taiwan, September.

Marquardt, Michael and Berger, Nancy O. (2003) 'The Future: Globalisation and New Roles for HRD', *Advances in Developing Human Resources,* Vol. 5, No. 3 August.

Marsick, V.J. and Watkins, K.E (1999), *Facilitating Learning in Organisations: Making Learning Count,* Gower: Aldershot, U.K.

Marsick, Victoria J and Watkins, Karen E. (2003) 'Demonstrating the Value of an Organisations Learning Culture: The Dimensions of the Learning Organisation Questionnaire', *Advances in Developing Human Resources,* Vol. 5, No.2, May.

McClernon, T.R. and Swanson, R.A. (1995) 'Team Building: An Experimental Investigation of the Effects of Computer Based and Facilitator- Based Interventions on Work Groups', *Human Resource Development Quarterly,* Vol. 6, No. 1.

Mirza S. Saiyadain (1991) ' HRD- Currency Vs. Concept', *Indian Journal of Training and Development,* May-June.

Orasanu, J. and Salas, E. (1993) 'Team Decision Making in Complex Environments' in Klein, G.A, Orasanu, J., Calderwood, R. and Zsambok, C.E (eds.) *Decision Making in Action: Models and Methods,* Norwood, NJ.

Pedler, M., Boydell, T. and Burgoyne, J. (1989) 'Towards the Learning Company', *Management Education and Development,* Vol. 20, No. 1.

Quinn, J.B., Anderson, P. and Finkelstein, S. (1996) 'Making the Most of the Best", *Harvard Business Review,* March-April.

Rao, T.V (1986) 'Integrated Human Resource Development Systems', in Rao, T.V and Pereira, D.F (ed.) *'Recent Experiences in Human Resource Development',* Oxford and IBH, New Delhi.

Rao, T.V (1995) 'Changing Role of HRD in the Liberalized Economy' in Rao, T.V, Silveira, D.M, Srivastava, C.M and Vidyasagar, Rajesh (eds.) *HRD in the New Economic Environment,* Tata Mc Graw – Hill Publishing Company Ltd., New Delhi.

Russ-Eft, Darlene, Preskill, Hallie and Sleezer, Catherine (1997),*'Human Resource Development Review- Research and Implications',* Sage Publication: London.

Senge, P. M. (1990) The Fifth Discipline: *'The Art and Practice of Organisation Learning',* Doubleday: New York.

Shukla, Madhukar (1997) *'Competing Through Knowledge-Building a Learning Organisation',* Response Books, Sage Publications, India.

Silveira, D.M. (1988) *'Human Resource Development – The Indian Experience,* News India: Bombay.

Sodhi, J.S. (1993) 'New Economic Policies and their Impact on Industrial Relations,' *Indian Journal of Industrial Relations,* Vol. 29, No.1.

Stracher, G. (1999) ' Socially Responsible Enterprise Restructuring', in Enterprise Forum, Geneva.

Venkataratnam, C.S (1996) 'Welfare to Money Fare: A Study of Social Security Clauses in Collective Bargaining', International Management Institute, New Delhi

Venkataratnam, C.S and Verma, A. (1997) (eds.) *'Challenge of Change: Industrial Relations in Indian Industry'* Allied Publishers Pvt. Ltd., New Delhi.

Venkataratnam, C.S. (1999) (ed.) *'HRD for Adjustment at the Enterprise level,* Participants Manual, International Labour Organisation.

Verma, Madhurendra K. (2000) *'Nurturing Change Through Your Human Assets'*, Sage India.

Vince, Russ (2003) 'The Future Practice of HRD', *Human Resource Development International,* Vol. 6, No. 4, December.

Watkins, K.E. and Marsick, V. (1992) ' Building the Learning Organisation: A New Role of Human Resource Developers' *Studies in Continuing Education,* Vol. 14, No.2.

Yang, Baiyin (2003) 'Identifying Valid and Reliable Measures for Dimensions of a Learning Culture', *Advances in Developing Human Resources,* Vol. 5, No. 2.

Yorks, Lyle and Sauquet, Alfonso (2003), 'Team Learning and National Culture: Framing the Issues' *Advances in Developing Human Resources,* Vol. 5, No. 1, February.

2

DEVELOPING THE HRD PROFESSIONAL FOR A CHALLENGING FUTURE

*Dr. Geoff Chivers**

Introduction

This paper brings together longstanding interests of the author in the fields of HRD and professional development more generally. All professionals are being faced by significant and sometimes quite daunting challenges in a rapidly changing world. However, as the profession with responsibility for developing other professionals, managers and the workforce generally, the HRD profession faces the greatest challenge of all. I have many years experience in developing HRD professionals, as well as a whole variety of other types of professionals and managers, and I am writing from the perspective of a practioner in the first instance.

The paper is also informed by the research I have carried out with colleagues interested in the world and learning of HRD professionals, and in the broad issues of professional competence and professional learning. My own development has benefited from involvement in various European and wider international organisations and projects in the fields of adult education, HRD and continuing professional development (CPD). Discussions with colleagues from around

* Professor in Business School, Loughborough University England.

the world who are concerned with developing HRD practioners convince me that even the most experienced colleagues feel themselves still to be pioneers exploring a jungle of complex strands of thought and experience. I am sure that nobody believes that they have the ideal approach to developing HRD professionals. Indeed in such a rapidly changing world it would be foolish to attempt to 'set in concrete' a definitive curriculum for the aspiring HRD professional. No sooner would we come to some agreement around the world, or even in one country, as to what this curriculum should be than it would be outdated.

This paper will certainly not be attempting to generate such a curriculum, but rather to offer some insights into underpinning concepts, frameworks and processes which may be of value to those trying to develop such a curriculum in a particular place and time, for a particular group of aspiring (or even experienced) HRD professionals.

Why is it so Difficult to Develop a Definitive Curriculum for Developing HRD Professionals?

As is discussed in other papers in this volume, controversy continues about what the HRD field covers, indeed whether there is any such field at all. Similarly, there is still debate about whether HRD is a field of professional work as such, or just a collection of tasks carried out by particular managers, or particular trainers (Mankin, 2001).

Clearly, these debates and uncertainties create challenges enough for those of us working to develop HRD professionals. However, as they are discussed extensively in this volume and in the literature more widely I will largely side step these issues in this paper. All well established professions have gone through the same phases of uncertainty that the HRD profession is passing through, even law, medicine and engineering. The fact remains that there are many workers who are defined by their work organisations or by themselves as HRD professionals. These people need and deserve support in regard to their development so that they can carry out their work as well as possible. Study programmes of many kinds already exist specifically for this purpose, some offering qualifications. I have myself been instrumental in developing a postgraduate course leading to a Diploma or Masters Degree in Training and Development, aimed at HRD staff, which has been offered for nearly 20 years in UK universities. There are university programmes of equal or greater longevity in the HRD field in North America.

So while theoretical debates continue about whether HRD exists as a discrete discipline (Swanson, 1999) those involved in its practice, or in developing HRD professionals need to move on. Otherwise we can become bogged down in theoretical debates, which are perceived by those we seek to help as 'paralysis by analysis'. Indeed, it could be argued that professions such as medicine and engineering established themselves in the 18th and 19th centuries through vigorous action to raise competency standards of those seeking to work in these fields, rather than by endless striving to set some definitive curriculum onto tablets of stone.

Kuchinke (2001) is firm that HRD is not an academic discipline. McLean (1999) argues that we can never have a well-defined core for a discipline for which we do not even have a common definition – nor should we! So, we must understand that HRD professionals need to be developed specifically to cope with uncertainty, ambiguity and change in their own profession. Mankin (2001) contends that 'it is this very ambiguity which provides HRD with its distinctiveness'; and that 'HRD practioners and academics should embrace HRD as an ambiguous concept. They should act as role models to help others embrace change and ambiguity.'

While most readers would doubtless applaud the sentiment here, neither those aspiring to become HRD professionals, nor society more generally, is likely to be satisfied to leave matters here. Indeed clients of professionals, and funders of professionals, in all fields, seek ever yet clearer understandings of what these professionals should be able 'to deliver' in terms of competent performance. No busy manager is willing to turn for help in solving a serious and urgent problem at work to a professional about whom they feel ambiguous in terms of the role, the competences, and the confident commitment of that professional. Nor can we leave the HRD professional with the view that they must try to be all things to all people, a view that I have found at times amongst some of my own post-experience students on the HRD courses I have managed and taught.

So there must be either a compromise between those that seek a theoretical basis for the HRD discipline, upon which to build a curriculum, or we must look at the whole issue of becoming an HRD professional from a different perspective. The attempts to produce a theoretical foundation for the discipline of HRD have been many and various. Swanson (1999) has determined 'at this point in time' that 'HRD's unique integration of psychological, economic and systems theories' constitutes the theoretical foundation of the discipline of HRD. Others have looked towards the practice of HRD in work organisations as a basis for understanding the competences that HRD professionals need. Kuchinke (2001) argues that there are three foci for the work of HRD professionals, person – centred HRD, production centred HRD and principled problem – solving HRD. He argues that 'each encompasses a range of theories, authors and schools of thought; is rooted in different philosophical traditions; and makes assumptions about the nature of human beings and the nature of organisations and society'.

Grieves and Redman (1999) in contrast boldly state that 'HRD is living in the shadow of OD (organisational development) because it is slow to recognise its roots in the debates of that discipline'. Mankin (2001) places his HRD model firmly within the work organisation, and sees its parameters as lying within the overlapping areas between the organisation's strategy and structure, culture and HRM practices. This approach leaves HRD to be defined as the field of work at the margins of strategic management and of human resource management, and subject to the whims of the organisation's existing culture. While this 'squeezed' position doubtless reflects the reality of the workplace for many HRD practioners today, I would argue that HRD professionals must have a strong influence on organisational strategy and HRM practices to justify their claim to be professionals rather than technicians (for example instructional trainers). The research by McLean and Suhadolnik (1989) for the American Society for Training and Development identified 35 areas of competence for those involved with HRD. These are much at variance with the competences identified for the training and development specialist in the UK (Wilson 1999).

It seems that the quest for a curriculum for HRD professionals based on understandings of HRD in principle, and its theoretical underpinnings is not well advanced. Swanson (1999) and McLean (1999) agree that theory-building research in the HRD field must go on. Meanwhile I believe we need to look to research carried out in recent years into professional competence development for a better understanding of how to develop HRD professionals.

A Model for Professional Competence and its Development

Initial and continuing professional development have been considered from a number of theoretical standpoints in modern times. Much of the debate about the most appropriate

HRD curriculum comes out of what Cheetham and Chivers (1996, 1998) have termed the 'technical-rational approach'. This focuses on underpinning professional knowledge and theory, rather than its day-to-day application in everyday life. Donald Schön (1983, 1987) above all has challenged the hegemony of this standpoint, with his emphasis on the 'reflective practitioner' approach. This foregrounds tacit knowledge built up from reflection on professional practise, and its re-application day-to-day via 'repertoires of solutions'.

Other theoretical standpoints address functional work competence, personal competence and so-called meta-competence, which stresses the importance of competencies that enable individuals to monitor and develop other competencies, enhancing or mediating them, Graham Cheetham and I (Ibid) have argued that these approaches are partial and tend to emphasise one area of overall professional competence at the expense of others. Further, we have considered that these theoretical approaches are complementary and overlapping rather than competing. Such considerations have led us to develop a model of professional competence, which places stress on the four key areas of professional competence, which are drawn upon in performance and mediated by the professional's meta-competences, which include learning how to reflect on performance, learning how to learn, problem identification and resolution, higher level communication skills, etc.

These four key areas of professional competence are (i) knowledge and understanding (especially of concepts), (ii) functional skills (which are occupation specific), (iii) personal or behavioural competence, and (iv) values and ethical competence (personal and professional). These four areas of professional (and personal) competence interact in complex ways during learning and during professional performance. We argue that, however they interact to produce the performance, the learning from reflection on performance, and the will to improve performance from recognition of weaknesses and limitations from such reflection, are of crucial importance for initial professional development, and especially for continuing professional development.

In initial professional development, the competence 'boxes' are filled by a mix of methods, but with a strong emphasis on filling the knowledge and conceptual understanding 'box' via formal education and training. (See for example Ehrlich, 1999). The functional competence 'box' is partially filled by formal practical training, and then 'learning by doing' in the real workplace. However, the novice professional usually has much more development to undergo in this area in the early years of professional practice. At this stage workplace supervisors and coaches often play an important part, and reflection on practice may be actively encouraged by others.

The personal/behavioural competence 'box' may not be much thought about in initial professional development, the tendency being to rely on earlier 'upbringing' to part fill this 'box'. The values/ethics 'box' with its strong influence on professional judgement and behaviour may or may not be subject to formal education and training influence. Certainly in some professions 'the way we do things round here' may be brought to the novice professional's attention at an early stage.

Dreyfus and Dreyfus (1986) argue that, in regard to skills acquisition there are five levels running from Novice, via Advanced Beginner, Competent, and Proficient to Expert. At one end the novice performs within rigid taught rules or plans, while at the other end the expert no longer relies on rules, guidelines or maxims, but on an intuitive grasp of situations based on deep, tacit understanding. Analytical approaches to the planning of performance, based on first principles, are only used in novel situations. The expert professional has a strong grasp of what is possible in performance under a wide range of circumstances.

Cheetham and Chivers (2001) have established that on average professionals believe that it takes six years for a professional entering the profession to become competent from the initial novice stage. Whether professionals move beyond 'competent' to 'expert' then depends on the extent and nature of their continuing professional development.

Formal and Informal Professional Learning

It is clear from the patterns emerging in the rapidly expanding higher education system, that those with the highest levels of education are those who tend to look for more advanced formal learning opportunities throughout their careers. This phenomenon explains the almost explosive development of postgraduate level taught courses offered by universities, colleges, professional bodies, and private training providers. These may be full blown Masters Degrees, full and part-time diplomas and certificates, across to short courses that carry no award. In the UK for example the numbers of part-time postgraduate students in higher education has risen from just less than 50,000 in 1982 to just over 250,000 in 2002 (HESA, 2004). In some cases progression in the profession makes it essential or valuable to obtain further qualifications following entry to the profession. In other cases there is a stronger focus on learning to increase competence for its own sake, and even on learning for its own sake without any obvious tie to professional competence improvement.

While such formal courses and learning programmes are important today, research by Graham and myself has revealed that, for many professionals, across 20 representative professions, competence development via informal learning methods was considered of greater fundamental importance in terms of developing from novice to competent to expert (Cheetham and Chivers, 2001).

Given that busy professionals cannot reasonably be expected to attend one formal qualification course after another, or even get along to numerous 3- to 5-day short courses each year, the area of informal learning, with all the opportunities and flexibility offered, must be very significant for professionals to consider.

In-depth interviews with 80 professionals from twenty professions, and a questionnaire survey of 372 professionals from six variegated professionals, have revealed a wealth of qualitative and quantitative data on the informal learning methods adopted by these professionals as they move on through their careers.

The approaches raised in interviews could be classified into broadly 12 learning mechanisms. This was no easy task, as many professionals have limited conceptual understanding of how they learn informally, and indeed may not even command sufficient relevant terminology to articulate their thoughts in this area. Often concrete examples were offered of how they had learnt to do tasks, and these examples needed to be elaborated to fit them to a broader framework of ways of learning informally.

The twelve general informal learning methods have been 'tweaked' into a list based on 'PROFESSIONAL', by Graham as follows:

1. Practice and repetition
2. Reflection
3. Observation and copying
4. Feedback
5. Extra-occupational transfer

6. Stretching activities
7. Perspective changing/switching
8. Mentor/coach interaction
9. Unconscious absorption or osmosis
10. Use of neurological or psychological devices/mental tricks
11. Articulation/teaching
12. Collaboration/networking.

Proposing these options, with some elaboration as to their meaning in the survey questionnaire with the six selected and very varied professions, enabled us to determine which informal learning methods were, or had been, of particular importance to these professionals. Indeed, a clear ranking was established as follows in terms of their contribution to competence development:

1. On the job learning
2. Working alongside more experienced colleagues
3. Working as part of a team
4. Self analysis or reflection
5. Learning from clients/customers/patients, etc.
6. Networking with others doing similar work
7. Learning through teaching/training others
8. Support from a mentor of some kind
9. Use of a role model
10. Pre-entry experience.

In considering this list some important points must be stressed. Firstly, as with all research in rapidly developing fields, the empirical research generating this data was done six years ago. Secondly, the professionals involved were broadly in mid-career and looking backwards into past experience to a large extent. Thirdly, some approaches to informal learning may have scored lower in terms of past value simply because they were not available to many professionals historically. Finally, the variation between the six professions in their scoring of these options was sometimes significant.

In regard to the first two points, the absence of e-learning (or any form of distance/open learning) from the list is perhaps less of a surprise than at first sight. In the interview work some professionals had reported that they simply never had the opportunity of benefiting from a mentor. So this may well explain the rather low position of this approach to informal learning. Finally, the variation between professions may be due to a mix of opportunity and perception of role. For example, 'trainers' were a profession included, and unsurprisingly they rated 'learning from teaching' highly. The clergy was a profession included and overall they rated role modelling and mentoring relatively highly as learning methods, probably because most clergy have mentors provided, and many put an emphasis on modelling appropriate professional character and behaviour of pastoral support.

The Role of the HRD Professional and its Relationship to Learning

Traditionally HRD professionals have been regarded as concerned with the organisation and delivery of training, within work organisations. During the last 10 years a number of empirical studies have been carried out to examine the changing roles of HRD practitioners in work organisations. For example, the 1990s saw a series of surveys carried out to compare the nature of the HRD profession across several European countries (Hytönen, Poell, and Chivers, 2002). These surveys concerned self-evaluations by HRD practioners of the actual work roles, outputs, and professional competences considered important and beneficial to their everyday work practice. The survey questionnaires adopted the descriptive model for the work of HRD practioners established by the American Society for Training and Development (McLegan and Bedrick, 1983; McLegan, 1989; McLean, 1996). A comparison of the results from five of the participating countries (Valkeavara, 1998) suggested that the roles of organisational change agent, instructor, HRD manager and programme designer appeared to best define the current activities of HRD practitioners.

Typical HRD roles in the Netherlands were distributed quite evenly across the role alternatives presented in the survey questionnaire. The 'change agent' aspect of HRD practice was highlighted, particularly in Finland and the United Kingdom. The Finnish survey results based on returns from 164 Finnish HRD practioners showed that 51 saw themselves primarily as change agents, 37 as designers (those who organise specific HRD interventions), 50 as managers (who spend most of their time managing, marketing, consulting and administrating the HRD function), and only 26 as trainers (who deliver training, carry out training needs assessment, research, instruct, or offer careers advice).

The role of 'change agent' is especially of interest given that it does not fit to the common (indeed stereotypical) understandings of the role of the HRD professional. In the Finnish study the 'change agents' were involved in the resolution of conflicts in the workplace; achieving changes in group norms, values, and culture; planning organisational change; implementing change strategies; identifying or following up sales and business leads; and data analysis and interpretation. Few of these roles would have been reflected in a curriculum to develop HRD professionals ten years ago, indeed many may still not do so.

Poell and Chivers (1999) in an interview based survey of 19 HRD professionals in the UK found that not only were the roles of HRD professionals very much changed compared with a decade before, but that looked at organisation by organisation these changes were by no means all taking the HRD role in the same direction. For example while 9 of these interviewed thought that in their respective organisations learning and development were considered to be more important than training these days, 5 participants saw no tendency at all towards self directed learning in the organisations they work with. Nor did the study find that the problems or barriers faced by HRD professionals were reducing. Ten participants reported resistance to change in trainers and in managers, especially in regard to getting managers to take more responsibility for the training and development of their subordinates. Managers resented being made responsible for training issues that were formerly dealt with by trainers. Some trainers were resisting taking on a more facilitative consultant like role. Eight participants experienced a lack of recognition for training issues in their organisations. They referred to a lack of a 'training culture' with not enough money spent on staff development. Some managers were seen as ignorant about training issues, resulting in a lack of training and development policy. Both training needs assessment and training evaluation are sometimes considered to be missing from standard operations.

HRD Strategies of HRD Professionals in the Poell and Chivers (1999) UK Survey

A particularly interesting aspect of the Poell and Chivers (1999) survey was the list of strategies that HRD professional reported using to deal with the problems and barriers they were facing. These can be summarised under three headings.

Firstly 13 of the 19 participants interviewed were actively trying to develop the learning climate of organisations. For instance, they attempted to create an 'empowered' climate for staff throughout the company. They encouraged learning at all levels and in all places. They developed learning programmes incrementally rather than by blueprint. They also tried to get employees to recognise the important learning opportunities that are available in everyday work situations.

Secondly, ten participants highlighted the importance of negotiating with the various stakeholders involved in HRD processes, especially with managers. An important aspect of this work concerned attempting to influence strategy, by influencing the definition of an assignment or forthcoming project at an early stage. Participants tended to stress the group's rather than just their own responsibility for taking forward certain learning processes. Sometimes they tried to 'educate management' rather than simply 'train the workforce', initially seen to be the 'problem' in terms of learning deficits.

Thirdly, some of the participants (8) were undertaking activities which would make them more marketable as professional consultants. To do this they worked with associates, developed their consultancy skills, and developed HRD services and products that they could market.

Valkeavara (1999) carried out a qualitative study of 20 Finnish HRD practioners, who worked mainly in HRD management positions within public sector organisations and private enterprises. She found quite similar results to the Poell and Chivers (1999) study in the UK. The ideals of the learning organisation, such as open communication, collaboration and management involvement, constitute the primary source of problems for these HRD developers in their everyday work practice. Furthermore, taking on the role of change agent caused HRD professionals notable unease and uncertainty. 'As much as HRD practitioners sensed the expectations and possibilities to act as challenge or change agent, they also perceived the resistance to this activity as problematic to their professional practice' (Valkeavara, 1999). This author goes on to question to what extent HRD professionals can really be involved in shaping organisational change. She herself questions the cost in becoming so involved to their position as professional experts on HRD issues.

This is a crucial question for all professionals within work organisations where there is a separate line management structure, that is where the professionals are to a large extent not responsible for managing the organisation's assets and are therefore not the final decision makes about the disposition of the organisation's resources. In such cases, which would typify the UK National Health Service for example, major ethical issues arise where professionals step out of their expected advisory and facilitation roles and take on management decision-making responsibilities, or are seen as 'colluding' with management at the expense of professional standards.

What Does all This Mean for Developing HRD Professions?

First, Cheetham and Chivers (1996; 1998) have developed a generic model for professional competence, into which can be added a whole variety of methods of formal and informal learning at professional level. This model has been utilised and adopted by a wide variety of experts and organisations, (including some professional bodies) as a basis for rethinking professional development for the professional fields they are concerned about. This model seems to have proved of particular interest and value to those concerned with 'emergent' professions or those subject to rapid and often dramatic change. To this extent the model provides a sensible template for thinking about HRD professional competence and its development.

Studies of HRD practice seen through the eyes of well-qualified and experienced practitioners indicate that:

- Roles are very varied, and make significantly different competence demands in different work organisations.
- For this reason, HRD professionals moving from one organisation to another could find themselves regarded as lacking key competencies because of the expectations of the new employer.
- We cannot produce an initial professional development curriculum for the HRD field, which will equip young/ inexperienced professionals on completion of their studies for any eventuality that they will meet throughout their career, or even in their first post.
- HRD professionals need to live what they espouse, that lifelong learning is necessary to gain and retain sufficient learning to be regarded as generally competent in all reasonable work circumstances.
- Much further learning will be necessary to achieve expert status, and even then it would be easy to get out of date quickly if learning is not ongoing.
- The relationship between the HRD professional acting as a specialist consultant and advisor, and as an HR (or general change) line manager is thin and problematic, not least from an ethical viewpoint.
- Within a job role in a particular organisation, or as a particular type of HRD consultant, it is possible to find sufficient repetition of tasks to build up a 'repertoire of solutions' to everyday problems and challenges. However, the rapid changes of role which typify HRD work for many professionals today mean that they are forced back on the technical – rational approach, involving command of infrequently utilised concepts and knowledge.

- The range of functional skills that HRD professionals are called upon to utilise at a high level is very wide. On the one hand, the integration of HRD professionals into the detailed work of modern manufacturing and service sector managers and their teams requires strong IT skills, while the sheer range of people that HRD professionals seek to influence places a premium on verbal and written communication skills, negotiating skills and interpersonal skills more generally. Consulting skills will be at a premium for the future and require formal development as will project management skills.
- At the level of personal skills much is also expected. Because of the inevitable multi-tasking required, skills of 'keeping all the balls in the air' and meeting deadlines while maintaining quality in a calm environment are at a premium. HRD professionals need to be strong team players and have a good understanding of group dynamics in the workplace. At the same time they must really care for the welfare of all the individuals that they come in contact with and seek to develop.
- Professional ethics loom large as an area for formal and informal learning and development for professionals. Indeed the whole area of values and beliefs must be given ongoing attention and remain a strong focus for professional bodies in the HRD field.

So I would argue that we can recognise all four of the 'boxes' in the Cheetham model as needing filling for HRD professionals. Some of this filling can be achieved through formal, (and today often accredited) learning. However, the HRD professional, more than most, has to work to develop their meta-competencies, the high level competencies that monitor all other competencies across the four boxes, and plan how to improve these more task and role specific competences. But how can the HRD professional improve their meta-competencies relating to professional performance, so that they become competent, proficient and ultimately expert practioners?

The Role of Reflection on Practice

Cheetham and Chivers (1998) argue that the key to development and honing of meta-competencies is reflection on professional practice. While such reflection will benefit all aspects of professional learning and competence, and is the basis for developing Schön's 'repertoire of solutions' and lower level 'tacit knowledge', its crucial importance comes when reflection goes deeper and impacts the level of meta-competencies. Reflection on practice is a mantra in some areas of initial professional development today, for example in teacher and nurse training. However, although most professionals in practice seem to understand the concept, research by Cheetham and Chivers involving interviews with 80 professionals revealed that 20 percent of our sample (from 20 professionals, four from each) did not consider that they reflect on a regular basis. Less than half of the sample considered that they often modified their professional practice as a result of such reflection. While HRD professionals may be stronger in learning and changing their practice from reflection, the results are concerning.

If the Cheetham and Chivers model is valid, then this empirical research suggests that for many professionals the potential power of reflection on performance in terms of learning and competence improvement is at best only partially exploited. Indeed, in times of rapid change in many fields of work, one can imagine professionals who are neither learning by highly structured purposeful means, (such as course progression by attendance at classes, or via e-learning), nor by meaningful reflection, actually becoming less competent over time.

I have argued elsewhere (Chivers, 2003) that some professionals have learning styles which make them unsuited to learning from reflection on their practice (or indeed the practice of other professionals). These professionals need opportunities to reflect on their practice in a group practice or on a one-to-one basis. Those developing as HRD professionals are often doing so in relative isolation and might well benefit from joining 'learning from experience' groups. I have also made the case in previous writing (Ibid) for reflective practice one-to-one interviews with appropriate learning facilitators. Experienced HRD professions, with some further training, would be well suited to acting in the role of interviewers, or indeed stepping up as mentors for inexperienced HRD 'beginners'.

Conclusions

HRD professionals hold the development of other professionals, managers and members of the general workforce in their hands to some extent. It is essential that their development follows best practice, and is imaginative and offers very wide ranging learning experiences. The roles of HRD professionals are today very varied within work organisations, and HRD professionals may be employees in larger or small organisations, or indeed be self-employed. Their roles may change rapidly within a work organisation grappling with rapid external changes. Indeed HRD professionals may change jobs quite rapidly from one organisation to another, act as temporary staff, consultants or take a part-time job in the HRD function, while working part-time in one or more other jobs outside the HRD field.

Thus a 'one curriculum fits all' approaches is not appropriate for developing a nation's HRD profession, and no HRD professional can 'rest on their laurels' in terms of believing that their existing professional competence will be sufficient to see them through their career (or even the next 5 years).

Looking at the components of the Cheetham and Chivers model, it seems clear that HRD professionals will need to draw on well topped up 'boxes' under all the four competence headings proposed. The cognition 'box' will need to include knowledge and understanding drawn from the disciplines of occupational psychology, organisational development, psychology of learning (especially adult learning), sociology (for example of the workplace, and of diversity), human resource management (and relevant legislation, including equal opportunities law), business studies and management (including management of people, finance and other resources, management of information, marketing, etc), as well as specialise knowledge relevant to the sector of the economy in which they are working (e.g. the chemical industry, health service etc). Clearly, not all of this learning relating to disciplines from which HRD professions draw in their work can be achieved at the initial professional development stage. Hence the protracted debates about what knowledge is core and what 'nice to have'. Given the diversity of roles I see no difficulty with different curriculum content in this 'cognition box' for different HRD qualification courses. Indeed, it would be disastrous if all HRD professionals took their careers forward from the same basis of cognitive knowledge, due to the danger of 'group think'.

However, as HRD professions look to progress from 'novice' to 'expert' it is essential that they seek ways to fill the 'cognition box' to cover more and more of the gaps which become evident in moving from role to role and job to job. Combinations of formal and informal learning are needed for this CPD effort.

As regards the 'vocational competence box', it would be easier to find agreement, not least because functional analysis has been applied to the 'trainer' and 'training manager', resulting in the development of competency statements and standards in the UK. Such competences cover skills as diverse as classroom lecturing, management of learning groups, and development of coherent learning materials, across to basic information technology skills. Informal learning (Marsick and Volpe, 1999), reflection and feedback are especially important in functional competence development.

The personal competencies box is very important for HRD professionals to pay attention to, because their credibility rests substantially on being able to draw on these competences in professional performance. The HRD professional who appears to be poorly organised at work, unable to keep to time for meetings or training sessions, who cannot work to deadlines, who is a poor listener, or who patronises subordinate staff and trainees is hardly likely to inspire confidence in those seeking to learn, not least by example. In this area of competence development, reflection on practise is of paramount importance, and constructively critical (as well as positive) feedback by stakeholders in the HRD process is vital. Inability to handle such feedback in terms of learning and behavioural change indicates an HRD professional whose overall competence is unlikely to progress satisfactorily.

The ethics and values/belief 'box' needs constant attention through the career of HRD professionals, because societal change throws up new issues in this area almost weekly. On top of one's personal beliefs and ethical framework, there are likely to be in the future policies around professional ethics coming from professional bodies in the HRD field, to say nothing of HR legislation bearing down upon employees. Reading, thinking, challenging oneself through reflection on ethical issues, and challenging other HRD professions concerning their beliefs and their practices from an ethical standpoint, are essential to new learning in this area.

Meta-competencies are honed by taking on challenging professional tasks, whether this might include for HRD professions planning learning for quite different groups of learners, shadowing managers or professionals in other fields, working in HRD in another country, publishing in the HRD field, or using totally new training techniques. As stressed above it is the extent of reflection, in-depth, on these novel experiences, especially on how unexpected problems were resolved, that generates learning and development at the meta-competence level.

In regard to reflection itself, for most HRD professionals, who are 'good all rounders' in terms of their preferred learning styles (Kolb, 1984; Smith and Kolb, 1985) then a mix of individual reflection on performance, reflection in groups on 'why I do it like this' and 'why do you do it like that?,' and one-to-one reflective practise interviews, from time to time, probably represents best practice.

Professional bodies have a role to play in many of these learning processes, whether they step forward with formal criteria for entry to the profession, or mandatory CPD schemes, or whether they simply provide opportunities for some of the formal or informal learning to take place. Further education and training institutions both public and private, have much to offer in terms of knowledge and skill development, while higher education can take this work forward, but especially has a key role in developing HRD professionals as researchers, and authors in the field.

Many of the issues around the development of HRD professionals are of common international concern (Kuchinke, 2001) and the growth of the Academy for Human Resource Development from its American base to become a truly international body is important in this respect. Similarly the European Forum for HRD is playing a valuable role in drawing together those leading in HRD research and professional development across both Eastern and Western/Europe. It is also pleasing to see the growth in titles and subscriptions for HRD journals of international appeal such as Human Resource Development International, since these publications are feeding the requirements of HRD professionals for new knowledge and understanding about their complex but intensely rich and rewarding field. As Mary McAlease (1999) wrote, as President of Ireland, global HRD leaders need to share current thinking and developments.

REFERENCES

Cheetham, G. and Chivers, G. (1996) 'Towards a holistic model of professional competence', Journal of European Industrial Training, Vol. 20, No 5, pp 20-30.

Cheetham, G. and Chivers, G. (1998) 'The reflective (and competent) practioner: a model of professional competence which seeks to harmonise the reflective practitioner and competence-based approaches', Journal of European Industrial Training, Vol. 22, No.7, pp 267-76.

Cheetham, G. and Chivers, G. (2001) 'How professionals learn in practice: an investigation of informal learning amongst people working in professions', Journal of European Industrial Training, Vol. 25, No.5, pp 248- 292.

Chivers, G. (2003) 'Utilising reflective practice interviews in professionals development', Journal of European Industrial Training, Vol. 27, No.1, pp 5 -15.

Drefus, H.C. and Drefus, S.E. (1986) Mind over Machine: The Power of Human Intuition Expertise in the Era of the Computer, Basil Blackwell, Oxford.

Ehrlich, D.B. (1999) 'Case: developing a Competence -Based Exam for an HRD Graduate Program', Academy of Human Resource Development, 1999 Conference Proceedings, Arlington, Virginia, Vol. 1, 14-1, AHRD, Baton Rouge, LA.

Grieves, J. and Redman, T. (1999) 'Living in the shadow of OD: HRD and the search for identity', Human Resource Development International, Vol. 2, No.2, pp 81-102.

HESA (2002) statistics of the Higher Education Statistical Agency, reported in the Times Higher Education Supplement, 11 June 2004, London.

Hytönen, T, Poell, P. and Chivers, G. (2002) 'HRD as a professional career? Perspectives from Finland, The Netherlands and the United Kingdom', Chapter 14 in Nijhof, W., Heikkinen, A and Nieuwenhuis, L.F.M (Eds.) Shaping Flexibility in Vocational Education and Training, Kluwer, Condon.

Kolb, D.A. (1984) Experimental Learning, Prentice -Hall, Eaglewood Cliffs, N.J.

Kuchinke, K.P. (2001) Metaphors and paradigms for HRD research and practice', Advances in Developing Human Resources, Vol. 3, No.3, pp 366-378.

Kuchinke, K.P. (2001) 'HRD university education: an international research agenda', Human Resource Development International, Vol. 4, No.2, p 253-261.

Mankin, D.P. (2001) 'A model for human resource development' Human Resource Development International, Vol. 4, No.1 pp 65-85.

Marsick, V.J. and Volpe, M (1999) 'The nature and need for informal learning', Chapter One in Marsick, V.J. and Volpe, M. (Eds.) Informal Learning on the Job, Advances in Developing Human Resources, No 3, AHRD and Benett-Koehler Communications, University of Minnesota, pp 1-9.

McAleese, M. (1999) 'Revitalising HRD for the New Millennium, in Marquardt M. (Ed.) Developing Human Resources in the Global Economy Advances in Developing Human Resources, No.4, pp 1-2.

McLagan, P. (1989) Models of HRD practice: The models, American Society for Training and Development, Washington D.C.

McLegan, P. (1996) 'Great ideas revisited', Training and Development Journal, 20(1), pp 60-65.

MacLegan, P and Bedrick, D. (198) 'Models for excellence: the results of the ASTO training and development competence study', Training and Development Journal, 7(b), pp 10-20.

McLegan, P.A. and Suhadolnik, D. (1989) Models for HRD practice: the Research Report, ASTD Press, Alexandria, VA.

McLean, G.N. (1999)' Get out the drill, glue and more legs', Human Resource Development International, Vol. 2, No.1, pp 6-7.

Odenthal, C. and Nijhof, W. (19996) 'HRD roles in Germany', Studies in Human Resource Development, 13, Academisch Boekencentrum, De Lier.

Poell, R. and Chivers, G. (1999) 'Experiences of HRD consultants in supporting organisational learning', Chapter 14 in Facing up to the Learning Organisation Challenge, volume II by B.Nyhon, M. Kelleher, P. Cressey and P. Poell (Eds.), CEDEFOP, Office for Official Publications of the European Communities Luxembourg.

Schön, D. (1983) The Reflective Practitioner: How Professionals Think in Action, Maurice Temple Smith. London.

Schön, D.A. (1987) Educating the Reflective Practioner, Jossey -Bass Inc., San Francisco, C.A.

Smith, D. and Kolb, D.A. (1985) User Guide for the Learning Style Inventory, McBer and Co., Boston, M.A.

Swanson, R.A., (1999) 'HRD theory, real or imagined', Human Resource Development International, Vol. 2, No.1, pp 2-5.

Valkeavaara, T. (1997) 'HRD practioners analysing their work: what does it tell about their present role in working life?'. In R. Remes, S. Tosse, P. Falkenkrone and B. Bergstedt (Eds.) Social Change and Adult Education Research: Adult Education Research in Nordic Countries 1996, University of Jyväskylä, Institute for Education Research, Jyväskylä, Finland, pp 14-40.

Valkeavaara, T (1998a) 'Human resource development roles and competences in five European countries', International Journal of Training and Development, 2(3), pp 171-189.

Valkeavaara, T. (1998b) 'Exploring the nature of human resource developers' expertise' European Journal of Work and Organisational Psychology, 7(4), pp 533-548.

Valkeavaara, T. (1999) 'Sailing in calm waters doesn't teach: constructing expertise through problems in work: the case of Finnish human resource developers', Studies in Continuing Education, 21 (27), pp 177 -196.

Wilson, J.P. (Ed.) (1999) Human Resource Development: Learning and Training for Individuals and Organisations, Kogan Page, London.

3

HRD IN THE NEW CONTEXT—CHALLENGES AND OPPORTUNITIES

*Dr. J. R. Dhotra**

HRD function has got a good deal of attention in the recent pas and is continuing to get more. The instruments of HRD are many. The HRD instruments should lead to the generation of HRD processes like role clarity, performance, planning, development climate, risk-taking, dynamism etc., in employees. Such HRD processes should result in more competent satisfied and committed people that would make the organization grow by contributing their best to it. Such HRD outcomes influence the organizational effectiveness.

In this era of professional management where managers as well as Chief Executives are being professionally developed, systems interventions is the only way to develop and institutionalize processes and new culture. HRD processes and climate cannot be developed in any simple way in organizations that are already in existence and have already evolved a way of life. Process changes can be brought in through systemic interventions faster if the interventions are designed properly, taken seriously and are monitored constantly--designing of the system should be based on a

* Professor, Department of Management Studies, University of Jammu, J&K.

clarity of processes. In sum, the following can be postulated about the linkages between HRD mechanisms and processes:

1. HRD departments and mechanisms are useful instruments for initiating and strengthening development processes and culture and achieving HRD outcomes.
2. HRD mechanisms and sub-systems should be designed, keeping in view the HRD processes and culture to be achieved.
3. These mechanisms should be periodically reviewed to examine whether they are facilitating the institution of HRD processes and culture or not, and whether the mechanisms should suitably be changed
4. Irrespective of how well the mechanisms are designed and implemented if the top management does not have commitment to HRD and communicates such commitment to all employees, the HRD mechanisms may become more rituals resulting in wastage of managerial time rather than leading to the development of HRD processes.
5. Even when the HRD mechanisms are well designed, the top managemnet is committed and the implementation process is well monitored, generation and internationalization of HRD process and culture is a slow process and may take some years.

In view of these, the HRD mangers have a complex role to perform. In order to make an impact, the HRD manager should:

(a) be a person with a high degree of commitment to HRD and HRD philosophy:

(b) have a high degree of preservance:

(c) be closer to the Chief Executive and be able to get and communicate the top mangement's commitment to employees;

(d) be given enough time (a minimum of 5 years) to work as HRD manager without being transferred.

In addition, the top mangement should be sensitive to the organizational process and be able to preserve the incremental changes occurring in the development climate of the organization.

Indian Industry has come of age and is now ready to compete with foreign industry and cooperate with it. These decontrol measures and global economic environmental can only be faced by gaining competitive advantage. Competitive advantage means providing unique features in product or service, offering the customer some advantages. The competitive advantage has three important dimensions for HRD professionals to usher into the organization.

1. Evolving need based HRD strategies to develop a world-class organization.
2. Creating an urge for excellence at all levels in the organization by ensuring employee participation.
3. Developing an enabling culture for organized change through mission, vision, and core values.

To achieve these objectives calls for holistic and integrated view of HRD with specific reference to organization analysis, HRD strategy formulation and careful implementation.

1. Evolving Need-based HRD Strategies

For HRD Strategies to be viable in an organization, it is crucial that they are isolated from the realities and problems of the orgnaization. HRD Strategies must arise out of corporate objectives goals and broad competitive strategies adoped by the organization. A critical review of HRD efforts in many organizations reveal that organizational diagnosis has been neglected and HR efforts are centred around organizational processes and peripheral issues. HR processionals should also be able to process certain unmeasurable aspects of the organizational working by developing good insights into issues of power and conflicts. The tendency to propose HR interventions to suit knowledge and limitations of internal and external change agents thereby ignoring to define output variables and long-term strategies of organizational objectives may result in short term enviable efforts.

2. Ground Realities or Organisations

These are three major aspects of understanding organizations which focus HR Strategies viz, structure, process and culture. Organization structure defines the shape, autonomy and Framework, which holds, the various systems together. The organization processes describe what is to be done to the information generated at each stage. The extent to which the processes are effective will be partly determined by the rationality of the strcture and partly by the culture it develops. The third critical aspect of orgnaization analysis is culture. It can be understood through norms and value systems that govern the behaviour of the majority of the people. Therefore, it is essential that before designing HR Strategies, particularly with regard to Flat and lean organizations unless an integrated approach is evolved, the HR interventions will be counterproductive.

3. Selection of HR Interventions

HR interventions are specifically designed to achieve the intended results through planned change and are not something that happens to the organizations by chance. Black and Mouton have contrasted this planned systematic change with both revolutionary change. It has been reported that people seem to dislike both the change sequences because in revolution, an element of force is present, while in evolution, a sense of pious hope is noticeable - Research and experience indicate that they way in which the particular HR technology has been selected and implemented can have a major effect on the ultimate aim of organizational change. The success of HR efforts is directly related to the accuracy and appropriate use of HR knowledge of various HR technologies, but the experts must have a good understanding of organizational functioning.

HRD is a key to achieve a better organization. For it be effective in the new context of HRD, the management must:

- Have the total faith in the HRD philosophy.
- Give due emphasis to create an atmosphere of mutual trust and confidence by adopting open management concepts.
- Develop tripartite core groups to implement long-term HRD plans in consultation with specialized agencies.
- Ensure participation of unions and associations at the execution stage. A sense of shared purpose and team spirit will lead to the development of the organization as a whole.
- Have regular machinery for feedback and analysis of organizational problems and to suggest remedial action.
- Create an atmosphere in which workers do not think that there are two conflicting sides. Workers should feel that managers and workers in the organization sail or sink in the same boat.

Role of External Agencies in HRD

In a country like India, there is a vast reservoir of latent talents in workers, which, if nurtured carefully, will increase organizational synergy. External agencies like educational and professional institutions; the government and political parties, which control trade unions and associations have a critical role to play in promoting HRD.

Educational and professional bodies need to study the functioning and needs of organizations and identify areas for HRD, and to develop intervention strategies and monitor their implementation.

In today's context in India, political parties also have a role to play in HRD. They can help to influence in a positive way policies and practices at the organization level. They can also act as watch guards to monitor the formulation and implementation of human practices. With their influence over workers, they can help mould suitable attitudes. Finally, they can institute activities of their own to develop leadership and competence for HRD.

New Challenges of HRD

Liberalization has thrown up many challenges especially to the HRD professionals. There is unemployment on one side and a tremendous dearth of competent people to man the industry on the other. Financial sector is glaring example of this. However, shortage of competent people is by no means limited to any one sector. This shortage faced is attributable to the failure of HRD in the past, both at the national and corporate level. HRD professionals have not used a long-term strategy. There were only responses to immediate needs. The present day HRD professionals, under strain, is behaving no differently. He is concentrating on recruitment and sometimes recruiting people at any cost. He is focusing on short-term needs of the company and not on the long-term capability requirements. If he focuses on long-term needs, his approach and focus will be different. He also would focus more on utilizing the existing talents and developing a number of them.

In addition, increasingly the executives from other functions complain about the irrelevance of HRD professionals in their organization. They do express sometimes that the

HRD managers do not understand the issues - people as well as process of their department. They feel that the HRD managers interfere in their work, and take decisions on their behalf on HR related issues.

It is high time for HRD professionals in India to take a re-look at their activities and effectiveness of their role in their organizations. Some of the new challenges of HRD managers are :-

1. To develop an integrated approach. By integrated approach is meant that the HRD managers should try to have in-depth knowledge on various departments- the people, processes, and performance and the functional importance these departments have in relation to the overall objectives of the organization.
2. Further, he should strive to facilitate the HR processes rather than imposing them on the line managers. He should, in fact try to use his acquired knowledge to strengthen the hands of the line managers.
3. A continuous introspection of his role alongwith organizational objectives will required to an effective HRD manager in the ensuring days. It is strongly felt; only an integrated approach will help an HRD manager to be a true professional.
4. One of the best ways to develop an integrated appraoch is through ``Networking'' meeting of HRD managers to share their experiences with one another, and to learn from each other. This provides an opportunity for him/her to have insights into various issues being faced by fellow managers in different organizations. The National HRD Network, and the Academy of HRD are two institutions set up by HRD professionals of repute for this purpose. It is necessary to balance internal networking with external networking.

5. The development of each HRD managers is interrelated to the development of the field staff, and the movement of HRD, like the development process, has to be a continuous and vibrant one.

These HRD institutions provide the best information and forum for developing the HRD professionals to meet the new challenges. However, it is upto each one of us to make use of the facilities of these institutions by closely interacting with them, and also help these institutions to grow to their full potential.

Opportunities :

The new environment has thrown many challenges and opportunities to industry. The opportunities are of new ventures. The challenges include a fast movement to become customer driven, cost effective, quality oriented, quickly responding, service-centred and technology adopted organization. All these challenges require employees at all levels to change. It is clear by now that it is people, who can make the difference. If there is a fast change in these directions by such organizations, they are likely to survive and even emerge as future corporations.

The HRD staff has a key role to play in this direction. The first and foremost role is continuous education of employees about the changes and challenges facing the industry. It is important that an employees should understand and locate India on the global map in terms of its share in global business, its standing in the global economy, its standing in terms of the quality of life its people.

The second task is in terms of educating employees about the company. It is important that all employees know a lot more about the company, where they work than other, who do not work there. The HRD managers should prepare material to educate all employees through small booklets, papers, video films, lectures etc. They could use a group of trainers from their own staff. Alternatively, they could use outside trainers.

The thrid task is to assess and to keep re-assessing the core competencies required by the corporation at different level with the changing environment. The new competencies required by various groups and teams need to be assessed and strategies of developing these competencies may be evolved. Some of the competencies (attitudes, skills, perspectives etc.) may cut across all levels and departments in the company.

The fourth task, therefore, is to plan and implement strategies to develop new competencies at all levels. This could again be through training, appraisal system. Seminar and Workshops, participative discussions, quality circles and other forms of group work.

The fifth task is to review, revamp and rejuvenate the existing people management systems, and the HRD manager has a significant role to play. The systems may include reward systems, in centre schemes, reporting relationships and organizational structures, promotion policies, transfer policies, rotation systems, training policies etc. They all need to be made more dynamic, effective and in tune with the changing situation. Organisational restructuring, to create a responsive and entrepreneurial organization is an important task.

These five roles, of HRD managers are critical in the new environment, these require the HRD manager to also develop people to be internal and external customer oriented, highly responsive, cost conscious, technology driven and entrepreneurial. Training, performance appraisal and OD interventions seem to emerge as the three important system HRD managers have.

Training could be enlarged to include education activities and focused to develop new skills at all levels to meet the new challenges. Appraisal system should be refocused on the new attitudes and competencies needed to perform new roles as well as to help people understand the new roles and tasks they are to perform. OD interventions should focus on evolving new structures and culture that make the corporation competitive and customer responsive.

4

EXPATRIATION: THE CROSS-CULTURAL ISSUES AND DESIGN OF TRAINING FOR COPING

*Amit Pande**
*Sandeep Krishnan***

Introduction

The trend of globalization is providing opportunities for Indian firms to reach foreign markets. The business model of many upcoming industries like the information technology sector is dependent heavily on the foreign markets. This increases the need of professionals working in foreign cultural settings. The merger and acquisition activity especially the cross-border acquisitions have reached much higher levels. The trend of acquisitions is not only restricted to the new sectors like Information Technology, Telecom and Business Process Outsourcing, but core sector companies like Manufacturing (For Example: Bharat Forge acquiring Carl Dan Peddinghaus in Germany) and Mining (For Example: Sterlite group acquiring mines in Australia) have observed spurt in such activities too. The sheer size of certain deals in the range of 200-300 Million dollars (acquisition of Tetley,

* Fellow in Management, Personnel and Industrial Relations Area, IIM Ahmedabad.

** Fellow in Management, Personnel and Industrial Relations Area, IIM Ahmedabad.

UK, Flag Telecom in Bermuda) indicates global aspirations of the Indian firms. The Pharmaceutical companies have widened their reach in world market with examples like Ranbaxy and DRL having presence in many countries. The globalization dreams present a new challenge for the Indian firms; the challenge to develop competent managers who would be able to work in new environments efficiently and will act as a bridge between the parent company and its subsidiaries. The globalization will also bring new employees to the Indian firms, the ones with different origin, language and national culture adding complexities to the culture of Indian organizations. The firms thus need to develop systems and processes not only to train managers for expatriate assignments but also to handle cultural diversity. This task can be achieved by well designed cross-cultural training programs which will help employees in coping up with the stress and cultural shock while dealing with a new culture. The need for cross-cultural training will be for both: Indian expatriates and employees dealing with expatriates of other origins. The cross-cultural training will also be required for the Indian companies getting into Business Process Outsourcing as the clients belong to culturally different environments. Working effectively in cross-cultural context is becoming vital competence for aspiring managers (Harris and Kumra, 2000). The present article attempts to define the possible sources of cross-cultural differences, its impact on business practices, competencies required for the expatriates, evolution of cross-cultural training, issues to be considered while developing cross-cultural training and different ways of training the employees.

Determinants of Cultural Differences

There have been many attempts to define cultures and what differentiates them. The study by Hofstede (1981,in Hofstede, 2001) defined and differentiated between cultures on various dimensions – viz. collectivism vs. individualism, power distance, uncertainty avoidance, masculinity vs. feminism and long vs. short term orientation. The author classified a number of countries on these parameters. These parameters can be defined as:

1. Power distance: *degree of inequality in power between a less powerful individual and a more powerful one in which they belong to same social system.*
2. Masculinity vs. feminism: *refers to the distribution of emotional roles between the genders. It opposes a tough masculine to tender feminine society.*
3. Uncertainty avoidance: *is the extent to which a culture programs its members to feel either comfortable or uncomfortable in unstructured situations.*
4. Individualism vs. collectivism: *is the degree to which individuals are supposed to look after themselves or remain integrated into groups usually around the family*
5. Long term vs. short-term orientation: *refers to the extent to which a culture programs its members to accept delayed gratification of their material, social and emotional needs.*

The differences in cultural values were shown by the study of Hofstede (2001), which involves 60, plus countries where each one of them was classified on these parameters.These cultural differences may effect motivational factors, collectivism at work place, organizational structure design etc.Various studies have tried to study these differences. The difference in cultures has been associated with perceptions and paradoxes. The study by Osland and Bird (2000) lists down the paradoxes and the reasons for them. The paradoxes arise because of perceptual schemas (cultural myopia and lack of experience), theoretical limitations emic and etic studies which present one sided views of the cultures (From inside and outside the culture while ignoring the other ones.). The other reasons for misunderstandings are tendency for observers to confuse individual and group values, unresolved cultural issues, role differences and real vs. espoused values. The cultural differences and varying approaches lead to significant difference in business practices which must be recognized by the trainers and employees receiving expatriate assignment.

How do People and Practices Differ Across Cultures

The differences in cultures lead to significant differences in the way people react to a stimulus. The motivational needs of the managers and executives vary across the cultures. The motivational factors that work in India may not be relevant in China, hence the expatriates will need to understand the basic differences in the employee behavior. The production facilities of firms may be similar across all the subsidiaries but the employee behavior in these facilities may not remain the same. One of the relevant examples in this context is failure of Japanese management technique like Quality Circles in India. The study by Neelankavil, Mathur and Zhang (1999) that analyzed India, Philippines, USA and China for managerial performance and motivational factors in two different studies found different managerial values, value dimensions and comparative management. India was found closer to USA than China although the geographical distance is much lesser. For example for American managers drive and ambition were important for success which is not the case in China. These countries differ in their scores of individualism with USA (91) and china (7) and the other two falling in between. Similarly the study of motivational factors found opportunity for advancement and financial rewards to be least important while these factors were nearly very important for employees in the other countries. The study by Peters and Lipit (1978) found USA employees different from those in Latin American countries like Columbia, Peru and Chile,even within the Latin American countries there was a difference between Columbia and Peru (good pay as the highest ranked motivator) and Chile (creativity as the highest ranked motivator). The culture differences effect the managerial decisions related to performance appraisals in multicultural workplaces and decisions in international business context (Lee and Karakowsky, 2001).

Along with the business practices and values significant amount of research have been conducted in the context of cross-cultural negotiations. The cross-cultural differences in the negotiation game can be conceptualized along four basic dimensions: collectivism-individualism, power distance, communication context, and the conception of time (Cohen, 1997- as cited by Bazerman, Curhan, Moore and Valley, 2000). The time factor becomes important in the context of cross border acquisitions as people belonging to different cultures have different perceptions related to time, while in some cultures people prefer to start and finish meeting on time (Example: USA), in other people may prefer to take time of their own (Example: Latin America)(Mayfield, Mayfield, Martin, Herbig, 1997). The time factor also refers to relationship dynamics of negotiations. While in a more collectivist culture, people may prefer to develop relationships during negotiations, people in more individualistic culture like USA may not prefer to bring relationship dimension in the negotiations (Mayfield, Mayfield, Martin, Herbig, 1997). The study by Gulbrow and Herbig (1999), found that the negotiators from more collectivist culture would devote more time to non-task negotiating activities and positioning activities. Similarly the people from high power distance cultures were found to spend less time compromising and less persuasion was observed in people from more masculine culture. The analysis by George, Jones and Gonzalez (1998) lists three categories of differences which can affect the negotiator emotions, these include: individual differences (affective dispositions, experiences in previous cross-cultural negotiations), cross-cultural differences (Internalized cultural values and norms, Emotional expressions, Linguistic style) and contextual differences (Relationship between the negotiating partners, level of trust and conditions surrounding the negotiations). The norms and values related to the negotiations differ according to the culture, for example the study by Weiss and Stripp (1985, as referred to by George, Jones and Gonzalez, 1998) lists differences in the negotiations norms as: perceptions about negotiation to be strategic or synergetic, criteria for selecting the negotiator, importance given to relationship building, concern for protocol and formality etc. The way emotions are expressed in the various cultures may differ, for example the face expressions and hand gestures may convey different meanings in different culture. The study by Weber and Hsee (1998), points towards significant differences in the risk perceptions across cultures that might play an important role during business negotiations across coutries.

Impact of Dealing with a Different Culture

The cultural change leads to cultural shock (McEnery and DesHarnais, 1990), which is a mental state of stress caused by acute changes in the culture. The expatriates tend to feel lonely because all of a sudden every thing changes including the work environment, peers, processes and to an extent organizational culture and value system. The employees react by comparing the new culture to their own values and beliefs and at times are unable to accept the vast difference between the two. The process of encountering and accepting the new changes or in other words process of acculturation can be classified in four stages (Nicola, 1993)

- *Initial stage of elation and optimism*
- *Period of frustration, depression and confusion*
- *Gradual improvement of mood leading to optimism and satisfaction*
- *Mastery stage*

Oberg (1960, cited by Caligiuri et.al. (2001)) described four stages of adjustment: Stage I, the initial, or honeymoon stage; Stage II, the disillusionment, or culture shock stage; Stage III, the adjustment, or adaptation stage; and Stage IV, the mastery stage. The honeymoon stage is a period lasting less than two months. Here the employee is thrilled with the new experience. The culture shock stage occurs as the individual copes seriously with living in the new culture on a daily basis, as a lack of understanding of the culture inhibits awareness of what is appropriate, or inappropriate, behavior in the new cultural environment, resulting in confusion, frustration, tension and depression. The frustration occurs as the person begins to realize that past behaviors are inappropriate in the host culture but has not yet learned what behaviors to substitute. The adjustment stage is characterized by increased ability to adapt in the new culture; and, in the mastery stage, adjustment is about as complete as possible, and anxiety is largely gone. Rhinesmith (1970), classified reactions to a different culture in three categories that are flight, fight and adaptation. The flight here characterizes reactions like rejecting new culture and people and withdrawing from any opportunity of interacting with new people or situations that cause discomfort. The Fight is approaching new culture with hostility and term adaptation is used for people who undertake the process of understanding the difference and adjusting to the new culture.

Defining Expatriate Competencies

The expatriates need to perform the same set of functions but in a completely different environment which can cause lot of stress to the person. The cultural stress will have significant impact on various aspects of the job related behavior. Most of the expatriate failures are related lack of adjustment in new culture. Hence while defining the competencies for the expatriates human resource professionals also need to assess the soft skills of employees which will be handy in the new environment like tolerance of cultural difference, ability to adapt new culture and interpersonal relationships. The cross-cultural skills required for successful expatriate assignment can be listed broadly as (Hofstede, 2001):

- The capacity to communicate respect
- The capacity to be non judgmental
- The capacity to understand relativity of one's own knowledge and perception
- The capacity to display empathy
- The capacity to be flexible
- Tolerance for ambiguity

The focus is clearly on the soft skills and emotional maturity. The people undertaking foreign assignments must be mature and stable enough to accept the existence of cultural differences. They should also be able to understand the context of various situations and happening, which calls for objective evaluation of a situation without bringing in one's own biases and perceptions. The cross-cultural competencies can be viewed as combination of three different dimensions (Black and Mendenhall, 1990) that are self-maintenance dimension (mental health, psychological well-being, stress reduction and self confidence), relationship dimension (ability to foster relationship with the people of host nations and perceptual dimension (perceptions of host nation's culture and its social systems. Thus perceptions have been given an important role in defining competencies. Most often employees tend to make perceptions based little information they receive through the media or stories. This leads to general stereotyping causing formation of wrong notions about the host culture. The employee should instead form opinions and beliefs related to the host nation only after spending considerable amount of time over there. The events which are used to form these perceptions should be seen in depth using the back ground information like social value system, political system and cultural values. Only then a clear picture of host nation culture will emerge. The employees on expatriate assignments must be able to decode various verbal and non-verbal ways of communication used in the new culture and work in unstructured and ambiguous situations (Demers, 2002). The expatriate employees should have capabilities to deal with alienation and isolation, willingness to communicate and empathy for people of other cultures (Mendenhall and Odou, 1986). The competencies required for expatriate assignments have been classified under categories of stable and dynamic competencies in the paper by Sullivan (1999). The author has broken the dimensions proposed by Black and Mendenhall (1990) in stable and dynamic components. The components are listed in the following table:

Type of competency	*Self Maintenance*	*Relationship*	*Perceptual*
Stable	Emotional stability	Extraversion, agreeableness	Openness to experience, Conscientiousness
Dynamic	Cultural Knowledge, self maintenance and self-efficacy, stress management skill	Conflict resolution skills, Conceputal cultural knowledge	Perceptual questioning skills

Hence the employees should have the ability to question the perceptions and resolve conflicts arising out of the cultural differences. The stress management skills have been given importance because the cultural differences and lack of proper socialization along with cultural shock causes stress on the expatriates. The stress might also arise from living at a distance from the family.

Defining Cross-Cultural Training and its Objectives

The cross-cultural training in general can be defined as "Any intervention aimed at increasing an individual's capability to cope with and work in foreign environment" (Tung, 1981, in Zakaria, 2000). Hence cross-cultural training involves all the methods like lectures, simulation etc. used to make the person familiar with a different culture. The term cross-cultural training hence is broad enough to include differences in areas like language abilities, business etiquettes, beliefs and values, social system, negotiating styles etc. of any culture. The cross-cultural has also been defined as "Formal methods to prepare people for more effective interpersonal relations and job success when they interact extensively with individuals from cultures other than their own" (Brislin and Yoshida, 1994). The term job success here seems to be slightly ambiguous, as the factors defining success on an expatriate assignment can include organizational values, earning respect from peers and subordinates, technical skills, interpersonal and relationship management skills etc. The advantages from cross-cultural training have been listed as following (Zakaria, 2000: 2):

1. A means for constant switching from an automatic, home culture international management mode to a culturally adaptable and acceptable one
2. An aid to improve coping with unexpected events and cultural shock in a new culture
3. A means to reduce uncertainty of interactions with foreign nationals
4. A means for enhancing expatriates coping abilities

Hence cross-cultural training can be seen as a tool for improving the corporate culture and practices by constantly learning through induction of foreign nationals in the organizations. Further the cross-cultural training will help to reduce the psychological stress and cultural shock which often lead to failure of expatriates.

The process of expatriation - the cultural issues: A model for analysis

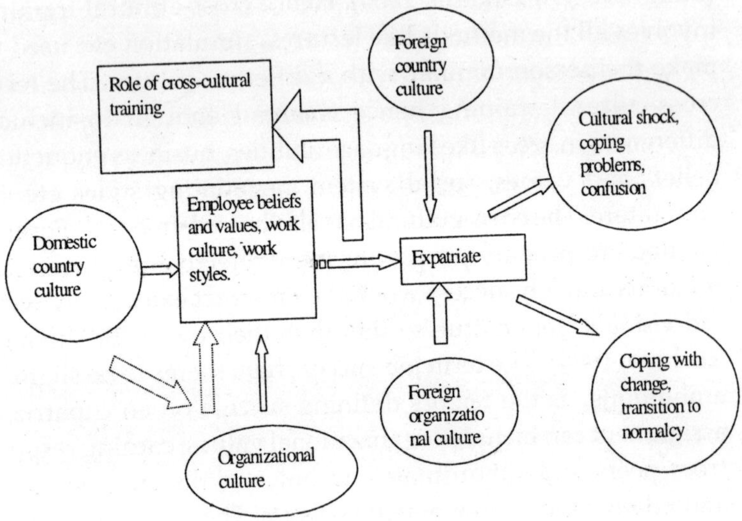

Design of cross-cultural training

The issues or focus points are very important in the cross-cultural as it is required to choose between culture specific or culture general training, which areas of the culture to focus upon and what are the personal requirements of the person who might have to deal with a situation like this or who is shifting to a different culture for work. The study by Hun and Jenkins (1998) mentions following issues for the cross-cultural training:

- Different aspects of time like punctuality- The time factor here involve two dimensions that are punctuality and relationship dimension. While in some cultures like USA starting and ending on time are very important in others like South American countries that may be considered exceptional. Some cultures prefer to take time for relationship building, which may not be acceptable at all in others. Hence cross-cultural barriers related to time need to be taken care of.

- Linguistic barriers- The English is being used for most transactions but then usage of English tends to change with the country contexts. For example the pronunciation in India is significantly different from the American way. Secondly certain terms may have different meaning in different languages; hence context also plays an important role. In case of countries with different language the expatriates must be trained in opening dialogues and discussions with the help of translators.
- Different business practices, like conduct in meeting and unstructured and open discussion. Hofstede's (2001) dimensions like power distance can play an important role in situations like conduct during the meetings. In cultures with lower power distance the employees may tend to call their bosses with their first names while this may be impossible in cultures with higher power distances. Hence developing a first hand knowledge about the practices is very important.
- Cultural stress (ambiguity and difference of perceptions)- The training should also involve methods to counter stress and to interpret situations. The expatriates will have to understand the situations on their own and then form perceptions. The training should avoid any kind of stereotyping where trainees may be lead to believe certain things about any culture. The culture may broadly explain value system of a community or country but every individual is different. Hence any individual with a pre-formed notion about the culture will be shocked to see people different from his beliefs leading to lot of confusion and stress.

- Body language and greetings- The way emotions are expressed in the various cultures may differ, for example the face expressions and hand gestures may convey different meanings in different culture.

The cross-cultural training should have components related to both general orientation and specific skill development (Harrison, 1994). The component of general orientation here consists of self assessment (dealing with change, stress management and identifying attributes) and cultural awareness (general dimensions, national values and work place incidents). The specific development on the other hand consists of knowledge acquisition (area studies, language studies and host attitudes) and skills training (case studies, area simulation and behavior modeling). Hence the training should focus on providing trainee the knowledge about national cultures and attitudes in the host country in the first phase while in second phase the trainee should be made to go through a rigorous process of handling the situations in a simulated environment. This will help the trainee to acquire hands-on experience. The paper by Nicola (1993) suggests following issues for cross-cultural training:

- Feed back
- Getting beyond culturally determined stereotypes
- How to raise and deal with cultural stereotype
- How to counsel employees
- Coaching and team building
- Resolving conflicts (those including various ethnic groups at work place)
- Counseling so as to go beyond all kinds of stereotypes and perceptions.

After the internet revolution things have vastly changed for various organizations. For example many firms use internet as a medium to coordinate between different employees working in different locations as a team like one of the team members would be in India, other one might be in Europe and third one in North America. The group dynamics in these situations becomes very important; hence the employees must also be trained at handling people from diverse cultures at the same time ensuring equal treatment and opportunities for all. One of the most important factors that is often forgotten while designing the training programs is the requirement of the employees, the design of training program should be made keeping in mind the length of stay in the host country, type of function he will have to perform, degree of socialization required by the employee and the personal characteristics of the employees (extraversion, interpersonal skills etc.). Hence cross-cultural training program should be customized for each employee to certain extend. It's not only the employee who needs to be trained; the family of employee should also be trained on certain issues like cultural differences. Many firms have started giving due importance to the training of spouse because the socialization of expatriate and job success to a large extent will depend upon socialization of his family.

The Training Methods

The cross-cultural training evolved with usage of lecture method (originated from university of Illinois- as referred by Bhawuk and Brislin, 2000). This development was followed by usage of contrast American method which was named as this method was used to train for contrasting cultural experiences. The scenarios and cultural assimilators were later additions to the methods. The self reference criterion method was developed from cultural analysis system developed in 1966. The first usage of the cultural assimilators was on the American soldiers in 1972. The existence of cultural general assimilator is relatively new with usage starting in 1986. The experiential and area simulation were developed in 70's.

The various cross-cultural training methods can be explained as follows (as described by Bhawuk and Brislin, 2000):

- *Cultural assimilator*: The cultural assimilator is a tool that consists of a number of real life scenarios describing puzzling cross-cultural interactions and expectations. The scenarios here can be defined as critical incidents which describe interactions between host and expatriates which involve misunderstanding related to cultural differences.
- *Contrast American method:* This method involves demonstration of behaviors that are completely opposed to what is seen in the current context of culture. This was used by Stewart in America to train people going abroad hence was named contrast American.
- *Self reference criterion (SRC):* Unconscious reference to one's own cultural values in communication with people who are from other cultures. This method was developed by Lee (1966), who proposed 4 step procedure to overcome self reference criteria. The first step involves defining any problem of situation in terms of the expatriate's own culture, followed by definition in the terms of host culture. The bias created by SRC is analyzed and removed in third stage which is followed by solution of the simplified business problem.
- *Area simulation:* The simulation is creating natural situation of interaction with people from other culture. This can be achieved using some actors who will interact with the trainee according to some predefined script.
- *Cultural self awareness model:* The cultural awareness model includes usage of video tapes with themes and role plays. If the trainee is able to understand how his culture is different he would be able to accept the

differences encountered in the real life interactions in a better manner.

The study by Caligiuri et. al.,2001 refers to the study by Brislin et al(1983) outlined the frequently used cross-cultural training methodologies during early 90's: "(1) fact-oriented training; (2) attribution training, associated with the culture assimilator to enable trainees to internalize values and standards of the host culture; (3) cultural awareness training, the study of the trainee's home culture and its effect on his/her behavior to enable the trainee to understand the nature of cultural differences; (4) cognitive-behavior modification, to assist trainees to be able to obtain rewards and avoid punishment in the host culture; (5) experiential learning, active participation learning about a specific host culture; and (6) interaction learning, for trainees to feel more comfortable with host nationals and to learn details about life in the host country. Language training aids in communications demonstrate an attitude of attempting to learn about the host culture enables one to be polite and permits understanding".

The Impact of Cross-Cultural Training on the Employee Performance

Many research studies have focused on the impact of cross-cultural training on variables like adjustment and performance of the employees. The Meta analysis by Morris and Robie (2001) found the correlation of cross-cultural studies to be 0.26 for performance and 0.13 for adjustment. This has been totally opposite to the results of the earlier studies like the one by Deshpande and Vishwesveran (1992, in Morris and Robie) found the correlation with performance to be .39 and 0.43 with adjustment. The study by Morris and Robic(2001) examined 16 studies for expatriate adjustment and 25 studies for performance. The authors also cites the results of studies by Black (1988) and Earley (1987) who found the correlation to be 0.42 and 0.57 for adjustment. The correlation with performance in the same studies was 0.08 and 0.79. Hence there is lack of consistency in the results.

The study of Gullahorn and Gullahorn (1966, cited by Caligiuri et. al. 2001) "found that cross-cultural adjustment process leads to a U-shaped curve of adjustment where the bottom of the curve is the strongest point of culture shock. This U-Curve Theory of Adjustment (UCT) has been one of the most consistently used theories, a rare case of theoretical perspective applied to cross-cultural research, although no in-depth and comprehensive reviews of the empirical literature related to UCT exist". Grove and Torbiorn (1985 cited by Caligiuri et al, 2001) proposed that cross-cultural, or intercultural, training should attempt to bring about changes in three psychological constructs, 'applicability of behavior, clarity of mental frame of preference, and level of mere adequacy'. The study by Worchel and Mitche (1972, cited by Bhawuk and Brislin, 1992) found use of cultural assimilator to be effective on the American soldiers(in Greece) in enhancing there productivity, adjustment, enjoyment of tour of duty and interpersonal behavior. The literature review by Zakaria (2000) found substantial positive relationship between cross-cultural training and adjustment. He cites works of Bochnar (1982) and Backer (1984) who found cross-cultural training to be useful for cross-cultural interaction. The paper by Caligiuri et.al. (2001) suggests development of training programs that will ensure that expatriates have realistic expectations. The study by Brewster and Pickard (1994) found that cultural training was more effective for younger people and people with no prior experience. Some studies like study of American expatriates in Mexico (Edmund, 2002) did not find a significant relationship between cross-cultural training and expatriate failure rate. Similarly the study by Selmer (2001) of didn't find relationship between the pre-knowledge about culture and practices of Hong Kong and their ability to get along with their host country subordinates. In contrast the study by Eschbach, Parker and Stoeberl (2001) found cross-cultural training effective in reducing time required to adjust and achieve cultural proficiency. Hence the studies broadly support the effectiveness of cross-cultural training in improving the expatriate efficiency.

Conclusion

It is imperative that employees who are to be expatriated are well informed regarding the challenges they might face in a foreign land. Coping with a foreign culture both organizational and national needs well-planned preparation. A well structured cross-cultural training will help the employees to prepare for coping with the changes in the working styles, beliefs and values they are expected to face. A large degree of uncertainty which an employee might face while moving to a foreign land and culture can be reduced through organizational support in terms of training. The huge costs that an organization might face due to expatriate failure is of high concern. Preparing the employees for a foreign assignment is mutually beneficial to the organization and the employee. For the employees, a well delivered training can help in managing with the new situations, while for the organization this helps in getting the best of the employee in terms of work output through maintaining the employee morale and motivation. With the growing influence of foreign markets and increasing growth prospects for multinational business models, it is of high importance that companies prepare their employees to be fit for global assignments.

REFERENCES

Bazerman, M.H., Curhan, J.R.,Moore, D.A., & Valley K.L.(2000). Negotiation. *Annual Review of Psychology*, 51 (1): 279-314

Bhawuk, D. P. S. (1996). Development of a Culture Theory-Based Assimilator: Application of Individualism and Collectivism in

Cross-Cultural Training. *Academy of Management Proceedings,* 147-151

Bhawuk, D. P. S., & Brislin, R. W. (2000). Cross-cultural Training: A Review. *Applied Psychology,* 49 (1): 161-192

Black, J.S., & Mendenhall, M. (1990). Cross-Cultural Training Effectiveness A Review and a Theoretical Framework for Future research. *Academy of management Review,* 15 (1): 113-136

Brewester, C., & Pickard, J. (1994). Evaluation of Expatriate Training. International *Journal of Management and Organization,* 24(3): 18-35

Brislin, R. & Yoshida, T. (1994). *Intercultural Communication Training: An Introduction.* Thousands Oaks: Sage publication

Caligiuri, P., Phillips, J., Lazarova, M., Tarique, I., & Burgi, P. (2001). The Theory Of Met Expectations Applied To Expatriate Adjustment: The Role Of Cross-cultural Training. *International Journal of Human Resource Management,* 12 (3): 357-373

Demers, J. (2002). Crossing the Cultural Divides. *CMA Management,* 76 (6): 27-30

Edmund, S. (2002). Exploring the Success of Expatriates of U.S. Multinational Firms in Mexico. *The International Trade Journal,* 13 (3): 233-257.

Eschbach, D. M., Parker, G. E., & Stoeberl, P. A. (2001). American Repatriate Employees' Retrospective Assessments of the Effects of Cross-Cultural Training on Their Adaptation to International Assignments. *International Journal of Human Resource Management,* 12 (2): 270-288

George, J.M., Jones, G.R., & Gonzalez, J.A. (1998). The Role of Affect in Cross-Cultural Negotiations. *Journal of International Business studies,* 29 (4): 749-72.

Gulbrow, R.D., & Herbig, P. (1999). Cultural Differences Encountered By the Firms When Negotiating Internationally. *Industrial Management and data systems,* 99 (2): 47-53

Harris, H., & Kumra, S. (2000). International Manager Development. *Journal of Management Development,* 19 (7): 602-615.

Harrison, J.K. (1994). Developing Successful Expatriate Managers: A Framework for the Structural Design and Strategic Alignment of Cross-Cultural Training Programs. *Human Resource Planning,* 17 (3): 17-37.

Hofstede, G.S (2001). *Culture's Consequences: Comparing Values, Behaviors, Institutions and Organizations Across Countries*, 2nd edn, Thousand Oaks: Sage publications

Hun, B. J., & Jenkins, M. (2000). International Peer Group Development. *Industrial & Commercial Training*, 32 (4): 128-132

Lee, J., & Karakowsky, L. (2001). Do We See Eye-to-Eye? Implications of Cultural Differences for Cross-cultural Management Practices and Research. *The Journal of Psychology*, 135 (5): 501-517

Mayfield, M., Mayfield, J., Martin, D., & Herbig, P. (1997). Time Perspectives of Cross-Cultural Negotiation Process. *American Business Review*, 15 (1): 78-86.

McEnery, J., & DesHarnais, G. (1990). Culture Shock. *Training & Development Journal*, 44 (4): 43-48

Mendenhall, M., & Odou, G. (1986). Acculturation Profiles of Expatriate Managers: Implications for Cross-cultural Training Programs. *Columbia Journal Of World Business*, 21 (4): 73-80

.Morris, M. A., & Robie, C. (2001).A Meta-Analysis of the Effects of Cross-Cultural Training on Expatriate Performance and Adjustment. *International Journal of Training & Development*, 5 (2): 112-126.

Neelankavil, J.P., Mathur, A., & Zhang, Y. (1999). Determinants of Managerial Performance: A Cross-Cultural Comparison of the Perceptions of Middle Managers in Four Countries. *Journal of International Business Studies*, 31 (1): 121-140.

Nicola, P. (1993). Spotlight. *Journal of European Industrial Training*, 17 (2): 1-4

Osland, J. S., & Bird, A. (2000). Beyond Sophisticated Stereotyping: Cultural Sensemaking In Context. *Academy of Management Executive*, 14 (1): 65-80

Peters, E. B., & Lippitt, G. L (1978). The Use of Instruments in International Training. *Journal of European Industrial Training*, 2 (7): 24-26.

Rhinesmith, S.H. (1970). Training for Cross-cultural Operations. *Training and Development Journal*, 24 (3): 20-25

Selmer, J. (2001). Antecedents of Expatriate/Local Relationships: Pre-Knowledge vs. Socialization Tactics. *International Journal of Human Resource Management*, 12 (6): 916-925.

Sullivan, S. L. (1999). The Distinction between Stable and Dynamic Cross-Cultural Competencies: Implications for Expatriate

Trainability. *Journal of International Business Studies*, 30 (4): 709-725.

Weber, E.U., & Hsee, C. (1998). Cross-cultural Differences in Risk Perceptions. *Management Science*, 44 (9): 1205-1218.

Zakaria, N. (2000). The Effects of Cross-Cultural Training on the Acculturation Process of the Global Workforce. *International Journal of Manpower*, 21 (6): 492-511.

5

UNDERSTANDING MANAGEMENT DEVELOPMENT AND LEARNING BEYOND THE WESTERN CONTEXT: THE CASE OF A SMALL CHINESE BUSINESS FIRM

*Paul Hill, X-Jian Wu and Jim Grieves**

Introduction

This research attempts to understand the relationship between cognitive/cultural elements and learning/application of management ideas. The research seeks to address, in particular, the acquisition of knowledge in relation to the management of employee commitment and performance. Furthermore, we attempt to investigate the extent to which organisational commitment and performance, as understood in the West, flow naturally across geographical boundaries with different political, cultural and ideological perspectives.

Phrases such as globalisation or the global village often give the impression that the industrial world of contemporary capitalism is developing, if not in the same way, then at least through the same concepts of management and entrepreneurial development. This is partly due to the development of modern

* Paul Hill, X-Jian Wu and Jim Grieves work at Newcastle Business School, Northumbria University.

communication technologies and particularly because of the spread of the Internet and World Wide Web. It is often assumed for example, as in the work of Davenport and Prozac (1998), that spontaneous transfer of knowledge take place as a matter of routine across organisational boundaries. Such work is reinforced by more recent research arguing "for example, when an employee from a subsidiary of a global corporation located in Korea, such as IBM, seeks pertinent information and knowledge on how to design a business plan from a colleague in the US headquarters, a transfer of knowledge across national borders occurs." (Bhagat et al, 2002: 204). However, Bhagat et al suggest, the transfer of knowledge is itself moderated by "the nature of transacting cultural patterns and the cognitive styles of the individuals" (Bhagat et al, 2002: 205). Consequently, the implication for management learning could be significant when considered at a cross cultural level.

At an organisational level, it is important to know the extent to which the management team are able to embrace change initiatives or other challenging management issues and ideas. They also need to know the extent to which management values and corporate culture could displace possible tensions as they come into contact with ideas that are not indigenous, such as knowledge from the West to the Eastern managers. Therefore, we are interested in understanding the way in which Western management ideas about performance and commitment are conceived, mediated and implemented in the context of Chinese organisations.

We explore the issues through an in-depth case study within a small Chinese business firm. In doing so we seek to ascertain and determine how the learning process has been shaped or outlined. In order to do this we investigate and explain in particular:

- the way the cognitive frameworks of managers are related to learning and managing employee performance and commitment.
- the extent to which Chinese assumptions of management knowledge and learning acts as either the mediator or inhibitor of ideas originated from the West.

This paper as such is structured in the following way. The next section outlines the theoretical ground on which our conceptualisation on knowledge absorption and management learning is oriented. Section three considers methodology whilst section four provides an account on an action research project in a Chinese business firm. Key findings and their implications for considering management learning and embracing knowledge from the West to the East in general is discussed and discoursed in the final section.

How Effective is Acquiring Management Knowledge Against Culture Diversity?

It is often assumed for example, as in the work of Davenport and Prozac (1998), that spontaneous transfer of management knowledge takes place as a matter of routine across organisational boundaries. Understanding the process of acquiring and accommodating knowledge from other cultural contexts is more of a problem than often suggested by the literature. For example, researchers and practitioners have taken various approaches that include the management of information approach and the management of people approach which seeks to assess, change and improve human skills (Fernandes and Raja, 2002). In this latter approach, individuals and social groups are investigated for their behavioural characteristics such as motivational dispositions, personality, and by territorial protection. In addition, the absorptive capacity (Lindsay et al, 2003) of recipients of knowledge will also be influenced by their shared values and characteristics. Where these are mediated by ideological or cultural differences then the communication processes implicated in the learning are likely to be influenced by very different cognitive outlooks of the organisational world as well as that of the individual managers.

The outcomes of management learning and competency development represent the critical competences of a firm's competitiveness (Hamel and Prahalad, 1989). In attempting to understand how effectively management knowledge has been acquired and accommodated across cultural boundaries, we need to establish whether the recipient of knowledge is able to interpret the knowledge presented, or in others words, has management learnt as expected and in the manner defined.

The interaction of Western and non-Western approaches to managerial work has been cited by various authors who wish to draw attention to issues that problematises the exchange or export of management ideas from one cultural domain to another. In China, for example, the proliferation of international joint ventures (JVs) should be seen in a political context (Wong et al, 2003) and a cultural context (Berrell et al, 2001). As Berrell et al, (2001) have pointed out, "the results of many commercial and non-profit collaborations between Western and Chinese partners have been uneven ...with negative outcomes attributed to a combination of operational, infrastructure, financial and knowledge factors" (Berrell et al, 2001: 28). Moreover, they indicate that "there are causal relationships between ideas about managerial work and culture" (Berrell, Wrathall & Wright, 2001: 28). Such research queries the extent to which Western management knowledge is easily transferable to or to be embraced in a non-Western setting.

Differences in worldviews of Chinese and Western managers indicate that Chinese workers value collectivism

(Hofstede, 1994), harmony and particularism (Mead, 1994) This can be contrasted with Western ideas about universalism and individualism whereby tolerance for ambiguity is less accepted (Trompenaars, 1993). Whereas the Western preference for personal achievement and development is seen as the source of motivation and performance the Chinese managers in emphasizing harmony attempt to reinforce the status quo. In this regard, Chinese mangers learning Western management concepts could embrace that in either way, to strengthening individual achievement and consolidating the outcome as Westerners do, or to leverage that for the interests of the whole organisation.

As asserted by Berrell et al (2001), focussing on the concepts of particularism and collectivism means that Chinese managers resist participative styles of management and leadership shown by western managers (Berrell et al 2001:30). They argue that the collective nature of Chinese society and the benevolent behaviour of the family predispose Chinese employees to view the workplace as akin to the family. Western ideas concerning individualism will support more participative styles of management and leadership whereas, given the influence of culture, Chinese managers could be more inclined to discard knowledge about participative styles of management and leadership, for example. Nonetheless, it is less clear from current literature what specific factors would push Chinese managers to go to the first way, while others make them more likely to go for the second.

Research Design and Method

Recognizing the complexity and potential confusion involved in the process of transferring management ideas or initiatives across national or language barriers, mostly in theoretical terms though, we consider it an illuminating experience to identify a practical issue of interests and closely examine the ramifications of being transferred or translated across other boundaries. How to effectively promote employee commitment via performance management has been a hotly debated issue in HRD literature in recent years and also caught the attention of Chinese business people because of the latter's growing ambition and prolific plans. Therefore, it would be a rewarding research experience to investigate how Western originated management ideas, as revealed in the employee commitment and performance research literature, have been introduced to the Chinese managers and what are the possible facilitating and prohibiting elements influencing their apprehension and application of such ideas or initiatives.

In this research, we rely on a single interpretive case study to gather relevant research material to understand the issue of cross border knowledge transfer. The case study approach has been conceived and conducted mostly in the tradition of qualitative ethnographic and sociological studies (Tellis, 1997: 2-3). It is the kind of method that tries to incorporate, consistently and consciously, the viewpoint of the "actors" in the case organisation. The first criterion of conducting a case study in this regard has been suggested to be the maximisation of what one can learn from the case (Stake, 1995:4-5). Yin's (1989: 23) conceptualisation of the case study as "an empirical inquiry that investigates a contemporary phenomenon within its real-life context when the boundaries between phenomenon and context are clearly evident, and in which multiple sources of evidence are used", although positions himself more towards a positivistic position, could fit into various research paradigms including interpretative investigation as our research intends, and accordingly provides the parameters of a good case study.

The case organisation facilitates a good understanding of the problem situation. The outcome of this case analysis is consequently one of the authors' narrative description and interpretation of the informant's experiences. One of the authors has for this purpose visited China on two occasions since 2002 and a brief account of the research background as well as preliminary findings is presented in the next section.

The Case of Kaihua: A Management Learning Experience in China

Background Introduction

Kaihua Bio-product & Service Ltd (KBS) is a small family owned business firm in Beijing, China, currently with 35 employees. Its business is to exclusively promote and sell "Meifeng Lotion", an immunization-enhancing drug targeting the Hepatitis B (HpB) carriers and patients within China. The managing director, Sam Zhu, founded this firm in 1993 to explore the market with this drug, invented and patented by his father in the previous year, which has promising and proved effects for Hepatitis B patients in improving their body immunization system, speeding up recovery time. In light of the huge population size of HpB patients in China, amounting to 22 million in the early 1990s with no signs of receding in the near future, Sam wasn't content with only licensing the drug to a local pharmaceutical manufacturing company as his Father had done for royalties and fees and gave up his own job in Beijing to start Kaihua to develop more substantial licensing arrangements.

For the first couple of years, Sam developed and managed KBS alone; mainly as a sales representative of "Meifeng Lotion" in Beijing for the licensed manufacturing company from Fuzhou in Southern China. Sam had mainly though his personal efforts established good working relations with the drug-dispensing network in some major hospitals in Beijing and via this network to provide the drug to patients. This was the main if not the only sales channel in urban China as retail sales of the product were minimal. It was apparent soon that to develop new contacts and maintain good relationships with key personnel in this network he had to expand employment to increase sales and promote more contacts. He therefore increased the numbers of sales assistants through direct invitation or recruitment, and by 1996, the firm had 10 staff with a sales' revenue of 5 million RMB.

Over the next 5 years, these same 10 staff worked with Sam to strengthen and expand contacts with the hospital dispensation network in Beijing. Sales, however only increased to 8 million RMB by 2001, not considered to be a large enough increase. Causes over this period for this could have been various market disturbances, some severely hitting small firms like KBS. Sam's employees were paid at an above average salary level and a result of this was the retention of all of his 10 employees through the economic downturn in the industry. All of Sam's sales staff had made a direct contribution to the sales revenue through his or her contact and maintenance work within the hospital network.

In 2002, Sam's personal and business life changed dramatically by marrying a former employee of Arthur Anderson in China and invited his new wife to join KBS looking after internal affairs. As a result of her participation and more importantly because of her ways of doing business, all 9 of the other employees were either sacked from or left KBS voluntarily within a very short period of his wife joining the organization.

KBS, by the end of 2003 had achieved a sales revenue of just over 20 million RMB, and had a 35-member workforce, predominantly recruited on short term contracts. Salary levels had seen a huge decrease to 20% of that of the original sales force.

Learning and Managing Employee Performance and Commitment in KBS

The following observations of Sam's experiences of learning and development as a manager were made by one of the authors of this paper based on the understanding of the case organisation resulting from his a personal relationship with Sam as both a long time personal friend and a business client. Some empirical findings were uncovered and reported through that author's last two field visits to KBS in 2002.

Learning in the early days- Despite having a big physical stature and a degree in 'Athletics and Body Training' in Beijing, Sam is known by others for his nice personality, quick thinking, 'openness' to new ideas and commitment. Shortly after setting up KBS in 1993, he invited one of the authors to advise him on organisational learning and performance management issues since this author had been a close friend of his and at the time, was teaching in a Business school in China on organisational analysis and performance management. For nearly a decade, they were very close in this respect and the author had advised Sam on contemporary western management thinking and practices relating to business, employee management and organisational study. Introductions to other Business School staff had helped provide Sam with other informal and 'consultancy' style advice. Therefore, even though Sam has never been formally educated in business or participated in any management development programme, he had over the years developed sufficient understanding through his relationship with the author, through actively socialising with other management scholars and experts, as well as his extensive private reading of traditional Chinese management texts together with 'bestsellers' in China from Harvard business professors.

Sam was particularly interested in exploring the ways of "managing people" by winning their souls and commitment, as he himself is a kind of person who likes to put emotional feelings ahead of effectiveness in the workplace. Sam, in the first round of sales staff recruitment had been very careful to identify and recruit appropriate associates and assistants, to reflect the above thoughts, to recruit committed staff to the firm. Since KBS relies heavily on the quality of personal contacts (nods) with various sectors in the hospital network systems in Beijing, it is very important for Sam to entrust his new recruits as good sources to maintain as high a standard of service as possible for existing or potential corporate customers. Sam in this regard perceived personal bond and commitment as the number one element for sustaining his company in a highly competitive business environment. Much influenced by some traditional Chinese writings on people management tactics, as well as contemporary western writings on organisation study, Sam developed KBS as a kind of family where all associates would be equally rewarded for their membership and with all employees being aware of each other's contributions in order to generate trust and transparency.

Managing commitment and performance in KBS- Sam believed that his father's invention could have a significant impact on the welfare of those HpB patients and what KBS should do is not just sell a product for profits, but also promote a kind of new knowledge and awareness about healthy ways of living and immunization enhancement. The staff Sam selected for KBS were mostly graduates from medical schools or business schools with sufficient professional understanding of their business conducts and well qualified in promoting this cause. KBS relied on their experience and expertise in effective liaison with the hospital network system to convey to or convince others of what "Meifeng Lotion" can and will do for its customers. The interaction involved combined elements of sales, publicity and consultancy and therefore provided a relationship which combined sales and advice. In return for his staff's contribution and commitment to this, he made all of them associates, sharing the profits and gains for their efforts. The relationship involved detailed business and financial knowledge of the transactions that they were generating with the hospital network which had good effect on employee satisfaction and commitment over the period 1996 to 2001, which as previously mentioned had witnessed turbulent changes in this highly competitive market and dramatic changes in government regulations. Sam was very happy with the relationship with his staff, which he thought was reciprocated, evidenced by good levels of satisfaction amongst the employees. He attributed such harmony to his understanding of how to treat other people and motivate them to work for a 'good cause' rather than just as salesmen working for a living. There was no clearly defined rules or steps to manage or monitor the performance of this small but 'closely-knitted' workforce, but Sam regarded all members as hard working and had contributed their best, since in Sam's words "we are friends working for each other, and one could benefit from others success or suffer together with others; so there is no reason for not contributing 'your best'". Even though the sales revenue for KBS only achieved 8 million RMB by the end of 2001, an average performance figure in the industry, both Sam and his associates were content with both the business itself, and the way KBS was organised and managed.

Learning in the new era - things in KBS changed in 2001 soon after Sam invited his newly wedded wife, Sally, to quit from her job at one of Arthur Anderson's Chinese subsidiary businesses and join in to help him in promoting the business of KBS. Firstly, Sally considered that KBS was not fully stretched, and had thus far overlooked a large customer group in rural China who couldn't afford to get access to the hospital system operating only in urban areas. She suggested to Sam a kind of shift in business strategy resulting in the restructuring of KBS in terms of: staff job definition, individual performance targets and performance appraisal linked to remuneration. The direct impact of such a change was to place less emphasis on the importance of an employee's expertise and experience of serving the hospital network systems and to explore and increase speed of supplies to rural areas at lower cost. The changes were opposed strongly by Sam's existing staff, and they considered that Sally didn't understand the unique business market served by KBS, and more importantly, Sally hadn't appreciated the special 'bonding' and understanding that all existing members, including Sam, had achieved since inception. Confronted with the dilemma of following his 'strongly willed' wife's suggestions, or accommodating resistance from his long serving workforce, Sam resigned to side with the former, out of the consideration that " I have to have a family in peace first, and besides to try something new as well". This resulted in a furious and undignified staff response and over a period of a month they all left the firm either voluntarily or were sacked by Sam at the request of Sally. At one point, KBS only had the couple themselves together with a number of casual workers.

However, Sam's feeling of unease resulting from removing his long term associates receded upon realising how effective Sally's policy had worked with the low cost casual workers and the firm's much improved performance. With those 'diploma level' short-term contracted employees, KBS has pushed them hard enough to achieve well defined and clearly communicated business objectives. As a result, by the end of 2002, at a staff cost similar to maintaining the previous team, KBS was able to recruit 35 employees, and fulfilled a sales figure of around 21 million RMB. A recent staff survey conducted by the author found that the majority of them were happy with working in KBS and no undue pressure had been reported. Sam was impressed and commented that he had learned much more in the last year about staff commitment and performance management than what he had understood in the previous decade. He attributed all this to his wife and her experience in the American subsidiary company. Though the long term implications of such change for KBS remains unknown, Sam is confident that he has more or less found an alternative pathway to manage both his business and his staff

Discussion and Conclusion

Through the narrative account outlined above relating to the learning experiences of Sam in KBS it is possible to identify a number of distinct features characterizing managerial learning and development practices in China to inform the discussion on management development or knowledge transfer across national boundaries. We argue that this short case could offer some specific viewpoints for discussing issues relating to the acceptance and application of western originated management thinking, and its interactions with unique cultural features as well as the cognitive systems of entrepreneurs like Sam in China.

Cognitive framework and management learning - A useful concept in the discussion on management development and learning is the cognitive maps of managers. This concept is important because a number of authors have "observed that in the West there is a predominant tendency to locate a causality of behaviour in the individual whilst in the East, particularly in East Asia, the predominant tendency is to locate causality in the whole context of behaviour"(Bhagat et al, 2002: 215). The holistic perception refers to the tendency to analyse the entire information system rather than to bits of information one piece at a time, as mostly noticeably displayed by managers from China or Japan (Maruyama, 1984). This corresponds with the Chinese preference for particularism by contrast to the British or Western preference for universalism as discussed earlier.

Sam's early learning experiences as a manager was featured mostly by his business ambition as well as his good awareness of the complicated problem situation in a holistic sense which itself presented a rich picture for interpretations. Rather than following any particular or dominating perspective in defining or understanding his business and that of his staff, as many business school trained managers would like to do, Sam had actually unwittingly embraced a conceptual model grounded in various "root definitions". What Sam had perceived as important were the diverse opinions and viewpoints that have to be considered in operating KBS. Issues or items captured in this cognitive framework include the position of key players in the hospital network system: do they endorse or at least experiment with his products? What are the governmental expectations from the drugs market as well as the drugs companies, given that the medical system in China needed to be improved on many fronts? What is at stake for those associates and assistants in KBS in light of the heavy competition and the small size of the business? The necessity or imperative for exploring all those varied, if not contradictory, views or perspectives had driven Sam to learn extensively at the early stage of his management career about how the market operates, government positions and propositions for change, etc, not in terms of the exact answer, but for what lay behind the responses and reactions. Therefore, when Sally joined KBS and suggested a strategic and structural change, Sam was quick to appreciate its necessity in spite of his initial unease, since his cognitive framework had been 'tuned' towards reflecting the integrative effects of various elements, including his wife's motivations for change and China's re-entry into the World Trade Organisation in early 2001 and its impact on national policy regarding the drugs market. The way in which Sam explored and experienced various management ideas and initiatives was in general supported consistently by his open-ended and all-embracing cognitive stance. Another example in this regard was that KBS had started operating a 'call centre' business model, tried and approved by Sam after being introduced to the idea two years previously when one of the author's advised him of such practices from the UK. Whereas it is less clear whether Sam's cognitive framework was shaped largely by his own personality, or by the way he accessed and learned management knowledge, as in his own words "very few people operate business like I do in KBS before 2001, and this could be I am a different type of businessman".

Nonetheless, it is reasonable to suggest that the cognitive approach (Kim, 1993) for management learning as implicated in Sam's experience was actually jointly defined by the business nature of his firm; the unique features of his customers and the general business environment which was and are always subject to changes in government regulations. The conceptual framework underpinning Sam's learning and managing interests has been drawn by political, ideological, cultural and personal features, and the resulting cognitive map had significant impacts on the learning ability and appetites of many entrepreneurs in China.

Cultural features and management development. - As a business firm, pre-2001 KBS was quite unique in terms of its corporate culture, especially for its management-employee relationship, and the way it serves the market. One reason could be that because of Sam's overindulgence in following the advice and consultancy of business school scholars, thus championing 'ideals' and experimenting with some contemporary management 'fads and fashions', rather than considering and conducting business pragmatically. What KBS displayed before 2001 was a system, co-developed by Sam and one of the authors, based on key Western management ideas like participatory management, flat organizational structure and emerged strategy. Though Sam learned about and subsequently designed and developed a corporate culture he liked and related to, and put it into practice with some success together with his nine original employees, he had underestimated the business context in which he operated, and underplayed the cultural context in which those Western-originated organizational concepts are exposed. However, overlooking cultural roots or assumptions in a business environment has been regarded widely as debilitating for business development, and practical cases or recommendations have been well documented in this regard (Chow et al, 2000; Mason, 2003). One key problem raised in KBS was that power attached to property ownership (i.e. Sam's power as the owner) has been consciously suppressed and the artificially created club-culture (Handy, 1988) was not well adapted and particularly effective for competing in the current Chinese business context, as revealed in its average financial performance. However the Power distance, (Hofstede, 1980, Hofstede & Bond, 1987) restored by Sally was an important feature in Chinese organizational life, and tampering with that in management learning could easily backfire. Sam's reflective learning on this was that " I initially did not pay too much attention, neither do I want, to how conventional business organisations have been run, since I want to create that bear my own features and still be effective. Now, with Sally's help, I've realised that one can not afford to be blind to the reality, why do I make an enemy of myself by fighting the tradition and culture rather than follow the rule?" He obviously was referring to former practices of equality of pay, participative decision making and collective identify in KBS, (in contrast to what the current low cost, highly structured employees' achievement).

Two distinctive culturally rooted issues could be identified from KBS's case relating to management learning and organisational development. Firstly, the overriding influences of power for family members; in this case, Sally's insistence on change, in private businesses in China with respect to management development and organisational learning. Though family owned businesses throughout the world demonstrate certain common features, the special consideration attached to the requirements of family members was quite apparent in Chinese small business firms. This might be the result of the traditional values on filial piety that made family members aware of the implications of one's concerns for others. Another issue is about how individual staff are treated and valued. In a cultural environment featuring collectivism like China, individuals can all be held either accountable for collective 'fate' as commonly expected, or be 'pushed' to concern only that of his or her business, and be strictly checked and monitored in that respect. This interesting contrast was exemplified in KBS after 2002 in terms of its 'hire and fire' practice and 'down to earth' management control style, brought in by Sally's experience of working in an American business subsidiary. This, to some extent resembles the claim that Taylor's 'time and motion' study in scientific management was mostly advocated not in a capitalist society like USA or UK, but in communist countries in the former Soviet Union. In a similar vein, we suspect that promoting individual contribution and accountability could have been outlined more clearly and strictly in a collectivistic community like China, rather than in a supposedly individual society like USA.

It has been suggested that Western management knowledge has often been classified in terms of the perspectives of the individuals and that of the organizations, while the Chinese tend to view the same body of knowledge from conceptual and social viewpoints respectively. The previous discussion indicated that Sam's experience of learning and leveraging Western management knowledge has been outlined, to a good extent, by his perceptual conditions and his power-relations implicated in KBS as well. More specifically, Sam's early stage of learning had been mostly associated with management concepts like leadership style, corporate culture, employee satisfaction and commitment, customer relationship management, organizational learning etc. Later on, with Sally's participation, Sam's learning horizon changed to incorporate reflection on organizational issues such as business strategy, business environment, modeling, performance management, rewards and benefit review, and the like. However, Sam picked up those constructs in a passive manner that did not meet his active quest for understanding and knowledge.

The Management learning process therefore required extensive power brokering between Sam and Sally, within and beyond KBS. Those constructs and the learning process are summarized in Table 1. In order make sense of Western concepts through his reading of Chinese versions of USA management texts he had to engage in informal discussion or consultation.

TABLE 1

Management learning process in KBS

	Content of Learning	*Conduct of Learning*	*Context of Learning*
Key Western management concept and constructs involved	*leadership style, corporate culture, employee satisfaction & commitment, customer relationship management, organizational learning*	Learning via Consultation Evolution Conceptuatlisation	Staff satisfaction and commitment, collectively-shaped identity Single decision power
	business strategy, business environment,	Learning via Negotiation	Clear business objective
	modeling, performance management, rewards benefit review	Experimentation Creation	A strong change agent Multiple decision powers
Sam's learning experi-ences	Individual-oriented	Cognitive Experiential	Strating biz Sustaining biz
	Organisation-	Experimental	Strengthening biz

Sam's passive acquisition of management concepts related to organizational commitment and performance management in KBS meant that he had to recontextualise the concepts.

The acquisition of Western knowledge was not a straight transfer process. This experience suggests that we do not really understand what happens when knowledge is transferred from one culture to another. We must therefore move away from the assumption that knowledge passed on from one individual to another without significant mediation, or knowledge from individuals could be extended to that at organizational level. For example, the concept of leadership from a western perspective is infused with individual images and historiographies of "great men" whereas in China the concept of leadership is mediated by political ideology and regulated by collectivist relationships, as illustrated by the previous harmonized relationship between Sam and Sally.

This was partly resulted from that Chinese managers contemplate development or management learning against a cognitive dimension as well as social-political dimension, rather than consider it at individual or organizational level as most Westerners do. For example, Sam's initial understanding and efforts in creating a committed workforce was grounded on his personal beliefs and cognitive framework that has been shaped out in his bid for sustaining KBS. While once Sally's proposal prevailed, KBS was changed to, with Sam's endorsement, a social-political arena whereby economic and political considerations had override cognitive framework, management learning thus became a process strengthening or promoting any particular objective instead of an approach broadening individual or organizational horizon.

There are some issues left unanswered by this case that deserve further attention and discussion. For example, in respect of Sally's experience at the Arthur Anderson subsidiary in Beijing, to what extent has Sally's proposal for organisational change and development been grounded on her understanding of American-made management thinking? Was Sally's learning experience qualitatively different from that of Sam's, even though they both have made references to Western management ideas. In light of the limited contribution that an interpretative case study like this one could offer in promoting understanding of management learning, it is desirable to explore other research designs for better insights and more comprehensive ideas. In many aspects, the issue of considering management learning and development across national boundaries is inherently problematic and challenging, thus rendering it an arena whereby research contributions from various disciplinary and cultural traditions are desirable.

REFERENCES

Ahlstrom, D., and Bruton, G.D. (2001) 'Learning From Successful Local Private Firms in China: Establishing Legitimacy', *The Academy of Management Executive*, November, 15 (4): 72-83.

Bhagat, R.S., Kedia, B.L., Harveston, P.D., and Triandis, H.C. (2002) 'Cultural Variations in the Cross-Border Transfer of Organisation Knowledge: An Integrative Framework', *The Academy of Management Review*, 27(2): 204-221.

Chow, C. W., F. Deng, & J. H.. (2000) 'The Openness of knowledge sharing within organisations: a comparative study of the United States and the People's Republic of China'. *Journal of Management Accounting Research*, 12: 65-96.

Davenport, T.H. and Prozac, L. (1998) *Working Knowledge*, Boston: Harvard Business School Press.

Fernandes, K. J. Raja, V. (2002) 'A practical knowledge transfer system: a case study' *Work Study*, 51 (3): 140-148.

Hamel, G., Prahalad, C, 1989, 'Strategic intent', *Harvard Business Review*, 66(3): 63-76.

Hofstede, G. & M. H. Bond. (1987) 'The Confucius Connection: from cultural roots to economic growth', *Organisational Dynamics*.

Hofstede, G. (1980) *Culture's Consequences: International differences in work-related values*, Beverly Hills, CA: Sage Publications.

Kim, D H. (1993) The Link Between Individual and Organizational Learning. *Sloan Management Review*, Fall: 37-50.

Leonard, D, (1995) *Wellsprings of Knowledge: Building and Sustaining the source of Innovation*, Boston: Harvard Business School Press.

Lindsay, V. Chadee, D. Mattsson, J. Johnston, R., Millett, B. (2003) 'Relationships, the role of individuals and knowledge flows in the internationalisation of service firms', *International Journal of Service Industry Management*, 14(1):7-35.

Maruyama, M. (1984) 'Alternative concepts of management: insights from Asia and Africa'. *Asia Pacific Journal of Management*, January: 100-11.

Mason, R. (2003) 'Culture-Free or Culture-Bound? a boundary spanning perspective on learning in knowledge management system', *Journal of Global Information Management*, 11(4): 20-36.

Mead, R. (1994) *International Management: Cross Cultural Dimensions*, Oxford: Blackwell.

Stake, R. E. (1995) *The Art of Case Study Research*, Thousand Oaks: Sage.

Tellis, W. (1997) Introduction to Case study (68 paragraphs). The Qualitative Report (online serial) Vol.3 No.2. Available online from http://www.nova.edu/ssss/QR/QR3-2/tellis.html (accessed 22/08/2000).

Trompenaars, F. (1993) *Riding the Waves of Culture: Understanding Cultural Diversity in Business*, London: The Economist Books.

Wong. Y.Y., Maher, T.E., Nicholson, J.D., Bai, A.F. (2003) 'Organisational learning and the risks of technology transfers in China', *Management Research News*, 26(12), 1-11.

Yin, R. K. (1989) *Case Study Research: Design and Methods* Vol.5 Applied Social Research Methods Series, Newbury Park: Sage.

6

DO SMART PEOPLE FIND IT DIFFICULT TO LEARN ?

*Aquil Busrai**

I know a very large multi-national organisation that has a collection of some of the finest managers. These managers, bright as they are, often have a smirk on their faces in a training class. The general thought running through their mind is something like " I have an impressive academic track record, I work in a most challenging environment, I deliver and I am successful " – so what's there for me to learn from this ?

I also know another multi-national, not so large. Taking a training session with their management team is a pleasure. The class is like a bunch of school children. Eager to learn from each other and absorb any and all new ideas and concepts. These managers are, by no means less successful than their counter-parts in the earlier organisation that I quoted as an example.

The first set of managers suffers from, what I term as, intellectual arrogance. The second set of managers is embodying the spirit of a learning organisation.

---

* Director HR, Shell Malaysia, Malaysia and, Managing Director, Shell People Services Asia Sdn Bhd. He is based in Kuala Lumpur, Malaysia.

Any organisation aspiring to succeed in the ever-increasing competitive market place must first resolve a basic dilemma : success in the market place increasingly depends on learning; yet, most people do not know how to learn. What is more perplexing is that those members of the organisation that many assume to be best at learning are, in fact, not very good at it. I am referring to the well-educated, high-powered high-commitment professionals who occupy key leadership positions in the management hierarchy. Most organisations not only have tremendous difficulty in addressing this dilemma of learning; some are not even aware that it exists in their own organisation. The reason: they misunderstand the concept of learning. Consequently, these organisations tend to make two mistakes in their effort to become a learning organisation.

First, most people define learning too narrowly as mere "problem solving". The focus, therefore, is on identifying and correcting errors. Solving problem is important. But if learning is to be institutionalised then managers need to critically examine their own behaviour, identify the ways they often inadvertently contribute to the organisation's problems and then change how they act.

I recollect Chris Argyris propounding the theory of "single loop" and "double loop" learning. He gave an analogy of a thermostat that automatically turned on the heat whenever the temperature in the room dropped below 68 degrees. He described this as an example of single-loop learning. A thermostat that could ask " Why am I set at 68 degrees?" and then explore whether or not some other temperature might more economically achieve the goal of heating the room was an example of double-loop learning.

Highly skilled professionals are frequently very good at single-loop learning. After all, they have spent much of their lives acquiring academic credentials, mastering intellectual disciplines, and applying those disciplines to solve real-life problems. Ironically, this very fact explains why these successful professionals are often so bad at double-loop learning.

The second mistake organisations make about learning is the assumption that getting people to learn is largely a matter of motivation. These organisations assume that when people have right attitude and commitment, learning automatically follows. Thus the organisations focus on re-structuring, compensation, performance reviews and the like – that are designed to create motivated and committed employees.

Effective double-loop learning is more a reflection of how people think rather than how they feel. Taking this cue, organisations can resolve the learning dilemma by expecting and encouraging their managers to question the reasoning behind their behaviour. Teaching people how to reason about their behaviour in new and more effective ways help in breaking down defenses that block learning. Only concentrating on a motivating environment may be a faulty strategy to create a learning organisation.

How does one explain this defensiveness? These professionals have a positive attitude about change and continuous improvement. They really want to work more effectively. The only disconnect is how they reason about their behaviour and that of others. These successful professionals describe themselves as driven internally by an unrealistically high ideal of performance. They toy with thoughts like "Pressure on the job is self-imposed". "I want not only to succeed but also do so at maximum speed". They are thus totally preoccupied with success.

Being successful at what they do, these professionals very seldom experience failure. They therefore, never get down to learn from failure just because they fail so seldom.

Thus when their single-loop learning strategies do not work, they become defensive and put "blame" on anyone and everyone but themselves. Consequently, their ability to learn shuts down precisely at the moment they need it the most.

They also develop a somewhat "brittle" personality. When faced with a situation that they can not immediately handle, they tend to fall apart. Such brittleness leads to a high sense of despair when people do not achieve high levels of performance they aspire to. This despondency when combined with the defensive reasoning can result in a strong predisposition against learning.

If defensive reasoning is the malaise, then focussing on an individual's attitudes or commitment is never enough to produce real change. Neither is creating new organisation structures or systems. The point is to teach people to how to reason in a new way.

How can an organisation begin to turn this situation around, to teach its managers how to reason productively ? The first step is for the top management to critically examine their own behaviour, to examine what is their espoused theory and what they really practice. If they become aware of and actually accept their defensive behaviour then only will they contribute to an ambience that leads others in the organisation to examine their own behaviour. In absence of this blessing from the top, all change activities are likely to be a mere fad.

Organisations thus have to promote a climate where open feedback becomes an accepted norm. Where questioning some one's reasoning is not seen as a sign of mistrust but a valuable opportunity to learn. Where failures are not viewed as final condemnation but a step in having learnt something new out of the experience. Where managers reason productively and not carry on a task based only on skill-sets they have learnt.

The key to any educational experience designed to teach senior management how to reason productively and non-defensively is to connect the programme to real-business problems. Once the managers realise that this reasoning makes a quantum difference to their own performance, the buy-in would be complete. This will not happen over night. Managers need plenty of opportunity to practice new skill. However, once they realise the powerful impact of productive reasoning on actual performance, they will start practicing the same, not just in a classroom but also in their real-life work relationship.

The insight that the process will produce will allow these managers to act more effectively in the future. They will not merely solve problems but develop a far deeper understanding of their role and the role of others. They will move in a direction of continuous improvement that will truly be continuous. They will learn how to learn.

7

NURTURING SOCIAL CAPITAL: THE PRINCIPAL LEVER IN DEVELOPING HRD'S CONTRIBUTION TO ORGANISATIONAL SUCCESS?

*David P Mankin**

Introduction

The aim of the paper is to argue that the future success of human resource development (HRD) lies in the ability of practitioners to develop strategies, policies, processes and practices that can nurture or cultivate social capital, rather than continue to focus on human capital only. The two forms of capital need to be developed in combination as part of a holistic HRD strategy. An underlying premise of the paper is that it is a fallacy to believe that all aspects of organisational knowledge and learning can be managed formally. Informal processes, such as social networks and communities of practice, elude formal structures and management interventions; and, heuristic knowledge, developed by individuals while carrying out their job, cannot be managed formally in the same way as other types of knowledge and information (Tsoukas & Vladimirou, 2001). As Von Krogh et al (2000) observe: "the

* Business School, Oxford Brookes University, Wheatley Campus, Wheatley, Oxon, OX33 1 HX.

term *management* implies control of processes that may be inherently uncontrollable or, at least, stifled by heavy-handed direction" (p.4).

Informal processes, which have been described as the "central nervous system" of organisations (Kracardt & Hanson, 1993: 104), are more stable than formal processes (Wenger et al, 2002) and are seen as providing a conduit for *working* knowledge to be shared within an organisation (Davenport & Prusak, 2000). Based on the findings from a study of business units of a large multinational electronics company, Tsai and Ghoshal (1998) concluded that informal social relations play an important role in creating value for an organisation. This raises challenges for the HRD practitioner. On the surface these appear to be new and perhaps more daunting than those faced in the past. But underneath the language and rhetoric they are little different; they simply require a greater degree of subtlety and sophistication, and a great deal of determination and perseverance on the part of the HRD practitioner.

Most of the literature on HRD and a great deal of that on knowledge management (KM) and organisational learning (OL) are predicated on human capital theory. Using the lens of social capital theory to analyse organisational processes provides an opportunity to better understand the relationship between HRD and KM and OL, particularly given the view that the knowledge of an organisation is socially embedded (Lam, 2000). This offers new ways of developing the role of HRD in knowledge formation and learning processes within an organisational context. Mainstream HRD literature has tended to ignore the concept of social capital until only very recently. Harrison and Kessels (2004) make some attempt to address this deficiency by arguing that "the focus of HRD investment should be on building social as well as human capital" (p.17). This is a welcome development but much more work needs to be done.

The paper posits that HRD should be used as an *umbrella* term that incorporates processes that focus on learning, knowledge, change and improved performance at individual, group, organisation and societal levels. Utilising and adapting a conceptual framework for human resource development (Mankin, 2001; 2003) it will be argued that a focus on social capital can result in an improved understanding of the relationship between individual, group and organisation. The nature of these relationships has still not been satisfactorily addressed in the literature as the lens of human capital has resulted in a focus on the individual rather than the relationships between individuals.

Although the arguments within this paper are of a conceptual nature they are seen as being relevant to both theorist and practitioner. HRD is still struggling to establish an academic identity and the credibility that goes with this (Mankin, 2003). HRD practitioners are also struggling for the status and profile associated with a mainstream, rather than downstream function (Mankin, 2003). Newell et al (2002) argue that unlike human capital, which can be possessed by many people, social capital is unique and is therefore a potential source of competitive advantage. Granted, the 'competitive advantage card' has been played before, with limited success for practitioners. The theoretical position set out in this paper can guarantee nothing for the practitioner; it can only act as a catalyst for debate. That debate may lead to something or it may not. Only time will tell.

The paper is structured in four sections. The first is a review of some of the relevant literature on human and social capital. The second explores a conceptual framework as a vehicle for better understanding the relationship between

HRD and social, as well as human capital; and for highlighting the criticality of social capital to the future role of HRD within organisations. The third makes a range of proposals on how HRD practitioners can develop social capital within the organisational setting. It must be said, though, that these ideas, and the assumptions underpinning them, are there to be 'shot at' especially given the view that there is still limited empirical evidence of the existence of HRD strategies, processes and practices within many organisations (Gibb, 2002) and "a lack of tangibility in quantifying and qualifying what constitutes HRD practice" (Gold *et al*, 2003: 451). The fourth section will summarise key points and, hopefully, act as a catalyst for further debate.

Human and Social Capital

Appreciating the value of human capital within an organisation is well established (Geroy & Venneberg, 2003). Becker (1975) popularised Schultz's (1961) human capital theory that organisation's derive economic value from employees' skills, competence, knowledge and experience. The theory assumes that both management and employee have a joint interest in investing in labour as an asset (Rainbird, 2000). It is a theory that underpins the bulk of literature on human resource management (HRM) as well as HRD and although this falls outside the scope of this paper, there is a clear need for further discussion and analysis of the relationship between HRM and social capital theory. This is because human capital theory does not consider the social processes that underpin human activity in the workplace which is somewhat ironic given that we are often described as social animals.

HRD literature has tended to focus on human capital theory in which the emphasis is on "the value employees bring to the organisation, encompassing the whole range of human abilities and potential" (Scarborough & Carter, 2000: 56) or as put more prosaically by Bertels and Savage (1998:

18) it is "the knowledge and experience in people's heads and hands". It is this perspective that allows investment in HRD processes and practices to be seen as a process that adds value to the organisation (Swanson & Holton, 2001; Harrison, 2002). Yet this has not been paralleled by an acceptance of human asset accounting as a mainstream financial process (Walton, 1999) (although it is has to be noted that the financial community has been reluctant to embrace other financial innovations, such as the cost-of-poor-quality in the late 1980s and early 1990s). The role of HRD in developing human capital has been characterised by direct training interventions, such as courses and workshops, designed to "boost quality, efficiency or marketing success, to increase technical skills or contribute to professional or managerial development" (Reynolds et al, 2002: 3). It has tended to be associated with a provider role; although clearly this is a generalisation. Ultimately, this reliance on human capital theory reflects the reality that "[a]lthough organisations are more than economic entities, they are nonetheless economic entities" (Swanson, 1998: 285). But in other ways they are more than this; they are also social institutions (Kogut & Zander, 1992); and, it is through this alternative lens that new possibilities for HRD practice can be identified.

The emergence of the concept of intellectual capital (Edvinsson & Malone, 1997) and subsequent refinements which have made the social capital aspect explicit (for instance, Scarborough & Carter, 2000), provides an opportunity to perceive HRD in new ways. Research reports published by the Chartered Institute of Personnel and Development (CIPD) have acknowledged the role that social capital plays in knowledge sharing processes (Swart et al, 2003) and in promoting learning in organisations (Stewart & Tansley, 2002). Social capital naturally builds upon human capital as it provides the opportunities to use human, and also financial, capital (Burt, 1992). It both reinforces the economic arguments underpinning HRD and facilitates a better understanding of how HRD can add value through the development of organisational knowledge and learning processes.

Social capital has been defined as "the sum of actual and potential resources within, available through, and derived from the network of relationships possessed by an individual or social unit" (Nahapiet & Ghoshal, 1998: 243). Consequently, social relations (or networks of relationships) constitute a resource (Leana & Van Buren, 1999). Not surprisingly, social capital has also been described as 'networking' capital (Anderson & Jack, 2002: 196). It is a fluid process as relationships between individuals change over time. Anderson and Jack (2002) arrived at the following conclusion as a result of their study into social capital in entrepreneurial networks:

"Social capital is not a 'thing' but a process. It is the process of creating a condition for the effective exchange of information and resources. It can only exist between people; accordingly it is a relational artefact which we can only observe as one or other of its dimensional manifestations. From this perspective social capital can be envisaged as a bridge-building process linking individuals, so that networks are a series of bridges that link numerous individuals" (p. 207).

Social capital provides the missing link in understanding how individuals interact and organise themselves to generate growth and development for an organisation (Huysman & de Wit, 2002). The social networks created by individuals are based on trust and reciprocity and this has important implications for HRD practitioners and organisational managers. The danger is that organisational managers may (continue to) perceive social capital as an artefact and apply actions to control it directly rather than recognise the subtleties required to nurture the process itself through indirect means. HRD practitioners and organisational managers need to be wary of suggestions that these social networks and related processes can be manipulated or engineered in some way. The problem with social capital is that it is messy, slippery and difficult to pin down precisely in the same way the value of more traditional assets can be. If organisations have struggled with placing a financial value on people as individuals imagine the heartache involved in persuading accountants to place a value on something as intangible as a network of relationships. There is also the problem of ownership. Who owns social capital? Coleman (1990) and Nahapiet and Ghoshal (1998) argue that social capital is a resource jointly owned by the individual and the organisation. This will have implications for the psychological contract between the individual and the organisation (thus returning to the need for more research into the relationship between HRM and social capital). In order to counter the issue of management control terms such as 'nurture' (Ichijo et al, 1998), 'foster' (Scarborough & Carter, 2000) and 'cultivate' (Wenger et al, 2002) have entered the literature as a way of articulating how managers can "implicitly manage the implicit" (Huysman & de Wit, 2003: 53).

A Conceptual Framework for HRD and Social and Human Capital

The earliest definition of HRD can be traced to the American theorist Leonard Nadler (Walton, 1999; Swanson & Holton, 2001) and the term has been defined in a variety of ways since 1970 (Swanson & Holton, 2001). However, it is only in recent years that British theorists have started to use the term in preference to its antecedents, such as training and development. Whilst there are some differences between some of the British and American perspectives much of the British literature on HRD has been influenced by the debates in the American literature (paralleling the situation with HRM a decade or so earlier). For the purposes of this paper HRD shall be used as an *umbrella* term that incorporates formal *and* informal processes which focus on learning, change and improvement at individual, group, organisation and societal levels. The emphasis on formal and informal runs counter to other definitions or models of HRD which focus on the formal only (for instance, see Stewart, 1999).

Human capital theory focuses solely on the individual and yet so much of the literature on HRD and the related concepts of organisational learning, the learning organisation and organisational knowledge focus on collective and social processes; both at the group and organisation levels. HRD practitioners will need to shift their understanding of learning theory from an individual to a social focus. There is a need to move beyond the five orientations to learning described by Merriam and Caffarella (1999), and utilised by Swanson and Holton (2001), which remain firmly rooted in the mind of the individual, and to consider a sixth, learning through social participation. As Lave and Wenger (1991) argue, learning is an integral and inseparable aspect of social practice. This shifts the emphasis from individual cognitive processes to shared activity or practice in a social context.

The framework shown in figure 1 is an attempt to describe some (but not necessarily all) of the *current* 'components' of HRD. It incorporates three elements which have been described as the traditional domains of HRD – organisational development (OD), training and development (T&D), and career development (CD) (McLagan, 1989). These domains were predicated on a human capital perspective. They have been further developed in this model to reflect the role of social capital and the current emphasis on learning, with organisational learning being closely associated with organisational development, individual learning with training and development, and lifelong learning with career development.

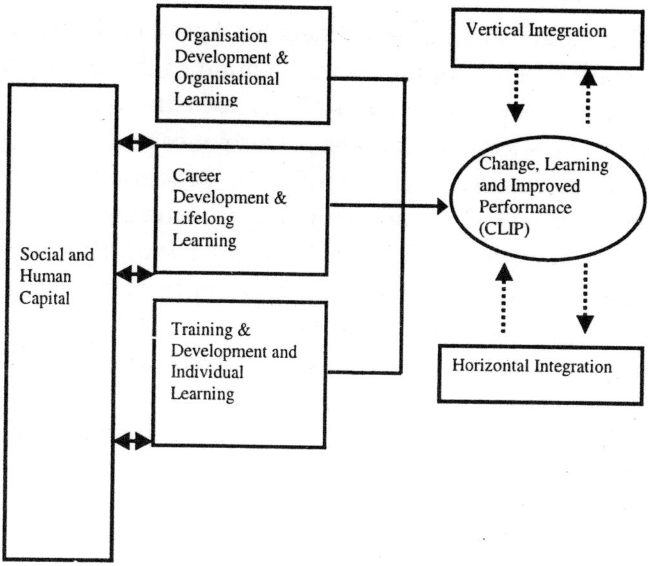

Figure 1: The components of Human Resource Development

In this framework organisational learning and individual learning are inter-related in a way that OD and T&D were not: through a common focus on knowledge sharing processes that rely on formal *and* informal learning processes; but particularly the latter. Knowledge sharing tends to take place between individuals who trust each other; and, collective knowledge exists between rather than within individuals (Lam, 2000: 491). This reflects the importance of the social context for such sharing to take place. Informal networks and groups, such as communities of practice, have emerged as an important locus for learning and knowledge sharing. The view that individuals and organisations share knowledge is largely predicated on an ICT perspective which tends to ignore the importance of interpersonal relationships and the criticality of face-to-face contact for the sharing of stories and insights (within which tacit knowledge is embedded). The new emphasis is on situated learning (Lave & Wenger, 1991) and collective processes. As Lave (1996:7) comments, "traditionally, learning researchers have studied learning as if it were a process contained in the mind of the learner and have ignored the lived-in world". By focusing on the social context there is no reason to see performance and learning as mutually exclusive outcomes of HRD processes. Learning and performance are complementary constructs (Callahan, 2003) as the purpose of HRD is "to bring about changes that cause the organisational and performance improvements necessary to enhance the firm" (Gilley et al, 2002: 13). In the 'traditional' model of HRD, OD and T&D were related to each other in an indirect manner. This is because human capital tends to relate to individual learning and does not necessarily contribute to organisational learning (Huysman & de Wit, 2002). In this framework HRD is not restricted to formal (direct) interventions but embraces informal (indirect) interventions which can be described as being more subtle than the former (the implications this has for the HRD practitioner's skills set is discussed below). It is this emphasis on social capital, on the 'bridges' between individuals, that offers a more coherent framework for HRD. If "the practice of HRD is dominated by positive intentions for improving the expertise and performance of individuals, work groups, work processes, and the overall organisation" (Swanson & Holton, 2001: 12), then extending HRD practice to encompass social capital is both consistent with, and a natural extension of this. As Callahan (2003) argues, HRD is a field of study that works with organisations as social systems. Consequently, developing an appropriate learning climate will be an important challenge for the HRD practitioner as this is both an input and an output of the processes embedded in the above framework.

Emphasising indirect and direct, and informal and formal processes when defining the role of HRD is captured in figure 2 below. HRD practitioners will need to strike a balance between processes that are designed to build on human capital and processes that develop social capital. This is not an either-or choice. It is about understanding the organisational context and being knowledgeable (and intuitive) in selecting a blend of direct and indirect HRD initiatives appropriate to the needs of the organisation. In developing social capital a spin-off or by-product will be the enhanced development of human capital as well.

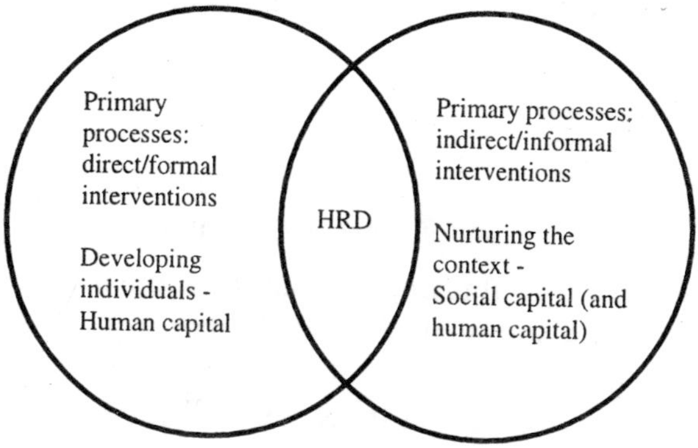

Figure 2: The 'balancing' role of HRD

The 'policy' choices that can be adopted by an organisation are illustrated in the typology set out in figure 3. These are not intended to be either-or choices but it is anticipated that an organisation would use a combination of these. This gives an indication of the theoretical impact on an organisation as a positive or negative rating. Empowered informal learning is seen to have the greatest positive impact because successful cultivation of social capital also brings enhanced development of human capital. Manipulation of learning will have a negative impact (and, again, this is likely to further impact on the development of human capital).

If informal learning *can* be deliberately *encouraged* by an organisation (Marsick & Watkins, 1990) through the use of action learning, communities of practice and action science

Learning as socialisation +	**Manipulation of learning --**
(delivering formal training & development	(engineering communities of practice and social networks)
Human capital	Social capital
Outcome	

Figure 3: HRD policy choices

(Raelin, 2000) then this implies that the same is true of social capital. Marsick and Watkins (1990) further argue that informal learning can take place despite an environment not highly conducive to learning. Similarly, social capital, in the form of networks and communities of practice, will always exist alongside the formal structure of an organisation – often people will get on and achieve things in spite of the organisation rather than because of it. The challenge for HRD practitioners is to understand how to tap into this asset and persuade organisational managers of the potential benefits in so doing - without falling into the trap of trying to manipulate the process (which is inherently self-destructive).

Proposals

Stewart and Tansley (2002) focus on the role of *training and development* professionals rather than HRD professionals in their analysis of the role of *training* in the knowledge economy. This distinction is an important one in the sense that it resonates with a central tenet of this section: that it is a return to basics that is needed if social capital is to be nurtured effectively within organisations. Get the basics of training and development right and social capital will take care of itself; that is, it will work in the interests of the organisation because the context is a positive one. Get the basics wrong and social capital is likely to work against the organisation. If an organisation seeks too much control over its employees then social capital may work against the organisation (see *manipulation of learning* in figure 3). Referring to the social science literature more generally and the role of social capital within societies, Portes (1998: 15) observes that "[t]he capacity of authorities to enforce rules (social control) can thus be jeopardised by the existence of tight networks whose function is precisely to facilitate violation of those rules". What this means is that 'traditional' training and development interventions (see *learning as socialisation* in figure 3) need to be effective as it acts as the bedrock for the further development of both human capital (see *devolved informal learning* in figure 3) and social capital (see *empowered informal learning* in figure 3).

In terms of operational activities the HRD practitioner will act in the role of both provider and facilitator. At a strategic level it will be a predominantly facilitator role. It is unfortunate that in much of the current literature the use of the term facilitator tends to have pejorative implications. HRD practitioners will need to improve and/or develop four skills' sets in particular. The first is those required to be an effective training and development practitioner, such as identifying training needs, designing interventions, evaluating such interventions. The second, is facilitating the learning of individuals at all levels within the organisation, such as raising awareness of how to learn and the importance of reflective practice, and the ability to identify and support informal learning in the workplace. The third is a combination of commercial and strategic acumen, for an HRD practitioner who is unable to converse comfortably and knowledgeably with senior managers and middle managers will rapidly lose credibility and influence. Fourth, an ability to handle ambiguity and uncertainty, and to be able to make sense of changing and complex-laden scenarios. In most respects this is little different to the advice that would have been given to a 'traditional' training and development practitioner a decade ago.

However, it will also be an immensely challenging role in which the HRD practitioner will need to be proactive, to take risks and learn to think 'outside the box' (Mankin, 2001). It is an indication of the gap between theory and practice and, therefore, between the academic and practitioner communities, that "there is little currently known about the training and development needs of training specialists associated with the knowledge economy" (Stewart & Tansley, 2002: 33). Stewart and Tansley (2002) make a range of pertinent proposals for the development needs of trainers; yet, strip out the knowledge terminology and their advice is consistent with the back to basics proposal above. The central issues remain the same as they have always been: how do HRD practitioners enhance their commercial acumen? How do they keep their core skills updated? How do they influence mangers at all levels of the organisation? How can they influence decision making at a strategic level? Whether the hot topic is social capital or knowledge management or the learning organisation, the questions and the challenges essentially remain the same. This is where more research by theorists would prove beneficial; firstly, in helping to support the efforts of practitioners; secondly, in helping to keep theorists grounded in reality, even if that reality may question the efficacy of the concept of HRD.

There is little doubt that developing 'networks of relationships' will be a difficult challenge for HRD practitioners who are more accustomed to focusing on the development of individuals. It will shift the focus and locus of much HRD activity away from formal structures and direct interventions to the informal and indirect; thus confronting the practitioner with the problem of how to tackle the vagaries and ambiguities of the elusive and intangible. But by focusing on social capital we are recognising the significant contribution that social relationships can bring to an organisation. This may be in the form of communities of practice and the socially embedded nature of knowledge (Lave & Wenger, 1991; Brown & Duguid, 1991; Wenger, 1998) or in the informal and social nature of workplace learning (Stewart & Tansley, 2002). Practitioners need to develop what Swart et al (2003: 60) describe as a "participative culture" and Tsoukas & Vladimirou (2001:991) as "a spirit of community". HRD, as well as HRM practices, need to be embedded in the social networks of such a culture. In many respects this strengthens the concept of a learning climate or community as it recognises that a collection of individuals is more than simply the sum of those individuals' knowledge, skills, abilities and experiences. The challenge is a difficult, if not a daunting one. Social networks are difficult to map as they tend to have 'fuzzy' boundaries (Johannisson, 1986) and HRD practitioners will need to develop what could be termed *cultural* or *network sensitivity*; an intuitive appreciation of the networks between individuals. This resonates with Scarborough et al (1999) who argue that the recognition that knowledge involves social relations has implications for HR practitioners as *enablers* of social interaction and social networking – both formal and informal. While others, such as Reynolds et al (2002) prefer the term *broker*. These terms reflect a shift in emphasis from the direct to the indirect. Both terms are predicated on a belief that knowledge sharing and related learning processes are critical to an organisation's competitive advantage. The concept of enabling "includes facilitating relationships and conversations as well as sharing local knowledge across an organisation or beyond geographic and cultural borders" (Von Krogh et al, 2000: 4).

These perspectives are a significant variation on the 'natural' tendency toward direct control that many managers and theorists display. Leana and Van Buren (1999: 539) hit the nail on the head when they comment that even "scholars generally regard social capital, like other forms of capital, as an asset that must be managed appropriately if its value is to be realised". The key word over which the turf war of academic debate rages is 'appropriately'. Rather than focus on direct, formal interventions to regularise the informal and bring this under the remit of the formal management structure there is a need for HRD practitioners to convince organisational managers of the need to do what Huysman & de Wit (2003: 53) describe as "implicitly manage the implicit". HRD theorists need to explore with HRD practitioners how this can be achieved. Both 'camps' need to challenge their own worldviews. There is a need to discard traditional management lenses as illustrated by Harrison and Kessels (2004) who argue that "left to itself, the learning that resides in communities of practice can become strategically irrelevant, thereby pulling the organisation back instead of driving it forward" (p.88). This is predicated more on a human capital and unitarist perspective that argues for a controlled congruence between individuals' actions and an organisation's strategic intent.

Attempts to 'regulate' social capital can pull the organisation ever further back (see *manipulation of learning* in figure 3). There is a need to resist the urge for direct control and to focus instead on the broader context. Getting this right should be the prime directive of HRD practice. However, an HRD practitioner's (in)ability to argue this point successfully is likely to be the result of a low level of credibility and status within the organisation. We are at the cusp of change and it is unfortunate that whilst there is a growing body of literature on how informal knowledge sharing processes, such as communities of practice, can be developed (for instance, Ahmed at al, 2002; Saint-Onge & Wallace, 2003) there is a lack of reference to the role of HRD in these processes. Leana and Van Buren (1999) argue that social capital can be managed through the adoption of appropriate employment practices, such as selection and compensation. This leaning, or bias, towards HRM rather than HRD processes is typical of much of the literature and suggests that a 'scientific-rationalist' perspective still dominates. This is contrary to the view that "cultivating communities of practice in an organisational context is an *art*" (Wenger et al, 2002: 14 – emphasis added). Fortunately, some theorists, such as Huysman and de Wit (2002) urge caution about using reward mechanisms for knowledge sharing. This advice should be noted as reward has become something of a misleading mantra in literature on communities of practice.

Conclusions

Research by Tsai and Ghoshal (1998) provides "strong support for the argument that social capital facilitates value creation"(p. 473). Such findings suggest that HRD theorists and practitioners should be more concerned about understanding the concept of social capital. As Wenger (1998: 10) stresses: "If we believe that people in organisations contribute to organisational goals by participating inventively in practices that can never be fully captured by institutional processes…we will have to make sure that our organisations are *contexts* within which the communities that develop these practices may prosper" (emphasis added). This will mean that as well as HRD practitioners, line managers will also need to acquire skills as knowledge enablers and learning facilitators. This is little different from the historic situation in which T&D practitioners have sought to develop line managers' skills as coaches or mentors and as evaluators of T&D activities. But, crucially, line managers need to understand the implications of nurturing or not nurturing social capital. This parallels Stewart and Tansley's (2002) argument that managers should become less concerned with control and more focused on leadership. Terms such as enabling, facilitating and leading remain elusive concepts for many managers. In many ways these remain an aspiration rather than a reality for many HRD practitioners who struggle to just to persuade managers to be more effective coaches and mentors and take a more active role in the development of their teams. Equally we need to be wary of the seductive influences of technology. Technology may help to overcome limitations found within communities (Eales, 2003) and may be useful in providing online environments within which social interaction can take place (Erickson & Kellogg, 2003); but technology is no replacement for face-to-face learning and knowledge sharing.

Staber (2003: 413) is prudent to warn that the adoption of "the most popular features of the social capital concept is risky and likely to lead to disillusionment". This is exactly the same mistake many organisations made when they (mis-)implemented TQM (as well as its antecedents). It is not about cherry-picking, it is about having the courage to embrace the whole concept, integrating it into the day to day workings of HRD processes and being prepared to challenge established orthodoxy. Failure to do so is an admission that it is training and development processes rather than HRD processes that are in place within the organisation. There is nothing wrong with this but we should be honest enough to admit that the re-labelling exercise is relatively meaningless and ineffectual in such cases.

Organisations can be viewed as many things; as economic entities, political entities, as rational entities. A wide range of lenses and metaphors exist in the literature which have been designed to help us make sense of organisations. In order to move away from a one or two dimensional picture of an organisation it is necessary to use more than one lens; but use too many and the analysis collapses under the (theoretical) weight of too many perspectives. The complexity of organisations ultimately defeats out ability to build a comprehensive, three or four dimensional picture. The integration of social capital with the HRD conceptual framework is an attempt to move beyond a one or two dimensional picture but it does place us on the cusp: in one direction lies confusion and failure, in the other lies improved understanding. Whether any improved understanding results in changes in practice only time will tell.

BIBLIOGRAPHY

Ahmed, P. K., Kok, L. K. and Loh, A. Y. (2002) *Learning through Knowledge Management*, Oxford: Butterworth-Heinemann.

Anderson, A. R. and Jack, S. L. (2002) 'The articulation of social capital in entrepreneurial networks: a glue or a lubricant?', *Entrepreneurship and Regional Development*, 14, pp. 193-210.

Becker, G. (1975) *Human Capital: A Theoretical and Empirical Analysis with Special Reference to Education* (2nd ed.), New York: Columbia University Press.

Bertels, T. and Savage, C. M. (1998) 'Tough questions on Knowledge Management' in G. von Krogh, J. Roos and D. Kleine (eds.) *Knowing in Firms: Understanding, Managing and Measuring Knowledge*, London: Sage.

Brown, J. S. and Duguid, P. (1991) 'Organisational learning and communities-of-practice: Toward a unified view of working, learning, and innovation', *Organisation Science*, Vol. 2, No. 1, pp. 40 –57.

Burt, R. S. (1992) *Structural Holes: The Social Structure of Competition*, Cambridge, MA: Harvard University Press.

Callahan, J. L. (2003) 'Organisational Learning: A Reflective and Representative Critical Issue for HRD' in A. Maycunich, J. L.

Callahan and L.L. Bierema (eds.) *Critical Issues in HRD*, Cambridge, MA: Perseus.

Coleman, J. (1990) *Foundations of social theory*, Cambridge, MA: Harvard University Press.

Davenport, T. H. and Prusak, L. (2000) *Working Knowledge: How organisations manage what they know*, Boston, MA.: Harvard Business School Press.

Eales, R. T. J. (2003) 'Supporting Informal Communities of Practice within Organisations' in M. Ackerman, V. Pipek and V. Wulf (eds.) *Sharing Knowledge: Beyond Knowledge Management*, Cambridge, MA: MIT Press.

Edvinsson, L. and Malone, M. S. (1997) *Intellectual Capital: The proven way to establish your company's real value by measuring its hidden power*, London: Piatkus.

Erickson, T. and Kellogg, W. A. (2003) 'Knowledge Communities: Online Environments for Supporting Knowledge Management and its Social Context' in M. Ackerman, V. Pipek and V. Wulf (eds.) *Sharing Knowledge: Beyond Knowledge Management*, Cambridge, MA: MIT Press.

Geroy, G. D. and Venneberg, D. L. (2003) 'A View to Human Capital Metrics' in A. Maycunich, J. L. Callahan and L. L. Bierema (eds) *Critical Issues in HRD*, Cambridge, MA: Perseus.

Gibb, S. (2002) *Learning and Development*, Basingstoke: Palgrave.

Gilley, J. W., Eggland, S. A. and Maycunich, A. (2002) *Principles of Human Resource Development* (2nd ed.), Cambridge, MA: Perseus.

Gold, J., Rodgers, H. and Smith, V. (2003) 'What is the future for the human resource development professional? A UK perspective', *Human Resource Development International*, Vol. 6 (1), pp. 437-458.

Harrison, R. and Kessels, J. (2004) *Human Resource Development in a Knowledge Economy*, Basingstoke: Palgrave Macmillan.

Harrison, R. (2002) *Learning and Development* (3rd ed.), London: CIPD.

Huysman, M. and de Wit, D. (2002) *Knowledge Sharing in Practice*, Dordrecht: Kluwer Academic Publishers.

Huysman, M. and de Wit, D. (2003) 'A Critical Evaluation of Knowledge Management Practices' in M. Ackerman, V. Pipek and V. Wulf (eds.) *Sharing Knowledge: Beyond Knowledge Management*, Cambridge, MA: MIT Press.

Ichijo, K., von Krogh, G. and Nonaka, I. (1998) 'Knowledge enablers' in G. von Krogh, J. Roos and D. Kleine (eds.) *Knowing in Firms: Understanding, Managing and Measuring Knowledge*, London: Sage.

Johannisson, B. (1986) 'Network strategies: management technology for entrepreneurship and change', *International Small Business Journal*, 5 (1), pp. 19-30.

Kogut, B. and Zander, U. (1992) 'Knowledge of the firm, combinative capabilities and the replication of technology', *Organisation Science*, Vol. 3, No. 3, pp. 383 – 397.

Krackardt, D. and Hanson, J. R. (1993) 'Informal Networks: The Company Behind the Chart', *Harvard Business Review*, July-August, pp. 104-111.

Lam, A. (2000) 'Tacit Knowledge, Organisational Learning and Societal Institutions: An Integrated Framework', *Organisation Studies*, 21(3), pp. 487-513.

Lave, J. and Wenger, E. (1991) *Situated Learning: legitimate peripheral participation*, Cambridge: Cambridge University Press.

Lave, J. (1996) 'The practice of learning' in S. Chaiklin and J. Lave (eds.) *Understanding practice: perspectives on activity and context*, Cambridge: Cambridge University Press.

Leana, C. R. and Van Buren, H. J. (1999) 'Organisational social capital and employment practices', *Academy of Management Review*, 24 (3), pp. 538-554.

Mankin, D. P. (2001) 'A model for HRD' *Human Resource Development International*, 4 (1), pp. 65 – 85.

Mankin, D. P. (2003) 'Ambiguity and elusiveness: the principal characteristics of the relationship between HRM and HRD' presented at the 'Innovating HRM Conference', University of Twente, The Netherlands (November).

Marsick, V. J. and Watkins, K. (1990) *Informal and incidental learning in the workplace*, London: Routledge.

McLagan, P. (1989) *Models for HRD practice*, Alexandria, VA: American Society for Training and Development.

Merriam, S. B. and Cafarella, R. S. (1999) *Learning in Adulthood: A Comprehensive Guide*, San Francisco, CA: Jossey-Bass.

Nahapiet, J. and Ghoshal, S. (1998) 'Social capital, intellectual capital, and the organisational advantage', *Academy of Management Review*, Vol. 23, No. 2, pp. 242 – 266.

Newell, S., Robertson, M., Scarborough, H. and Swan, J. (2002) *Managing Knowledge Work*, Basingstoke: Palgrave.

Portes, A. (1998) 'Social Capital: Its Origins and Applications in Modern Sociology', *Annual Review Sociology*, 24, pp. 1-24.

Raelin, J. A. (2000) *Work-based Learning: The New Frontier of Management Development*, Upper saddle River, NJ: Prentice Hall.

Rainbird, H. (2000) 'Training in the workplace and workplace learning: introduction' in H. Rainbird (ed.) *Training in the Workplace*, Basingstoke: Macmillan.

Reynolds, J. (General editor), Caley, L. and Mason, R. (2002) *How do People Learn?*, London: CIPD.

Saint-Onge, H. and Wallace, D. (2003) *Leveraging Communities of Practice for Strategic Advantage*, San Francisco, CA: Butterworth-Heinemann.

Scarborough, H., Swan, J. and Preston, J. (1999) *Knowledge Management: A Literature Review*, London: IPD.

Scarborough, H. and Carter, C. (2000) *Investigating Knowledge Management*, London: CIPD.

Schultz, T. W. (1961) 'Investment in human capital', *American Economic Review*, 51 (1), pp. 1-17.

Staber, U. (2003) 'Social capital or strong culture?', *Human Resource Development International*, Vol. 6 (3), pp. 413-420.

Stewart , J. and Tansley, C. (2002) *Training in the Knowledge Economy*, London: CIPD.

Stewart, J. (1999) *Employee Development Practice*, London: FT Pitman Publishing.

Swanson, R. A. and Holton, E. F. (2001) *Foundations of Human Resource Development*, San Francisco, CA: Berrett-Koehler.

Swanson, R. (1998) 'Demonstrating the Financial Benefit of Human Resource Development: Status and Update on the Theory and Practice', *Human Resource Development Quarterly*, Vol. 9 (6), pp. 285-295.

Swart, J., Kinnie, N. and Purcell, J. (2003) *People and Performance in Knowledge-Intensive Firms*, London: CIPD.

Tsai, W. and Ghoshal, S. (1998) 'Social capital and value creation: the role of intrafirm networks', *Academy of Management Journal*, 41 (4), pp. 464-476.

Tsoukas, H. and Vladimirou, E. (2001) 'What is organisational knowledge?', *Journal of Management Studies*, 38 (7), pp. 973-993.

Von Krogh, G., Ichijo, K. and Nonaka, I. (2000) *Enabling Knowledge Creation*, New York, NY: Oxford University Press.

Walton, J. (1999) *Strategic Human Resource Development*, Harlow: Financial Times/Prentice Hall.

Wenger, E. (1998) *Communities of Practice: Learning, Meaning, and Identity*, Cambridge: Cambridge University Press.

Wenger, E., McDermott, R. and Snyder, W. M. (2002) *Cultivating Communities of Practice*, Boston, MA: Harvard Business School Press.

8

HUMAN RESOURCE DEVELOPMENT: EMERGING PERSPECTIVES ON TRAINING AND EMPLOYABILITY

*Dr. Bhupen Srivastava**

India, like many other nation-states of the world, is at the threshold of transition from a largely centrally planned, tightly regulated and nation-bound economy to a relatively free market, deregulated global economy.[1] While the transition offers tremendous opportunities for organizations to gain competitive advantage based on their distinctive competencies, it also brings with it certain threats to the identity and continued survival of various organized sectors of human activity. The near demise of public sector undertakings, growing incidence of acquisition and merger, strategic alliances, arrival of MNC's, growing and potential sickness of several productive and service sectors coupled with unbalanced economic growth, rising consumerism and ever increasing unemployment have created uncertainties of a magnitude that Indian society had never confronted in the past. Organizations functioning within such a socio-cultural milieu seem to have no other option than to adapt or perish.

The impact of these changes has been most felt amongst

* Professor and Dean, International Management Institute (IMI), New Delhi.

the employees in both the organized and unorganized sectors of the economy. The pressure generated by the environment to transform a 'low performance – high cost' economy to 'high performance – low cost' economy will lead organizations to adopt the approach of downsizing of resources resulting in surplus manpower which will add to the already swelling pool of unemployed and underemployed workforce in the country. By doing so they would have created for themselves a social environment which will be unstable, hostile and volcanic. Economic growth and corporate success cannot obviously be achieved within such an environment.

Organization's Response to Change

It is in the backdrop of this scenario that organizations have to generate options to ensure their continuance and growth without sacrificing the goodwill of the people directly or indirectly engaged in contributing to their existence as producers of wealth and providers of services. In other words, organizations will have to develop active adaptive strategies and coping mechanisms to respond to the changes within and outside their boundaries.

In recent years, the changes have been characterized by unprecedented volume and increased pace. There is change in scale as also in diversity of human efforts. The value system of individuals, groups and societies have undergone changes and the direction of change is towards increased complexity. The trend is likely to continue and gain further momentum as we move towards the second decade of this century.

In a fast changing environment, the pace and direction of adaptation best suited to the individual organization is not easily identifiable. The task of anticipating and getting an organization to move towards change, thus, cannot be accomplished by one person. The difficulty arises on account of non-compliance, resistance and growing alienation not only among the workmen but also the middle ranks of management. The problems that organizations will face, therefore, relate to cost and effort needed to introduce change, gain acceptance for it and coping with its unanticipated consequences. Management of change, thus, must become the major thrust and preoccupation of HRD efforts.

In order to meet the challenges of change, which will play a decisive role in determining the continued survival of any system, the organizations need to adopt the following approaches:

1. Designing futures and developing a shared vision of the kind of future organizations will like to create for themselves.
2. Designing culture with articulated ideology, direction, priorities, value systems and norms conducive to excellence.
3. Positioning and gaining competitive advantage through distinctive competence.
4. Adopting strategic thinking mode of managing at all levels embracing units, departments, sections, and even individuals.
5. Broadening of perspectives and scanning wider horizons for anticipating and controlling unknown variable.
6. Designing decision structures for reduction in decision response time.
7. Progressive reduction in cycle and process time for greater speed.
8. Reducing time lag between the occurrence of deviation/ error, its detection and corrective action for ensuring quality, customer service, etc.

9. Developing communication system based on close loop principles of cybernetics.
10. Empowering employees by increasing involvement through team work dominated by strategic outlook.
11. Encouraging surprise-free management at all levels through decentralization of planning, goal setting, flexibility in deployment of resources and feedback mechanisms.
12. Creating a learning organization by providing opportunities for problem solving, innovation and continuous improvement in work spheres.
13. Aligning the structure, systems, processes and procedures with changing market forces.
14. Inculcating service orientation amongst organization members towards internal as well as external customers.
15. Integrating Information Technology enabled services with communication, problem solving and decision-making processes for easy and wider access with speed.

Positioning of HRD

HRD cannot be looked at as an activity separate from the challenges being encountered by organizations and their requisite responses to those challenges. Infact, HRD effort must inextricably be linked with strategic thinking and organization design and development efforts. The relationship among the three is interactive and dynamic characterized by directive correlation. The interrelationship among strategic planning, organization design and manpower development constitutes a major and perhaps a fundamental shift in the way organizations of the future will respond to environmental changes and justify their raison d'etre by meeting demands for which they were created. Developing appropriate designs of organization will be the key factor in providing competitive edge in the global market. It's not the technological superiority alone or abundance or scarcity of resources, but the way we organize various resources, in ultimate analysis, will account for success or failure of organizations.

A paradigm shift in the design of organizations is already evident in different parts of the world, the direction of which is mentioned below:

Traditional Paradigm	*Emergent Paradigm*
1. Fragmented Socio-technical System	1. Joint Optimization of Technical and Human Systems
2. Technological Imperative	2. Complementarity of Man and Technology
3. Maximal Task Break-down and Minimum Skill	3. Optimal Task Groupings and Multiple Broad Skills
4. One Man – One job with Individual Responsibility	4. Self-managing Groups with Joint/ Shared Responsibility
5. Design based on Total Specification	5. Design Based on Minimum Critical Specifications
6. Variety Decreasing	6. Variety Increasing
7. Control through Creating Redundancy of Parts	7. Control through Creating Redundancy of Functions within parts
8. Single Rigid Structure	8. Capacity to develop Multiple Structure
9. Interest/Goal Oriented System	9. Purposeful/Ideal Seeking System
10. Techno-economic Criteria of Evaluation	10. Techno-economic, Humanization and Environmentalization Criteria
11. Emphasis on External Coordination and Control	11. Control and Coordination through Shared Norms
12. Adaptation through Rules, Procedures, Uniformity etc.	12. Adaptation through Adjustment
13. Prediction of Environment and Developing Control Mechanisms to Respond/React	13. Decision/Actions Directed towards Designing Futures Appropriate to Achievement of Organization's Purposes
14. Management by Direction and Control	14. Management by consensus and Commitment
15. Sequential Operations/ Activities	15. Simultaneous/Concurrent Operations and Activities.

16. Centralized Monolithic Structure with Unity of Command, etc.	16. Decentralized Profit Centres with Internal Suppliers and Customers – Factories within Factory
17. Diffused accountability and Reduced Autonomy at Various Levels	17. Manager as an Entrepreneur, Work Group as a Small Business

Emerging Priorities of HRD

The success of creating and sustaining competitive edge depends on the sophistication of human infrastructure – and development of new technical and social skills in the workforce. The Human Resource Development Strategies must reflect the following:

1. Developing competence of employees enabling them to possess broad range of skills, more requisite knowledge and increased autonomy and discretion.
2. Awareness of the total system of production/service so that exigencies of the task requirements, changing priorities and variation standards can be responded to without time lag.
3. Appreciation of the flow of products and services in the market place and dynamic and interactive relationship with various stakeholders such as changing customer needs and expectations, suppliers and contractors etc.
4. Skills to manage cross-functional heterogeneous teams of workers in such a way as to create synergistic effect and to communicate internally with speed and clarity.
5. Increasing concerns over job security and career growth necessitating large investments in retraining and employability.
6. Continuous improvement in productivity of resources and quality of output at par with global standards.
7. Creating and sustaining a culture of excellence with

balanced emphasis on organizational effectiveness, quality of life of its members, and social responsibility.

8. In a turbulent environment not amenable to even probabilistic predictions, plans may become obsolete, subject to change and the planning cycle shorter and shorter. Strategic planning as a centralized activity loses much of its relevance. It is therefore, the process of planning itself that allows employee to develop alternative scenarios, articulate or validate their beliefs and assumptions and act as flexible guides for the future. "Strategic thinking", thus must percolate down to the lowest levels of the employee providing linkages between their responses and actions and the strategic objectives of the organization.
9. Plans for organizational revitalization, morale building, participatory management for mutuality of influence and individual renewal/revitalization though continuing education programmes.

Strategic HRD Issues

The strategic HRD issues of concern to organizations relate to the following:

1. Mutuality of Influence

The nature and extent of influence exercised by employees in the affairs of the company tends to vary from one organization to another. The trend, however, seems to be in the direction of enlarging the areas of employees' influence particularly in matters relating to their work, their careers, and personnel policies affecting their morale and commitment. Both formal and informal mechanisms have been developed to widen the span of influence such as open door policies, attitude and opinion surveys, employees committees, task forces, opinions and concerns expressed in training programmes, etc.

2. *Organizational Membership*

Yet another area where policies need to be formulated, concerns inflow and outflow of employees. The trend seems to be towards attracting and retaining talented and skilled manpower. The selection process, therefore, needs to be designed carefully for both the potential member and the organization so that they are able to enter into a longer term psychological contract through need alignment and goal congruence.

One organization, for example, designed a two-day training programme to assess the suitability of the candidates and also to allow them to decide whether they would wish to work in such an environment. In other cases, video-cassettes featuring the current employer talking about benefits, demands, stress etc. of the concerned work area are shown to candidates.

3. *Career Systems*

In traditional pyramidal structure, career growth of employees invariably means vertical movement with corresponding rise in status and wider span of control. With delayering of the structure, opportunities for vertical mobility will be highly restricted. Career growth thus would need to be redefined in terms of lateral and cross-functional movement of employees. Further, career growth prospects will have to be measured in terms of job/responsibility content and skill/expertise requirement rather than in terms of status or position in the hierarchy of an organization. The area and extent of vertical and horizontal specialization necessitated by the nature of technology and strategic considerations will be decided by the organization as career paths available to its employees. In other words, status will be delinked from the nature of job leading to situations where movement could be even downward. It's quite likely that in the event of technical obsolescence setting in faster, employees may have more than one career. In a couple of organizations, employees are encouraged to take responsibility for their own career. The organization's role is to provide more information to enable the employees make informed choice.

4. Job Security

Highly competitive and fast changing environment necessitates cutting down fats through downsizing resulting in threat to job security at middle, supervisory and workmen level. Organizations, however, do make use of multiple criteria for retention of employees in the face of imminent redundancy. Performance may not be the sole criterion; employee commitment and loyalty, impact of economic cycles on employment stability, social obligations, political compulsions, etc. are other criteria used in decision for retention.

Considering the unemployment situation in the country and availability of trained manpower in traditional skills, organizations do have the option of laying off surplus human resources. However, most organizations, even in the developed nations, exercise this choice only after other possibilitres have been explored and exhausted. The possibilities, some of which are being tried out in India include; Voluntary retirement scheme, shortened work weeks, transfers to other parts of the organization, planned reduction through attrition, replacement of casual and contractual workers, creation of innovative jobs, out-placement, counseling and support. If at all, lay off becomes inevitable, it is desirable to openly communicate and involve the concerned groups and / or their representatives so that various options are explored and the decision will thus acquire more credibility and acceptability.

5. Reward Systems

With the qualitative change in the nature of workforce who are professionally and technically trained, organization is viewed not as a source of supplementary income but as an instrument for growth and development of one's professional expertise and enhancement of one's quality of life. Consequently there has been a shift in emphasis from 'monetary reward' to 'intrinsic rewards' like responsibility, self fulfillment, social status, etc. In fact, in India, traditional source of one's identity based on caste, village, lineage etc. is being replaced by organizational identity. Inculcating a sense of belonging and commitment to organizational purposes and goals, therefore, is a potent reward as it instills pride in an individual and heightens his sense of achievement.

So far as tangible forms of rewards are concerned, the critical issue will be to find an optimum balance between individual excellence and collective performance. Most reward systems are heavily biased in terms of individual performance; while the output of any organized system is the result of collective efforts through interactive or synthetic teams. Individual excellence will have to be rewarded more on the basis of acquisition, sharpening and development of skills and special expertise relevant to the organization's needs. The above development together with redefinition of career patterns will necessitate delinking of rewards' from hierarchical position in the organization.

Individual skill-based reward can be supplemented with team-based performance rewards. Additional incentives can be provided to individuals for acquisition of new skills relevant to the current and future requirements of the teams and the organization.

With the restructuring of organizations in terms of semi-autonomous self-contained work groups being run as small business, it will be possible to decentralize the development of pay plans within the overall policy guidelines of the organization. Members of these small business units can be involved in deciding the quantum and distribution of rewards. In addition, there is an increasing trend towards financial participation by the employees in a variety of forms like gain-sharing linked to productivity/production, profit-sharing, stock ownership in companies, etc.

In nutshell, the reward systems will have to be flexible enough to attract and retain employees, reinforce learning and competence, encourage multiskilling and cross-functional expertise acquisition, inculcate team spirit and enhance collective performance, ensure long term viability and health of the system, and achieve need alignment through active participation in matters relating to financial gains.

6. Work System

It is the work system where interface between technology and human beings is more evident and its effects directly observable in terms of output. This is an area, therefore, that must become the central core around which HRD strategies and policies should be formulated. One-man-one job as the basic building block of the organization leads to elongated hierarchical levels, elaborated horizontal differentiation, compartmentalized operations along functions and authority levels resulting in increased decision response time, high costs of coordination and control, pressures for vertical movement, lack of flexibility in deployment of human resources to meet exigencies of work requirement and limits realization and utilization of human potentialities. Human resource development efforts do not always lead to enhanced organization success due to the nature of the design of the work system. There is, thus, a definite trend toward, redesigning the system of work in the direction of self-managing integrated teams responsible for the whole task, sub product or service with specified inputs and measurable outputs. While work system restructuring has gained momentum in the developing economies since 1980's , in India, we conducted successful redesigning of the work system to meet optimally the technical as well as human resource development requirements leading to improved productivity, multiskilling, team synergy, employee satisfaction, etc.

There is a world wide movement to organize work around integrated teams, diagonal teams, problem solving groups, productivity improvement groups, quality circles and the like to create learning organizations capable of responding with speed to the challenges of change and thus enabling organizations to maintain their competitive edge. Together with the shift towards team management and advancement in and adoption of information technology, managerial and supervisory levels are progressively being reduced or even eliminated.

The change in the organization of work will necessitate formulating HRD Policies directed towards, facilitating smooth transition to the new forms of work organization through training in technical, cross-functional, managerial and change management skills to concerned employees. It will also necessitate delineation of system performance criteria, redefinition of roles and career growth paths, evaluation mechanism for individual/group performance, restructuring of reward systems and mechanisms for training needs assessment.

7. Training and Retraining

Training and retraining activities, if planned properly, can prevent the occurrence of a crisis situation leading to retrenchment of the employees. Organizations both public and private – find themselves in this situation as they could not apparently anticipate changes and formulate plans to manage the change. Human resource is an asset and it is the management's responsibility to ensure their effective utilization and development by creating avenues and opportunities that the environment offers. Search for establishing linkages between the current and future requirements of the organization and manpower training needs must become an on-going process with the direct involvement of line managers, supervisory staff and the workmen.

Development efforts through training or continuing education programmes need to be integrated into the work system so that they contribute to enhanced organizational effectiveness and increased personal efficacy. The role of managerial and supervisory staff assumes far greater importance in providing opportunities for continuous learning on-the-job, identifying organizational and individual blockages hindering the learning process and formulating strategies and initiating actions to overcome those blockages.

Direction of Training

The training activities, to contribute meaningfully to the success of an organization, should take into consideration the following:

1. *Strategic Consideration*

The purpose of training and priorities of goals to be achieved through training will obviously depend on strategic options of corporations. Strategic considerations like, expansion, diversification, single product – single market, etc. would determine the direction of the training and development effort. The divisions, units, departments or work groups may widely differ on strategic goals in the same corporation. It will be desirable to identify and develop different cadres of employees to fit into the roles required by various strategic considerations.

2. *Organizational Culture*

The cultural factors like concern for employees comfort and welfare, commitment to internal development, dedication to social/community, responsibility, power and status differentiation in the organization will have influence in determining the direction the training and development effort might take.

3. Contextual Factor

The contextual factors such as sectoral changes, competitive threats, economic fluctuations, technological advancements and rising aspirations and expectations of workforce for career growth will also have implications for prioritization of various training efforts.

Training Activities

Based on these considerations, wide range of training activities can be identified and grouped under the following categories:

I. Task-Skill Training

(i) Acquisition

(ii) Socialization/Orientation of new entrants

(iii) Developing advanced skills not easily available in the labour market

(iv) Changing job responsibilities for given position

(v) Improving job productivity and quality

II. Career Advancement

(i) Attracting and retaining talent

(ii) Retraining dislocated workers

(iii) Providing skills to advancing managers

(iv) Reinvigorating burned – out workers

(v) Assisting the exit process - pre retirement counseling, out placement, etc.

III. Organizational Effectiveness

(i) Improving work-group effectiveness

(ii) Reinforcing a company culture and core values

(iii) Changing a company culture and inculcating new values.

(iv) Rewarding performance or long service

(v) Enriching the work experience of workers

IV. Interface Effectiveness

(i) Meeting statutory/non statutory requirements

(ii) Changing customers/user group's needs and expectations

(iii) Conflicting demands of the stakeholders and strategies / tactics for

reconciliations

(iv) Supplier/vendor development

(v) Entrepreneurial orientations and skill for the community/society

Thrust Areas for Retraining

The thrust areas for training and retraining will have to be organization – specific directed towards meeting the priority demands and major concerns of respective organizations. In one of the leading public sector undertakings, retraining of the staff and workmen on their promotion to executive cadre to enable them to meet the demands of the new role was identified as the thrust area. A comprehensive training package was developed which consisted of orientation programme and three modules spread over a period of one and a half to two years with continuous on-the-job evaluation between the modules. Participation in the modular programme was made compulsory. A series of seminars and workshops were organized for heads of the departments and controlling officers of the promotees throughout the organization to elicit their support in enabling the trainees transfer learning to their respective spheres of work. controlling officers and heads of the departments were required to formulate action plans for facilitating development of their subordinates and for ensuring the implementation of action plans developed by the latter. A full time co-ordinator was appointed at every plant to monitor the development efforts and to assist controlling officers in identification of technical training needs of each of the promotees.

In one of the private sector organizations, the major thrust was on creating a climate for improvement in productivity, quality and adaptation to modernization. An opinion survey was conducted among the employees to ascertain their views and to identify their major concerns. The findings of the survey were discussed with the trade union activists and it was jointly decided that training programmes for trade union and opinion leaders of the workmen should be conducted for equipping them with skills for improvement as also broadening their perspective and changing their orientation towards adoption of 'normative' rather than legal or administrative approach to issues confronting the organization. These training programmes created conditions wherein not only the industrial relations scenario underwent transformation, but changes introduced for productivity and quality improvement were accepted willingly.

In yet another organization professionalization of management process and change of organization ideology from 'power-centered' to 'Task excellence-centered' were identified as thrust areas for gaining competitive edge in the market place. To achieve this end, training in adoption of strategic thinking mode at all levels in the organization was considered appropriate intervention. Module and their implications were discussed in their top management group for obtaining their consent and support. The exercise has resulted in the decision to restructure the organization in accordance with the recommendations made in the modular programmes. The process of implementation has been set in motion and an organization – wide campaign will soon be launched to give practical shape to the 'priorities for action' for change.

A young unit of an old multi-national company has identified creating a culture of excellence with emphasis on high performance, high commitment and consensual mode of decision making as its thrust areas. A training package has been designed to involve managerial, supervisory staff as also the workmen and the union tenders, in developing a shared vision of the future and in redesigning their roles to contribute towards translation of that vision into reality. The exercise has begun with a training programme for the trade union leaders wherein they have developed their vision of the company and defined their roles and those of the workmen in operationalization of the vision. This is an illustration of bottom-up approach to designing futures of organizations.

Some of the examples mentioned above are illustrative of the fact that every organization, depending on its perception of current realities and future options, has to make a conscious and planned effort to identify thrust areas for training. In keeping with the kind of scenario that is emerging, the thrust areas for training and retraining are likely to be the following:

1. Multi-Skilling

In the face of rapid technological change and fluctuating market demands, employees need to upgrade, acquire and sharpen a broad range of technical skills to be able to respond to the demands of new products and processes and to the requirements of flexible work organizations. Multiskilling, in addition to harnessing of untapped potentials of the employees, provides flexibility in deployment of human resources to meet the exigencies of the work system. At managerial level, cross-functional training will assume far greater importance for ensuring speedy decisions with broader perspective, introducing innovations, and for reduction in the cost of co-ordination and control. Horizontal mobility at all levels in the organization will become an important factor for organization's success.

2. *Team Management*

As the skills and expertise required for achieving the purposes of an enterprise are widely distributed horizontally and vertically within the organization and outside its boundary as well, it is important to develop mechanisms for integrating these diverse potential contributions towards accomplishment of tasks. The teams provide the mechanism for achieving high level of vertical and horizontal integration and creating synergy. Managing through team serves the twin purposes of enhancing task excellence as well as contributing to the development of its members. Training employees to become team player and developing appropriate support system to inculcate team spirit will have to be accorded high priority to ensuring organizational excellence and employee development.

3. *Customer Orientation*

In a highly competitive environment, products, services, decisions and responses must be directed towards meeting the changing demands and expectations of customer and user groups. In fact there is already a visible trend to restructure organizations based on the concept of internal customer to enable the work groups orient their efforts and output for meeting their specifications and priorities. Customer satisfaction is a concern that has, by and large, been neglected by most organizations in India. In the changing scenario, customer orientation will hold the key for success of organizations regardless of their business interests. Training in customer orientation thus, is yet another thrust area towards which HRD efforts will have to be directed.

4. Productivity and Quality

Productivity and quality of products and services have already been recognized as a major thrust area for training by most organizations in India for gaining and retaining competitive advantage in national and global markets. When India became independent, it was among the two most industrialized nations in Asia; today, it is at the bottom of the top ten. About 40% of our educated are unemployed and 5% of workforce is literate. Our products and services are, in general much below the global standards. India is getting marginalized in a world which is becoming increasingly interdependent. Productivity and quality improvement programmes must get the utmost priority over any other activities in the context of existing and emergent global scenario. Most organizations in India have already made significant strides in training their employees in improving productivity and quality. Increasing number of organizations has qualified for certification in quality in terms of international standards. Training in quality circles, and productivity improvement techniques are already being conducted in a large number of organizations with the help of external as well as in house trainers and facilitators. The trend is going to continue necessitating changes in other aspects of organizational functioning and philosophy.

5. Out Placement

As a strategy to deal with surplus employees, a number of organizations in the U.S. and Europe, have begun to provide training in marketable skills and provide assistance in finding employment elsewhere sometimes even outside the industry. This sort of assistance is also being provided to managerial and supervisory staff who are to be laid off. The measures to encourage employees to look for alternative employment often include free training, reimbursement of expenses for attending interview calls, lien on the job for specified period, etc. By adopting these measures, the organization not only earns the good will of the employees and the community, but also saves the otherwise payable separation compensation.

6. Entrepreneurship

Training in entrepreneurial orientation and skills to employees is gaining importance due to pressures on organizations to adopt and manage innovations in product, process, operations, systems and procedures on a continuing basis. Entrepreneurial training will enable employees to manage their respective work groups as an entrepreneurial venture and small business, to take risks in trying out new ideas and be accountable for their actions / decisions. The skills acquired through training can also be utilized by employees in taking up subcontracting from the organization, setting up ancillary firms or establishing trade or business of their choice.

7. Empowerment

The organizations designed on the basis of traditional management principles create a divide between a few at the top who are perceived as powerful and a great majority at the bottom made to feel powerless with a sizeable chunk in the middle alienated because of identity crisis. This kind of scenario makes it difficult for the organization to achieve unity of action towards common purpose. It also gives rise to dependence. Counter-dependence syndrome at successive levels thereby creating conditions for wasteful expenditure of human psychic energies. To get best out of people and to elicit their willing support to organization's endeavour, the employees must be made to feel powerful, a mental and psychic state of being in command, releasing and using one's energy in productive pursuits and actively influencing and transforming situation conducive to achievement of one's goals and purposes. The workmen, their representatives and the managerial staff need to be given training in empowerment so that they are encouraged to make productive use of their potential power.

8. Perspective Building

The changes in the structure of organizations and their response patterns to transforming realities of the world of business must be accompanied by corresponding changes in employees' perceptual map and perspective through which they comprehend, understand and interpret the world around them and select appropriate and adaptive responses. As a consequence of functioning within an environment characterized by schism, centralized control, high power distance and growing inequity, organization members have tended to develop and perpetuate partial perceptions and narrow perspective based on sectional interests. As we seek to globalize our economies it is imperative for organizations to develop among employees broader global perspective based on corporate and national interests. Perspective building and enlarging the perceptual map of the employee at all levels incorporating various interest groups will increasingly become a major thrust area of training to enable them to think globally.

9. Desirable Value-set

In a world increasingly moving towards materialism, consumerism and individual competitiveness, organizations in their long term interest of sustained viability would need to inculcate desirable set of values in their employees for their continued support to organization's purposes and for creating a socio-cultural milieu conducive to furtherance of organization's objectives. Also, with the diminished role of the State in a free market economy, corporations will be required to contribute towards achievement of social objectives. Training employees to uphold certain universal socially desirable values and to fulfill their obligations to the community would need to be given due consideration.

10. The Untrainables

Based on the consideration of age, rigid attitudes, and / or obsolescence, it is not uncommon for organizations to brand a few employees as untrainables. The older employees are often classified under this category and based on the cost benefit considerations, organizations may not be willing to invest in training them. There are considerable number of organizations in India, who as a matter of policy do not invest in training or redeployment of workers nearing retirement. As a result of this, there is invariably a conflict between the older and the younger employees and an attempt to introduce change in the organization or the work system is resisted by the former. If the untrainables are not trained, they are likely to suffer job and income loss most. Uncertainties for them are likely to be more, leading to resentment and greater resistance to any change effort. In order to elicit their support and create a climate conducive to acceptance of change, the so-called untrainables including the older employees would need to be retrained not only in technical skills but also in attitude change and confidence building.

Conclusion

Managing through 'Values' and 'Vision' must become the main thrust area for HRD movement in the corporate world for success, excellence and competitive advantage in a turbulent environment. A management team has articulated and published its values as under:

- Meeting customer need is our obsession; their needs drive our actions.
- We work with all groups to serve our customers.
- Our work should create wealth for customers, stockholders, and employees.
- We balance short-term business needs with long-term business strategy.

- Everybody is a business partner.
- We eliminate artificial barriers so that each individual can make his or her maximum contribution.
- We take courageous actions.
- We add va ue and eliminate waste.
- We keep things simple and use common sense.
- We are anti-bureaucratic, we manage systems, policies, methods; we are not managed by them.

All HRD and training activities must be directed towards inculcating and reinforcing organization-specific and environment – relevant values amongst employees to ensure organization success – and to improve quality of life of its members.

REFERENCES

- Burton, Cary and Anton Frankeiss, 1994, Training for Total Quality Management, Gower Publishing Ltd. .
- Kleiman, Lawrence S., 2003, *Human Resource Management – A Managerial Tool for Competitive Advantage* (3rd Edn.), Published by Biztantra, New Delhi.
- Srivastava, Bhupen and Mamta Panda, 2003, *Paradigm Shift and Dimensions of Work Culture: Implications for Organizations* In *Global Business Review*, Vol. 4, No. 2, pp.285-310, July – December, Sage Publications.
- Srivastava, Bhupen, 1976, *Conditions and Organisation of Work.* National Labour Institute Bulletin, New Delhi 2.2 February pp 41 - 55.
- Srivastava, Bhupen, 2003, Chapter on *'Indian Environment – The Changing Scenario'* In Social Processes and Issues, Indira Gandhi National Open University (IGNOU), New Delhi, December.
- Srivastava, Bhupen, 2003, Chapter on *'Organization Values and Work Ethics'* – The Changing Scenario In Social Processes and Issues, Indira Gandhi National Open University (IGNOU), New Delhi, December.
- Srivastava, Bhupen, 2003, Chapter on *'Social Issues and*

Organizational Relevance' – The Changing Scenario in Social Processes and Issues, Indira Gandhi National Open University (IGNOU), New Delhi, December.

- Venkata Ratnam C.S. and Bhupen, Srivastava, 1991, *Personnel/ Human Resource Management*. Text and Cases; New Delhi; Tata McGraw Hill.
- Wexley, Kenneth, N. and Gary P. Latham, 2002, *Developing and Training Human Resources in Organizations*, 3rd Edition, Prentice Hall, New Jersey.

9

STRATEGIC HUMAN RESOURCE DEVELOPMENT: A TRANSFORMATIVE PERSPECTIVE

Dr. PS Yadapadithaya & Dr. Jim Stewart***

Introduction

Over the recent years, there has been a shift in scholarly interest from strategic human resource management to strategic human resource development (Thomson and Mabey,1994; Mabey and Salaman,1995; Harrison,1997; Rothwell and Kasanas,1989a and 1989b; Walton,1999; Wilson, 1999). The shift is partly motivated by the research on Japanese management practices that shows that business success based on high standards of performance is dependent on a highly trained and developed workforce (Brown and Read, 1984). In addition, Porter's (1980,1985,1990) competitive advantage and the excellence literature (Ouchi, 1981; Peters and Waterman, 1982) also call for a shift towards a developmental and transformative focus. The literature on competitive advantage underlines an organisation's need to identify the key elements of its value chain in order to earn and sustain competitive advantage. The excellence literature suggests that employees' values and philosophies should be guided by, and be consistent with, the strategies proposed by the organisation.

* Senior Reader, Mangalore University, Karnataka, India.

** Professor, Nottingham Business School, UK.

Strategic human resource development (SHRD) offers a proactive, value-adding, holistic, synergistic, and long-term perspective for "people-development" function in all forms of organisations (Yadapadithaya,1998). The basic philosophy (system of beliefs and values) is to help all employees recognise and realise their full potential as human beings, so that individuals, teams, and organisations can achieve their objectives both effectively and efficiently. The strategic goal of modern firms is to create organisations that are more intelligent and flexible than their competitors by hiring and developing more talented human resources and by extending their skill base. Towards this end, SHRD can play a critical transformative role in the people resources. The central purpose of this chapter is to provide an overview of the field of SHRD focusing on its evolution, underlying theories, conceptual analysis of HRD and SHRD, key components, and major challenges.

EVOLUTION

Human Resource Development (HRD) is a relatively new term, but not a new concept. The original roots of HRD can be traced directly to the earliest form of training, often referred to as vocational education, provided by the apprenticeship system in colonial America in the eighteenth century (Miller, 1987; Nadler and Nadler, 1989). With the advent of the industrial revolution during the late 1800s, the resultant factory system of production made it possible to increase production by using machines and unskilled workers. Eventually, many factories created 'factory schools' to train the engineers, machinists, and skilled mechanics who were needed in large numbers to design, build, and repair machines (Pace, Smith, and Mills, 1991). Later on, the introduction of the Model T cars by Ford in 1913 and the economics of mass-production through assembly lines necessitated the training of semi-skilled workers to perform several inter-related tasks. During

World War I many factories producing non-military goods had to retool their machinery and retrain their workers to meet a huge demand for military equipment.

By the end of the nineteenth century; Taylor's (1911) principles of scientific management stressed the managerial responsibility of job design, selection, training, and planning. Factories started training more and more employees in the art of "one best way" to do a job. The human relations movement ignited by the Hawthorne studies (1924-1932) of Elton Mayo and his associates broadened the scope of inquiry to the importance of human behaviour on the job (Mayo, 1933). The movement continued into the 1940s, with World War II as a backdrop.

During the fifties and sixties, the writings of Trist and Bamforth (1951), Argyris (1957), McGregor (1960), Likert (1961) and Herzberg (1966) had a tremendous impact on the behavioural science movement. This period can be considered as the true historical starting point of HRD (Stead and Lee, 1996) and it is because of the behavioural science movement that HRD has had such a dramatic impact on today's organisations.

In the USA the first professional association focusing exclusively on HRD issues was founded in 1942 as the American Society for Training Directors (Nadler and Nadler,1989). In 1945 the association published the first issue of *Industrial Training News*, renamed in 1947 the *Journal of Industrial Training*. In 1964 the association changed its name to the *American Society for Training and Development* (ASTD) owing to the realisation of a wider role and relevance of the professional trainers in such areas of employee development as coaching, counselling, and problem solving. Consequent to this development, in 1966 it renamed its publication the *Training and Development Journal*. During the late 1980s, the ASTD sponsored a two-year study to explore emerging models and to identify the HRD roles and competencies needed for an effective HRD function. The seminal work of McLagan (1989a and 1989b) had culminated in the ASTD's *Models for HRD Practice*. The Models sought to provide tools that are detailed enough to reflect the vast differences in the organisation of HRD content, but at the same time they sought to develop a common language about HRD so that people can communicate about it, recognise similarities across jobs and train and educate others for HRD work. The *Academy of Human Resource Development* (AHRD) was established in the early 1990s by a group of HRD academics and it emerged as a significant source of scholarly literature on HRD in the US. During the mid to late 1990s, AHRD sponsored two internationally focused and fully refereed academic journals: *Human Resource Development Quarterly* and *Advances in Human Resource Development*; and very recently it introduced '*Human Resource Development Review*' as its third journal. Gradually, many colleges and universities introduced HRD programmes in one of three academic departments: business/management, psychology, and education (Gerber 1987).

In the UK the development of career professionals came somewhat later. It was triggered by the Industrial Training Act 1964 which introduced a network of Industrial Training Boards for designated industries, and a compulsory training levy/training grant system for all but small organisations (Walton 1999). It led in the same year to the formation of the *Institute of Training Officers* which in the late 1970s was renamed the *Institute of Training and Development*. As in the USA it sponsored its own journal, entitled *Training and Development*. In 1994, the Institute of Training and Development merged with the Institute of Personnel Management to form the Institute of Personnel and Development, currently known as *Chartered Institute of Personnel and Development* (CIPD).

National vocational education and training (NVET) systems constitute an integral part of the economic environment of most nation states, particularly advanced industrial countries (Stewart 1999). The National Council for Vocational Qualifications (NCVQ) was set up in 1986 – a landmark development in the creation of the present national VET system in the UK. This led to the development of National Vocational Qualifications (NVQs) in England and Wales, and Scottish Vocational Qualifications (SVQs) in Scotland. The introduction of the NVQ system offered Britain for the first time in its history a structure of occupational qualifications comprising agreed national standards of competence across every recognised occupational area.

The business-led and government-supported *Investors in People* (IiP) was established in 1991 to promote the IiP standard nationally. It is a national standard which provides a framework for establishing corporate goals and targets, communicating with employees, and training them to meet those goals and targets. It provides a framework tool for bringing about organisational change and development, and for benchmarking against other organisations. The UK IiP standards framework has been influential in encouraging UK organisations to develop an explicit commitment towards training and development and an implicit commitment to learning (Walton 1999).

In the UK, HRD courses are more recent with the first professionally recognised HRD Master's programme being validated at South Bank University, London in 1991. The *University Forum for HRD* was established in 1992 as a national network of higher education institutions offering Master's degree in HRD, and the first UK professor in HRD was established at Liverpool John Moores University in 1993 (Walton,2001; cited by Kuchinke, 2002). In 1993 the university of Twente, the Netherlands (de Rijk, Mulder and Nijhof,1994) co-ordinated a pan-European survey of HRD professionals and their practice by replicating the ASTD's study. The essential difference is that the ASTD study focused on future idealistic profiles, while the practitioner study in Europe focused on current HRD practices. The European results provided a contemporary view of the HRD role in Europe (Valkeavaara, 1998). During this period, HRD academics and practitioners witnessed the launch of internationally focused and fully refereed academic journals: *International Journal of Training and Development*, and *Human Resource Development International* are UK based; and the *Journal of European Industrial Training* is based in Ireland and has been established for nearly two decades.

In summary, historically, the development of HRD can be traced from training and instructional design, to training and development, to employee development, to human resource development (Jacobs 2000). Perhaps the main advance of HRD as a field of academic study has taken roots in the USA pioneered initially by the ASTD, and taken further forward by its academic offshoot – the Academy of Human Resource Development (AHRD). New technology, globalisation, drive for quality, cost containment, market volatility, workforce diversity, the importance of knowledge capital, and the speed of change acted as the precursors of SHRD in progressive and result-oriented organisations of both developed and developing economies. These trends posed both challenge and opportunity for organisations to earn and sustain competitive advantage through developing multi-skilled, flexible, and committed workforces. While all nations have systems of workforce development and workplace learning and exhibit an amazing range of differences in their purposes, values, policies, structures, stakeholders, and patterns of participation, the UK and US are probably the two western nations where systems of HRD are most clearly identifiable, including academic preparation, professional certification, and formal acceptance of HRD roles in virtually all sectors of the world of work (Kuchinke,2002). While comparing national systems of HRD in the US and UK, Kuchinke (2002:15) reports: 'a more centralised system of professional HRD accreditation and certification in the UK with an articulated link to the national system of vocational education. In contrast, in the US, there is no national level focus or coordination, no accreditation or certification scheme, and HRD education and training are decoupled entirely from the vocational system'.

Theoretical Framework

Theory is particularly important to a discipline such as HRD that is emerging and growing (Swanson, 2001). Some of the prominent theory-building efforts of HRD scholars include *Systems Theory Applied to Human Resource Development* (Jacobs, 1989), *Foundations of Performance Improvement and Implications for Practice* (Swanson 1999), *A Theory of Intellectual Capital* (Harris, 2000). A sketch of theoretical underpinnings of HRD contained in general systems theory, institutional theory, human capital theory, and the resource-based theory is given below.

General Systems Theory: In general systems theory, the unit of analysis is understood as a complex of interdependent parts (von Bertalanfly,1950). An open (vs. closed) system is dependent on the environment for inputs, which are transformed during throughput to produce outputs that are exchanged in the environment. According to a competence management model of organisations (Wright and Snell, 1991), skills and abilities are treated as inputs from the environment; employee behaviours are treated as throughput; and employee satisfaction and performance are treated as outputs. Extending the same logic, Kozlowski and Salas (1994) presented a multilevel organisational systems approach for understanding training implementation and transfer.

Institutional Theory: Institutional theory views organisations as social entities that seek approval for their performances in socially constructed environments. Organisations conform to gain legitimacy and acceptance, which facilitate survival (Meyer and Rowan,1977; Zuker,1977). Because multiple constituencies control needed resources, legitimacy and acceptance are sought from many stakeholders. Studies on institutionalisation (Scott,1987) focuses on pressures emanating from the internal (formalised structures and processes, informal or emergent group and organisation processes) and external (government laws and regulations, licensure and certification of profession, and existing practices within the industry) environments.

Human Capital Theory: In the economics literature, human capital refers to the productive capabilities of people (Becker,1964). Skills, experience, and knowledge have economic value to organisations because they enable it to be productive and adaptable; thus, people constitute the organisations's human capital. All costs related to eliciting productive behaviours from employees – including those related to developing, motivating, monitoring, and retaining them – constitute human capital investments made in anticipation of future returns (Flamholtz and Lacey,1981).

Resource-Based Theory: The resource-based theory of the firm blends concepts from organisational economics and strategic management (Barney 1991, Conner 1991). A basic assumption of this view is that organisations can be successful if they gain and maintain competitive advantage (Porter 1985). Competitive advantage is gained by implementing a value-creating strategy that competitors cannot easily copy and sustain (Barney, 1991) and for which there are no ready substitutes. Three types of resources available to organisations are (a) physical (plant, technology and equipment, geographic location), (b) human (employees' experience and knowledge), and (c) organisational (structure; systems for planning, monitoring, and controlling activities; social relations within the organisation and between the organisation and external constituencies). HRD greatly influences an organisation's human and organisational resources and so can be used to gain competitive advantage (Schuler and MacMillan, 1984).

There exists an ongoing debate surrounding the conceptual and theoretical foundations of HRD (Walton,1999; Lynham, 2000; McGoldrick and Stewart,1996; McGoldrick *et al.*,2002). Gourlay (2000:99) in attempting to clarify the nature of HRD states that ' it focuses on theory and practice relating to training, development, and learning within organisations, both for individuals and in the context of business strategy and organisational competence formation'. HRD is multi-disciplinary in nature and it draws heavy influence from other related disciplines such as adult education, instructional design and performance technology, psychology, business and economics, sociology, cultural anthropology, organisation theory and communications, philosophy, axiology (the study of values), and human relations theories (Willis, 1997; cited by Walton, 1999).

Human Resource Development (HRD)

The basic elements associated with the concept of HRD are education, training, development, and learning. *Education* is defined as ' activities which aim to develop the knowledge, skills, moral values and understanding required in all aspects of life rather than a knowledge and skill relating to only a limited field of activity' (MSC 1981, quoted in Reid and Barrington, 1997:7). The basic purpose of education is to develop in an integrated way an individual's intellectual capability (training the mind), conceptual and social understanding, and work performance (Harrison, 2000).

Training is learning that is provided in order to improve

performance of an individual to improve performance in the present job (Gilley and Eggland,1989). It is ' a relatively systematic attempt to transfer knowledge or skills from one who knows or can do to one who does not know or cannot do' (Megginson *et al*.1993: 10). Training is a planned process to modify attitude, knowledge or skill behaviour through learning experience to achieve effective performance in an activity or range of activities. Its purpose, in the work situation, is to develop the abilities of the individual and satisfy the current and future needs of the organisation (MSC 1981, quoted in Reid and Barrington, 1997:7)

Development is a long-term process designed to enhance personal potential and effectiveness (Megginson et al.,1993: 10). The term "development' is used to denote learning experiences of any kind, whereby individuals and groups acquire enhanced knowledge, skills, values or behaviour. Its outcomes unfold through time, rather than immediately, and they tend to be long-lasting.' (Harrison, 2000: 2)

Learning is ' a relatively permanent change in behaviour that occurs as a result of practice or experience' (Bass and Vaughan, 1967:8). It refers to the process of unlearning what has been wrongly (inappropriately) learnt over the years, relearning new things which are relevant for the current and future needs, and getting oneself committed to the continuous process of learning and development. Hence, learning involves change (Stewart, 1996).

Human resource development was originally conceived as a composite term incorporating three types of vocational learning activity that would contribute to making individuals more effective at work: (a) training, focusing on immediate changes in job performance; (b) education, geared towards intermediate changes in individual capabilities; and (c) development concerned with long-term improvement in the individual worker (Nadler,1970; Nadler, 1979; Weinberger,1998; McLean and McLean, 2001). In 1970, Nadler used HRD as a 'series of organised activities conducted within a specific time and designed to produce behavioural change' (p.3). In 1980, he applied HRD to ' the entire range of educational, training, and development facilities available in an organisation that enhance the learning processes essential to an organisation's capacity to change' (Nadler,1980; cited by Harrison, 2000:18). In response to the changing HRD practice, Nadler reformulated HRD in 1989 as 'organised learning experiences provided for employees within a specified period of time to bring about the possibility of performance improvement and/or personal growth' (Nadler and Nadler,1989).

McLagan's (1983:7) conception of HRD as the 'integrated use of training and development, career development, and organisation development to improve individual and organisational performance' and Swanson's (1995:208) interpretation of HRD as a 'process of developing and unleashing human expertise through organisation development and perscnnel training and development for the purpose of improving performance' are more focused but certainly more functional in scope.

McLean and McLean (2001:322) suggested the following integrated view:

> *Human resource development is any process or activity that, either initially or over the long term, has the potential to develop adults' work-based knowledge, expertise, productivity and satisfaction, whether for personal or group/team gain, or for the benefit of an organisation, community, nation or, ultimately, the whole of humanity.*

They conclude that HRD is influenced by a country's

value system, and the point of the life cycle of the field of HRD in that country, and that the perception and practice of HRD differ according to the status of the organisation, whether it be local or multinational.

Megginson et al. (1993) deem HRD as an 'integrated and holistic approach to changing work related behaviour, using a range of learning techniques and strategies.' In 1995, the University Forum for HRD (the UK and Europe) adopted a position statement on HRD implying that although HRD as a concept and as a practical discipline owes many of its roots to employer-driven learning activities, it is also beginning to encompass far more than traditional 'training and development.' As the strategic significance of organisational learning as a source of competitive advantage gains recognition, a strategic need arises for appropriately positioned 'learning architects' with the distinctive competencies to orchestrate learning initiatives on behalf of organisations (University Forum for HRD, 1995).

While highlighting the role and relevance of HRD in positively influencing the learning processes of individuals and organisations, Stewart and McGoldrick (1996:1) made the following observation: 'Human resource development encompasses activities and processes which are intended to have impact on organisational and individual learning. The term assumes that organisations can be constructively conceived of as learning entities, and that the learning processes of both organisations and individuals are capable of influence and direction through deliberate and planned interventions. Thus, HRD is constituted by planned interventions in organisational and individual learning processes'.

The hallmark of HRD is, therefore, a deliberate focus on 'learning' (intentional or accidental). Stewart (1998) differentiates between 'learning' and 'interventions,' which he considers to be two distinct processes contributing to HRD. 'Learning' can, will, and does happen, irrespective of the wishes or actions of anyone. It is as natural and inevitable as breathing. However, the practice of HRD is constituted by deliberate, purposive, and active 'interventions' in the natural process of learning. Such interventions can take many forms, most capable of categorising as education or training or development. Similarly, Hendry et al. (1991) see two distinct meanings implicit in HRD – (a) a methodology for learning, and (b) a philosophy for investing in people.

From this discussion it follows that HRD does not have any definitive form or definition, and instead takes diverse forms in different contexts and times (Mankin, 2001). As such, strategic human resource development must take a transformative approach to allow for the flexibility in education, training, development and learning.

A transformative approach to HRD allows it to be complementary to the conventional Human resource management, rather than relegating it as to a subservient role (Thomson and Mabey 1994; McGoldrick and Stewart, 1996). McLagan (1989) uses a human resource wheel to portray the distinctive role of HRD in relation to the human resource management, i.e. its focus on the 'development' issues – 'training and development,' organisation 'development,' and career 'development.' She identifies four human resource management areas as being closely aligned to the three Primary HRD areas: selection and staffing, performance management systems, human resource planning, and organisation/job design. These areas are linked as a set of processes for achieving a set of strategic results such as productivity, quality, innovation, human resource fulfilment, and readiness for change.

Strategic Human Resource Development (SHRD)

Strategic human resource development (SHRD) is the identification of needed skills and active management of learning for the long-range future in relation to explicit corporate and business strategies (Hall 1984:159). It refers to ' development that arises from a clear vision about people's abilities and potential, and operates within the overall strategic framework of the business (Harrison 2000:79). SHRD puts particular emphasis on the development of comprehensive, coordinated and dynamic approaches for major learning initiatives within and outside an organisation in order to facilitate the achievement of corporate objectives in a competitive environment (University Forum for HRD, 1995). According to Walton (1999:82) SHRD involves 'introducing, eliminating, modifying, directing and guiding processes and responsibilities in such a way that all individuals and teams are equipped with the skills, knowledge and competences they require to undertake current and future tasks required by the organisation.'

HRD is traditionally preoccupied with designing and delivering training and development programmes, and at times, it runs the danger of adopting a piece-meal approach to the overall development of the individuals, teams and organisation without an explicit coherence among its strategies and activities on the one hand and, on the other, an absence of vertical linkage and alignment with the business strategy and organisational vision. More often than not, the HRD practitioners may perceive their roles as passive providers and guardians of disintegrated HRD systems and processes without a sense of purpose, pride, direction, strategic awareness, and process ownership. SHRD brings a transformative focus to the HRD with its holistic orchestration of learning within organisations (Walton,1999).

SHRD goes beyond conventional HRD because of its thrust on transformative issues. In SHRD, people development and the supporting learning processes are one of the strategic capabilities and distinctive competences of those organisations that effectively undertake them. Learning and development initiatives are undertaken with full strategic intent, with an understanding of how they add to the coherence of the knowledge creation, development, and application at levels in the organisation, congruent with an explicit learning philosophy incorporated into the overall organisational vision and mission. Similarly, education, training, and development initiatives are undertaken with an explicit strategic intent and with the total commitment and involvement of those people who are supposed to benefit from them. As a result, SHRD is a strategically important partner assuming the same level of importance as the traditional core organisational processes: finance, production, and marketing. It is characterised by the presence of a credible, high-status, expert, and business-focused HRD department and HRD practitioners.

In sum, SHRD is concerned with the management of employee learning for the long-term, keeping in mind the explicit corporate and business strategies. It genuinely establishes strategic partnerships across the organisational spectrum ranging from influencing people development policy decisions at the board level to effectively collaborating with line managers and other personnel practitioners. It ensures that there exists an organisational strategy for the HRD effort that guides, unifies, and provides direction to 'planned learning' sponsored by the organisation. People at all levels in the organisation's chain of command willingly share responsibility and accountability for HRD. As such, SHRD demonstrably contributes to the long-term survival, growth, and excellence of the organisation by ensuring a favourable learning climate and encouraging the employees to challenge the status quo through innovation, change, and continuous learning and development. Also, organisations adopting a strategic approach to their HRD function continuously benchmark 'best practices' in HRD.

Characteristics of SHRD

The key characteristic features of SHRD are as follows.

1. **Business-led Approach**: SHRD function strives for constant alignment with the mission, goals and the genuine needs of the organisation (Zenger,1985; Barham *et al.*,1987; Burgoyne,1988; Garavan,1991).

2. **Analysis of the External Environment**: SHRD function builds capacity to analyse and understand the external environment in terms of the opportunities and threats it presents in the context of both the business and HRD strategy (Higgs, 1989).

3. **Formal Policy Statement**: SHRD policy statement serves many purposes such as guiding management in the identification and implementation of appropriate and relevant SHRD activities; spreading awareness among supervisors, line managers, and top managers about their individual and collective SHRD responsibilities on a regular basis; communicating to everyone in the organisation about the main reason why the organisation is investing in various SHRD programmes; clearly defining the relationship between the organisational objectives and its commitment to the SHRD function; helping continually to assess the learning needs required for releasing both the employee's and the organisation's growth potential; and finally, providing a framework for evaluating SHRD programmes.

4. **Top Management Support, Involvement, and Commitment**: SHRD function cannot be integrated into strategy unless senior managers want that to happen. The extent to

which SHRD becomes a feature of strategy, therefore, largely depends on the ability and willingness of top managers to visualise important environmental trends in SHRD terms (i.e., learning opportunities).

5. Competence of the Line Manager: The basic responsibility for continuous employee development is always resting with the immediate manager or supervisor. The line manager is best placed to assess, on an ongoing basis, the training and development needs of subordinates, and can facilitate in identifying development routes for subordinates and is ideally placed to offer advice, direction, and counselling to subordinates (Gunnigle and Flood,1990; Garavan,1987; Mumford,1989). In this context it needs to be appreciated that the competence of the line manager is vital to successful implementation of SHRD. Several research studies pointed out the competency deficiencies of line managers in such areas as inability to appraise performance, lack of counselling skills, inability to identify skill gaps, poor listening skills, and inability to empathise with their subordinates (Aston, 1984; Garavan,1987; Mumford,1989; Tjepkema et al., 2002).

6. Integration Between HRD and HRM activities: A strategic approach to HRD is fundamental to the adoption of a comprehensive human resource management approach in the organisation. Not only does SHRD provide an impetus for a more integrated HRM approach, but it is also necessary to have a close integration between HRD and other HRM activities. SHRD must view itself as one strategy available to an organisation wishing to attract, develop, motivate, and retain its human resources (Keep, 1989).

7. Marketing of HRD: For the SHRD policy to work, it must be known, understood, and accepted by those implementing it and affected by it. To make this happen HRD specialists should be good at marketing their services by educating and convincing the top management and line managers about the potential contribution of SHRD. A SHRD function needs a specialist who can be a perfect combination of trainer, provider, consultant, innovator, and manager (Bennett 1988).

8. SHRD is Context-specific: The philosophy, policies, processes, programmes, and practices of SHRD are influenced by a host of factors shaping and reshaping the internal and external environments of organisations. The internal contextual factors include technology, structure, size, life-cycle stages, existing and required competencies of individuals and teams, and business strategy.

Technology refers to a system's processes for transforming inputs into usable outputs. These processes can vary along many dimensions, including the degree of continuity in the production system, the types and levels of knowledge required by the system, the degree to which tasks are routinized and predictable, and the linkages and interdependencies among tasks and people.

Organisation structure describes the allocation of tasks and responsibilities among individuals and departments; it designates the nature and means of formal reporting relationships as well as the groupings of individuals within the organisation (Child, 1977). Structures for domestic firms include functional departmentalisation, product-based divisionalisation, geographical divisionalisation, and matrix organisation with dual reporting relationships. On the other hand, structures for organisations that span across national borders include multinational, global, international, or transnational forms (Phatak,1992). Each structural form probably faces some unique challenges that have implications for SHRD.

The trends and status of SHRD vary with *organisation size*. Compared to smaller organisations, larger ones are more likely to use more sophisticated training and development procedures (Saari *et al.*,1988), and have more highly developed internal labour markets (Ferris *et al.*, 1992).

The literature on *organisation life cycle* stages directs attention to the changing managerial priorities that characterise organisations in various developmental stages such as start-up, growth, maturity, and perhaps decline and revival (Baird and Meshoulam,1988). The life cycle stage may constrain and shape SHRD in organisations.

With regard to *strategy,* SHRD function has got definite implications within the framework of strategic analysis, planning, and implementation (Johnson and Scholes,1997). A strategic approach to HRD can be applied at three levels to produce a corporate strategy concerned with the organisation as a whole, a business strategy focused on significant elements or units within the organisation, and a strategy for HRD at the functional level. These three levels have a linear relationship in that SHRD functional strategies are derived from and contribute to business strategies, and business strategies are derived from and contribute to corporate strategy. All strategies in turn, at whatever level, derive from and enable achievement of the organisation's mission. In this context, it is, therefore, important that SHRD functional strategies are designed and managed in a coordinated way so that they interrelate with each other and at the same time collectively allow the competitive strategy to be implemented properly.

The external contextual factors are legal, social, and political environments; unionisation; labour market conditions; industry characteristics; and national cultures. The legal, social, and political environments are bound to impact SHRD initiatives. For instance, almost all aspects of HRM are affected by the legal and regulatory environment in the US, and in some European countries, organisations are obliged to set aside specific sums of money for formal training and development (Brewster et al 1993). The union-management relations within each firm may be adversarial or cooperative, which in turn may influence the successful implementation of various SHRD initiatives. One of the features of modern labour market is greater diversity in terms of gender, age, and ethnicity (Triandis *et al.*,1994). This increasing workforce diversity has clear implications for training, development, and mentoring (Powell and Butterfield, 1994). Industry characteristics (public vs. private sectors; regulated vs. unregulated; manufacturing vs. service; characterised by high vs. low stability or change) may have far reaching implications for SHRD. Finally, SHRD is country-specific and cross-national differences can be noticed in the way in which SHRD policies and programmes are being evolved and implemented (Tiepkerna et al. 2002). In addition to cultural differences (i.e., values, norms, and customs), differences in SHRD policies and practices may also be the result of differences in economic and political systems, laws and regulations, industrial relations systems, and labour market conditions.

9. Aligned with Corporate Strategy and Culture: A strategic HRD function must be matched with the corporate strategy and culture. It has to establish options, policies, and plans that fit the strategic logic and cultural web found in the organisation (Edwards and Kleiner,1988; Denison,1984). Hence, SHRD efforts cannot afford to ignore the prevailing and desired culture of an organisation.

10. Stakeholder-driven approach: Within the context of SHRD, a stakeholder is anyone whose actions can affect the management of SHRD activities within the organisation. Key stakeholders include: top management, line managers, training and development specialists, personnel managers/HR specialists, individual employees, external training providers, educational establishments, and trade unions. Stakeholders may have different values and expectations which will influence their reaction to various learning and development initiatives undertaken by the organisation. SHRD calls for a symbiotic and synergistic approach ensuring commonality of interests; mutual trust, confidence and goodwill; and a shared vision among the key stakeholders for the successful implementation of training, education, and development programmes.

11. Evaluation: Strategically-oriented HRD functions invest time, energy, and resources in evaluating their activities and they use measures that seem most relevant to the management of their own organisation (Zenger and Hurgis,1982; Stewart,1999). SHRD also advocates that managers, supervisors, and employees should be evaluated on how well they develop themselves and contribute to the development of others in the organisation.

12. Wider Scope: SHRD is different from the traditional training and development function in many ways. Megginson and Pedler (1992) clearly pointed out that HRD is not just confined to training, although training activities constitute an important component. There are certain perceptible differences between traditional training and development *and* SHRD (Beer and Spector,1989; Rothwell and Kazanas,1991). SHRD can be viewed as a proactive, system-wide intervention linked to strategic planning and cultural change. On the contrary, the traditional view of training and development consists of reactive, piecemeal interventions in response to specific problems. Further, SHRD advocates the involvement of many stakeholders such as supervisors, line managers, human resource colleagues, training and development specialists and top management rather than simply the training and development function acting as a provider. Also, traditional training activities provide individuals who are lacking in knowledge and skills with structured opportunities to receive the fruits of deskilled organisational experience. In this sense, training and development is a maintenance subsystem, intended to improve organisational efficiency by increasing routinisation and predictability of human behaviour. But SHRD advocates that individuals should anticipate knowledge and skills needed in the future rather than react after problems become apparent.

13. Universal Applicability: Principles of SHRD are applicable to any conceivable organisation - private, public, or MNE; for-profit or not for-profit; voluntary or employing - where people are found working together in groups for the effective and efficient accomplishment of organisational goals and objectives.

14. Micro and Macro-level Interventions: SHRD and its far reaching implications can be visualised at both micro and macro levels. SHRD interventions can take place within an organisation (micro) at the levels of individual, dyadic (interpersonal), team, inter-team, and organisation as a whole. SHRD aims at continuously improving personal competence, professional development, and continuous employability at the individual level; promoting better mutual relations and understanding at the inter-personal level; trust and teambuilding, communication and leadership styles, and creating and sustaining positive synergy among members at the level of teams; strengthening relationships, understanding, and a need to "see the forest through trees" between groups at the inter-group level; and at the organisational level, increasing the organisational capability to excel by transforming itself into a knowledge-based, knowledge-enabled, and knowledge-productive learning organisation.

SHRD can influence and also be influenced by the national and global developments (macro) in the field. Human capital, conceptualised as a stock of skills and knowledge, is perhaps a significant factor explaining the differential rates of economic growth of nations. SHRD, with its focus on humans, is heavily influenced by the context in which it is studied and practised. The public policy and strategy, educational and research infrastructure (primary and secondary education, adult education, vocational education, higher education), training and development infrastructure at the national level will influence the corporate policies and strategies of HRD at the organisational level (Yadapadithaya,2000). For instance, the German system of vocational education and training has been based on the duality of workplace and educational institutions, and it is seen as underpinning the post-1945 German economic miracle by providing both transferable skills and job-specific training (Lewis 1997). Similarly, since the French government is involved in setting HRD policy for companies, HRD takes on a national flavour in France.

Finally, global human resource development takes place across more than one culture or nation, and may occur on an international (between nations), multinational (many nations), and regional (e.g., European, Pacific Rim, Latin America) scale. Although global SHRD involves the same practice areas, roles, functions, and activities of domestic SHRD, it is shaped and reshaped by several factors such as the composition of the trainees (host country nationals, parent country nationals, and third country nationals), cultural differences among trainers and trainees, and physical and financial resources available to the global SHRD practitioner.

Components of SHRD

The concept of SHRD consists of four inter-linked and interdependent components: (1) employee training and management development; (2) career development; (3) organisational development; and (4) individual, team, and organisational learning (McLagan,1989; Marsick and

Watkins,1994; Swanson,1995; the University Forum for HRD,1995; Walton,1999; Simon and Streumer,2001).

Training and Development

Training and development of employees are essential to organisations which seek to gain competitive advantage through a highly skilled and flexible workforce as a major ingredient for high productivity and quality performance (Finegold and Soskice,1988; Streek,1989; Porter,1990). An appropriate and adequate provision of training and development may contribute to the organisational progress in many ways. First, a more highly skilled workforce may increase productivity by producing a higher level of output or by producing output of greater value. Second, a well-trained and motivated workforce may cut the costs of supervision, as they possess the skills to inspect their own work and become self-managed. Third, a skilled workforce can also improve the firm's functional flexibility since they are much easier to retrain owing to their relatively broad knowledge-base and multi-skills. Fourth, a technically competent workforce can also give management confidence in utilising new technology and provide employers with more scope for rapid adjustment in production methods, product requirements and technology. Fifth, management's commitment to training and developing the employees in an attempt to improve product quality and service delivery bears a symbolic significance in that it sends a signal to the workforce that they are valued in the organisation. Such a message may in turn raise the morale of the employees and encourage their commitment to the organisation.

The benefits of training and development can be realised only through the systematic implementation of employee training and management development policies and programmes. It is not enough to believe in training as an act of faith. This belief must be supported by a positive and realistic philosophy of how training contributes to the bottom line. Training and development should not be treated as an expenditure, but it needs to be clearly demonstrated that it is an investment which would pay rich dividends in the long run (Yadapadithaya,2001). The systems approach to planned training is underpinning this belief and it consists of the following five inter-linked steps: identifying training needs, defining learning requirements, planning training programmes (techniques, facilities, locations, and trainers), implementing training, and finally, evaluating training.

Career Development

A career is a pattern of work-related experiences that span the course of a person's life (Greenhaus,1987). Career development is an organised, planned effort comprised of structured activities or processes that result in a mutual career plotting effort between employees and the organisation. Within this system, the employee is responsible for career planning and the organisation is responsible for career management (Gutteridge and Otte,1983). Such planning needs to be appreciated that the relationship that binds individual and organisation is two-fold: legal contract (specifying duties, terms and conditions, and material rewards) and psychological contract (felt and perceived expectations, wants and rights). The challenge is one of matching the needs of the organisation with those of the people who work for it, and to do so from entry into the organisation, through each career transition-point thereafter, until exit, in order to achieve a mutually beneficial relationship over time (Schein,1978).

Two decades ago, when an individual was more likely to spend his or her entire work life with the same employer, most large and medium-sized organisations engaged in extensive employee career planning. Such planning focused exclusively on developing employees for career opportunities within the specific organisation. But as more and more organisations downsize their operations, reengineer processes, and restructure themselves to increase flexibility, they are shifting career development responsibility to their employees. It is increasingly recognised that today employees are operating in an age of discontinuity – either they are holding temporarily permanent or permanently temporary jobs. In this context of unstable employment environments, employees will not be able to make decisions and take action that will ensure continuous work life with a single employer. Furthermore, there is evidence that in such an environment employers are unable to commit themselves to long-term relationships with employees (Hutton,1995; Herriot and Pemberton,1995). The traditional concept of 'career' is now replaced by 'portfolio' of transferable skills and competences, and new ideas and understandings of careers place much more weight on the active agency of individuals (Watson and Harris, 1999). There is a breakdown in the 'old deal' of job security, a fair day's pay, and career development in return for loyalty, commitment and, at least, a fair day's work (Guest, 1998; Herriot,1992; Hiltrop,1995). Instead, they are being offered a 'new deal' involving less security but the chance to make themselves more employable in the future.

When employees are empowered to manage their own career, they have to take responsibility for planning their personal career track. It is not their manager's or the company's job to define their future. So, today's employees are becoming more concerned than ever with keeping their skills, abilities, and knowledge current, and preparing for tomorrow's new tasks. They are beginning to understand and appreciate learning as a lifelong process. As far as career development function is concerned, the individual employee is responsible for maintaining his or her employability and marketability both within and outside the organisation. On the other hand, the employer's responsibility is limited to providing support for employees to continually add to their skills, abilities, and knowledge (clearly communicating the organisation's goals and future strategies), creating growth opportunities (providing new, interesting, and professionally challenging work experiences), financial assistance (tuition reimbursement), and providing the time for employees to learn (paid time-off from work for off-the-job training). Many organisations are now offering opportunities for individuals to develop their skills and competencies to increase their marketability or employability (Viney, Adamson and Doherty,1995).

Organisational Development

Organisational development (OD) is a system-wide process of data collection, diagnosis, action planning, intervention, and evaluation aimed at: (1) enhancing congruence between organisational structure, process, strategy, people, and culture; (2) developing new and creative organisational solutions; and (3) developing the organisation's self-renewing capacity (Beer 1983). It is basically the process of enhancing the effectiveness of an organisation and the well-being of its members through planned interventions that apply behavioural science concepts (Beckhard, 1969; Alderfer,1977; Beer and Walton,1990).

Some of the OD techniques or interventions aimed at bringing about planned change include: sensitivity training (training groups that seek to change behaviour through unstructured group interaction); survey feedback (the use of questionnaires to identify discrepancies among member perceptions, discussion follows and remedies are suggested); process consultation (consultant gives a client insights into what is going on around the client, within the client, and between the client and other people, and identifies processes that need improvement); teambuilding (high interaction among team members to increase trust and openness); and inter-group development (OD efforts to change the attitudes, stereotypes, and perceptions that groups have of each other).

Learning

Being a highly complex human process, learning covers the acquisition of new or/and fine-tuning the existing knowledge, skills, attitudes, values, and habits. It encompasses individual, team, and organisational learning experiences triggered by failures, successes, and anything in between. Employees need to develop learning abilities as individuals, and work and learn as teams (Garrat,1990). It needs to be appreciated that employees are not only individual learners but also have the capacity to learn collaboratively (Hoyle, 1995). Learning is, therefore, a continuous process, and 'learning to learn' is the most fundamental learning of all (Honey, 1998; Armstrong,2001). Organisations do not perform the actions that produce the learning; it is individual members of the organisation who behave in ways that lead to it, although organisations can create conditions which facilitate such learning (Argyris, 1992). Recently, terms such as learning, learning organisation, organisational learning, and knowledge management and development have received much attention by HRD scholars and practitioners.

Senge (1990:3) defined a *learning organisation* as one 'where people continually expand their capacity to create the results they truly desire, where new and expansive patterns of thinking are nurtured, where collective aspiration is set free, and where people are continually learning how to learn together'. In the whole process, a learning organisation will develop the continuous capacity to adapt and change, it continually transforms itself and becomes more flexible and vibrant (Garvin, 1993; Wick and Leon,1995). Just as individuals learn, so too do organisations. Kim (1993:37) has rightly stated: 'All organisations learn, whether they consciously choose or not -it is a fundamental requirement for their sustained existence'.

Marsick (1994) defines *organisational learning* as a ' process of co-ordinated systems change, with mechanisms built in for individuals and groups to access, build and use organisational memory, structure, and culture to develop long-term organisational capacity'. It should aim at creating, developing, and sustaining organisational capability (Wenger and Snyder, 2000). Organisational learning occurs when an organisation achieves what is intended, and also when a mismatch between intentions and outcomes is identified and corrected (Argyris,1992). Organisational learning is basically concerned with the exploration of effective ways and means to develop and nurture individual and team learning, and translating into an organisational resource. In order to revitalise the practice of learning organisation and organisational learning, they should be integrated with knowledge management initiatives so that different forms of knowledge can be linked, fed by organisational learning, and used in adding value to goals and services (Burgoyne, 1999).

Scarborough *et al.* (1999) defined *knowledge management* as ' any process or practice of creating, acquiring, capturing, sharing and using knowledge, wherever it resides, to enhance learning and performance in organisations'. The organisational capability to gather, lever, and use knowledge effectively will become a major source of competitive advantage in many businesses over the next few years (Grant, 1991; Trussler,1998). There are two basic forms of knowledge: tacit and explicit (Nonaka, 1991; Nonaka and Takeuchi,1995). Tacit (implicit) knowledge resides in people's minds in such forms as scientific or technological expertise, operational know-how, insights about an industry, and business judgement (Hansen et al.,1999). On the other hand, explicit knowledge is codified, recorded, and available in the form of databases, corporate intranets, and other records. Fundamental to 'knowledge creation and development' is the bending of tacit and explicit knowledge to the strategic advantage of the organisation through processes of socialisation (tacit to tacit), externalisation (tacit to explicit), internalisation (explicit to tacit), and combination (explicit to explicit) (Nonaka and Takeuchi,1995; Scarborough *et al.*,1999).

Knowledge management is a relatively new, but still a very hot topic in management research and practice. The increasing relevance and strategic significance of knowledge management in modern organisations are due to the continuous rise of technological opportunities (internet and intranet, e-learning), new competitors and new requests by customers, demand for proactive strategies aimed at continuously renewing the sources of competitive advantage (Collis and Montgomery, 1995). The emphasis on the knowledge management and development process progressively went from mere information and knowledge exchange to knowledge embodiment and transfer for re-use and, finally, to the overall process of knowledge creation, diffusion and refinement over time. Today, leading companies are reshaping their organisations in order to increase their ability in managing knowledge sharing and transfer within and across their organisational boundaries.

The development of knowledge is repeatedly claimed to be an essential determinant of organisational profitability (Senge,1990; Huber,1991; Nonaka,1994; McGrath *et al.*,1995). In a knowledge economy, organisational success is largely hinging on the rapid generation and application of knowledge to achieve organisational objectives (Stewart and Tansley 2002). People are becoming knowledge workers, expected to know more, learn more quickly and cope with ever more frequent change. Knowledge workers (Drucker, 1993) are individuals who have high levels of education and specialist skills combined with the ability to apply these skills to identify and solve organisational problems. Furthermore, these knowledge workers are more mobile and challenging to manage, but fundamentally important to success.

The SHRD function should be able to effectively handle the challenges involved in successfully positioning and applying the management and development of knowledge within and across organisations such as the management of values and culture, providing clear direction to the people involved, ensuring aligned and measured processes to facilitate knowledge creation and development, encouraging the appropriate use of technology, obtaining collaboration and teamwork from knowledge workers. SHRD practices associated with creating the right environment for sharing knowledge will in particular promote organisational learning by creating a 'rich landscape of learning and development opportunities' (Kessels,1996).

Conclusions

SHRD is concerned with the provision of training, education, development, and learning opportunities for continuous transformative improvement in individual, team, and organisational performance. Organisational success is heavily dependent upon a skilled, flexible, and highly motivated workforce that is geared towards achieving continuous improvement. Transformative HRD policies and practices of an organisation must be driven by the business strategy. As Guest (1991) rightly stated, human resources can be integrated into strategic plans and the company's strategic plans are likely to be more successfully implemented only if HR policies cohere, if line managers have internalised the importance of human resources and this is reflected in their behaviour, and if employees identify with the company.

There are several challenges posed by SHRD as a transformatvie function for the HRD scholars and practitioners. There is a need to evolve a conceptually sound, analytically perfect, and operationally feasible model of SHRD reflecting ideological underpinnings and a holistic context. Closer and effective collaboration and interaction must be encouraged between HRD researchers and HRD practitioners in order to build more accurate empirical evidence of SHRD policies and practices in different types of organisations. This would help improve the competence and business credibility among SHRD practitioners. Also, one can enhance he credibility of SHRD by measuring and assessing its actual and potential contribution to organisational success.

To support SHRD, the firms must double up their efforts for fostering a learning and learner-centred organisational culture that encourages and supports individual, team, and organisational learning. It is critical to manage and develop knowledge and knowledge workers for the transformative role of the SHRD to work effectively. In addition, one must meet the training and development needs of special groups such as disabled and ethnic minorities. Tackling various ethical issues and dilemmas arising from the facilitation of continuous learning and development in the organisation would build confidence in the transformative value-addition of SHRD.

SHRD practitioners have to adopt a professional (expert and ethical) approach to the development of people at work. Efforts should be made to remove actual and potential barriers to the credibility and effectiveness of SHRD in organisations. Furthermore, SHRD is too important to be left only to HRD department; it calls for the total involvement, support and commitment of people at all levels in the organisation. Organisational culture is the single biggest vehicle to the creation of a knowledge-based and knowledge-enabled enterprise. The corporate philosophy about people, the values and styles of leadership and management, and the social system in the workplace will act either as enablers or inhibitors of transformative effects of SHRD policies and strategies (Harrison, 2001). In the age of globalisation and the knowledge economy, the ability to survive, grow, and excel in the long run would largely depend on the quality and level of SHRD in the organisation.

REFERENCES

Argyris, C. (1957). *Personality and organisation.* New York: Harper & Row.

____________ (1992). *On organisational learning.* Cambridge, Mass.: Blackwell.

Armstrong, M. (2001). *A handbook of human resource management practice,* 8th edition, London: Kogan Page.

Ashton, D. (1984). Current issues in iine/staff relationships. *Management Education & Development,* 10(2): 105-18.

Baird,L.,Meshoulam,I. (1988). Managing the two fits of strategic human resource management. *Academy of Management Review,*13: 116-28.

Barham,K., Fraser, J. and Heath, R. (1987). *Management for the future.* Ashridge Management College/FME.

Barney, J. (1991). Firm resources and sustained competitive advantage. *Journal of Management,*17: 99-120.

Bass, B.M. and Vaughan, J.A. (1967). *Training in industry: The management of learning.* London: Tavistock Publications.

Becker, G.S. (1964). *Human Capital.* New York: National Bureau of Economic Research.

Beckhard, R. (1969). *Organisation development: Strategies and models.* Reading, MA: Addison-Wesley.

Beer, M. (1983). What is organisational development?. In: Baird, L.S., Schneier, C.E. and Laird, D. Eds. *Training and development sourcebook.* Amherst, MA: HRD Press.

Bennet, R (1988). The nature and context of training for success. *Journal of European Industrial Training,* 12(2): 3-7.

Beer, M. and Spector, B. (1989). Corporate wide transformations in human resource management. In: Walton, R.E. and Lawrence, P.R. Eds. *Human resource management: Trends and challenges.* Boston, MA: Harvard University School Press.

Brewster, C., Hegewisch, A., Lockhart, T. and Holden,L. Eds. (1993). *The European human resource management guide.* New York: Academic.

Brown, G. and Read, A.R. (1984). Personnel and training policies – Some lessons for western companies. *Long Range Planning*, 17(2): 48-57.

Burgoyne, J. (1988). Management development for the individual and the organisation. *Personnel Management*, June: 40-44.

———————— (1999). Design of the times. *People Management*, 5(11): 39-44.

Child, J. (1977). *Organisation*. New York: Harper & Row.

Collis, D.J. and Montgomery, C.A. (1995). Competing on resources: Strategy in the 1990s. *Harvard Business Review*, 4: 118-128.

Conner, K.R. (1991). A historical perspective of resource-based theory and five schools of thought within industrial organisation economics: Do we need a new theory of the firm?. *Journal of Management*, 17: 121-54.

Denison, D.R. (1984). Bringing corporate culture to the bottom line. *Organisational Dynamics*, Autumn.

De Rijk, R.N., M.Mulder, and W.J.Nijhof. (1994). *The HRD profession in the 90's – Table report of a survey on the HRD profession in four European countries*. The Netherlands: University of Twente.

Drucker, P. (1993). *Post-capitalist society*. Oxford: Butterworth-Heinemann.

Edwards, J and Kleiner, B. (1988). Transforming organisation values and culture effectively. *Leadership and Organisations Development Journal*, 9(1): 13-16.

Ferris, G.R., Buckley, M.R., and Allen, G.M. (1992). Promotion systems in organisations. *Human Resource Planning*, 15: 47-68.

Finegold, D and Soskice, D. (1988). The failure of training in Briton: Analysis and prescription. *Oxford Review of Economic Policy*, 4:136-54.

Flamholtz, E.G., and Lacey, J.M. (1981). *Personnel management, human capital theory, and human resource accounting*. Los Angeles: Institute of Industrial Relations, University of California.

Garavan, T.N. (1987). Promoting natural learning activities within the organisation. *Journal of European Industrial Training*, 11(7): 18-23.

————————(1991), Strategic human resource development. *Journal of European Industrial Training*, 15(1): 17-30.

Garrat, R. (1990). *Creating a learning organisation*. London: Institute of Directors.

Garvin, D.A. (1993). Building a learning organisation. *Harvard Business Review,* July-August: 78-91.

Gilley, J.W. and Eggland, S.A. (1989). *Principles of human resource development*, Maidenhead: Addison-Wesley.

Grant, R.M. (1991). The resource-based theory of competitive advantage: Implications for strategy formulation. *California Management Review*, 33(3):114-135.

Gourlay, S. (2000). Knowledge management and HRD. *HRD Research and Practice Across Europe Conference Proceedings,* Surrey: Kingston University: 90-104.

Greenhaus, J.H. (1987). *Career Management*. New York: Dryden Press.

Guest, D.E. (1991). Personnel management: The end of orthodoxy. *British Journal of Industrial Relations*, 29(2): 149-76.

——————— (1998). Is the psychological contract worth taking seriously?. *Journal of*

Organisational Behaviour, 19: 649-64.

Gunningle, P and Flood, P. (1990). *Personnel management in Ireland: Practice, trends and developments.* Dublin: Gill & Macmillan.

Gutteridge, T.G. and Otte, F.L. (1983). *Organisational career development: State of the practice.* Washington, DC: ASTD Press.

Hall, D.T. (1984). Human resource development and organisational effectiveness. In: Fombrun, C.J., Tichy, N.M. and Devanna, M.A. Eds. *Strategic human resource management.* New York: John Wiley and Sons, 159-81.

Hansen, M.T., Nohria, N. and Tierney, T. (1999). What's your strategy for managing knowledge?. *Harvard Business Review.* March-April: 106-16.

Harris, L. (2000). A theory of intellectual capital. In: R.W.Herling and Provo, J. Eds. *Strategic perspectives on knowledge, competence, and expertise*. San Francisco: Berrett-Koehler: 22-37.

Harris, D.M. and DeSimone, R. (1994). *Human resource development.* Fort Worth, TX: The Dryden Press.

Harrison, R. (1997). *Employee development*. London: Institute of Personnel and Development.

——————— (2000). *Employee development*. 2nd edition, London: Chartered Institute of Personnel and Development.

Herriot, P. (1992). *The career management challenge. Balancing individual and organisational needs.* London: Sage.

Herriqt, P and Pemberton, C. (1995). *New deals: The revolution in managerial careers.* Chichester: Wiley.

Higgs, M. (1989). A strategic approach to training and development. *Training and Development,* November: 11-14.

Hiltrop, J.M. (1995). The changing psychological contract. *European Management Journal,* 13(3): 286-94.

Honey, P. (1998). The debate starts here. *People Management,* 1 October: 28-29.

Hoyle, E. (1995). The school as a learning organisation. *Paper delivered at the AERA Conference,* San Francisco, April.

Huber, G. (1991). Organisational learning: The contributing processes and literatures. *Organisation Science,* February: 88-115.

Hutton, W. (1995). *The state we're in.* London: Cape.

Jacobs, R.L. (1989). Systems theory applied to human resource development. In:

D.Gradous Ed. *Systems theory applied to human resource development.* Alexandria, VA: ASTD Press: 27-60.

———— (2000). Determining the boundaries of HRDQ and HRD. *Human Resource Development* Quarterly, 11(1): 1-3.

Johnson, G. and Scholes, K. (1997). *Exploring corporate strategy,* 4th edition, Hemel Hempstead: Prentice-Hall.

Keep, E. (1989). Corporate training policies: the vital component. In: Storey, J. Ed. *New perspectives in human resource management.* London: Routledge: 109-25.

Kessels, J. (1996). Knowledge productivity and the corporate curriculum. In: J.F.Scjhreinmakers Ed. *Knowledge management: Organisation, competence and methodology.* Proceedings of the fourth international ISMICK symposium, Rotterdam, the Netherlands, 21-22 October: 168-74.

Kim, D.H. (1993). The link between individual and organisational learning. *Sloan Management Review,* Fall: 37-50.

Kozlowski, S.W.J., and Salas, E. (1994). A multilevel organisational systems approach for the implementation and transfer of training. In: J.K.Ford and Associates, Ed. *Improving Training Effectiveness in Work Organisations.* Hillsdale, NJ: Erlbaum.

Kuchinke, P.K. (2002). Comparing national systems of human resource development: Role and function of post-baccalaureate HRD courses of study in the UK and US. *Third conference on HRD research and practice across Europe, Edinburgh, 25-26 January, 2002.*

Lewis, P. (1997). A framework for research into training and development. *International Journal of Training and Development*, 1(1): 2-8.

Likert, R. (1961). *New patterns of management*. New York: Harper & Row.

Lynham, S.A. (2000). Theory building in the human resource development profession. *Human Resource Development Quarterly*, 11(2): 159-78.

Mabey, C. and Salaman, G. (1995). *Strategic human resource management*. Oxford: Blackwell.

Mankin, D.P. (2001). A model for human resource development. *Human Resource Development International*, 4(1): 66-85.

Marsick, V.J. (1994). Trends in managerial invention: Creating a learning map. *Management Learning*, 21(1): 11-33.

Marsick, V. and Watkins, K. (1994). The learning organisation: An integrative vision of HRD. *Human Resource Development Quarterly*, 5(4): 353-60.

Mayo, E. (1933). *The human problems of an industrial civilization*. New York: Macmillan.

McGoldrick, J. and Stewart, J. Ed. (1996). *Human resource development: Perspectives, strategies and practice*. London: Pitman.

McGoldrick, J., Stewart, J and Watson, S. Eds. (2002). *Understanding human resource development: A research-based approach*. London: Routledge.

McGregor, D. (1960). *The human side of enterprise*. New York: McGraw Hill.

McLagan, P.A. (1983). *Models for excellence: The conclusions and recommendations of the ASTD training and development competency study*. Washington, DC: ASTD.

__________ (1989a). Models for HRD practice. *Training and Development Journal*, September: 49-59.

__________(1989b). *Models for HRD practice: The models*. Alexandria, VA: American Society for Training and Development.

__________(1989c). *Models for HRD practice: The HRD practitioners' application guide*. Alexandria, VA: American Society for Training and Development.

__________(1996). Great ideas revisited. *Training and Development*, January: 60-65.

McLagan, P.A. and D.Suhadolnick. (1989). *Models for HRD practice: The research report.* Alexandria, VA: American Society for Training and Development.

McGrath, R.G., Macmillan, I.C. and Venkataraman, S. (1995). Defining and developing competence: A strategic process paradigm. *Strategic Management Journal,* Vol.16: 251-75.

McLean, G.N. and McLean, L. (2001), If we can't define HRD in one country, how can we define it in an international context. *Human Resource Development International,* 4(3): 313-26.

Megginson,D., Joy-Mathews, J. and Banfield, P. (1993). *Human resource development.* London: Kogan Page.

Megginson, D and Pedler, M. (1992). *Self development: A facilitators guide.* Maidenhead: McGraw-Hill.

Meyer, J.W., and Rowan, B. (1977). Institutionalised organisations: Formal structure as myth and ceremony. *American Journal of Sociology,* 83: 340-63.

Miller, P (1987). Strategic industrial relations and human resource management: Distinction, definition, and recognition. *Journal of Management Studies,* 24: 101-109.

Mumford, A. (1989). *Management development: Strategies for action.* London: Kogan Page.

Nadler, L. (1970). *Developing human resources.* Houston: Gulf.

———— (1980). *Corporate human resources development: A management tool.* New York: Van Nostrand Reinhold.

———— and Nadler, Z. (1989). *Developing human resources.* 3rd edition. London: Jossey-Bass.

———— and Wiggs, G. (1986). *Managing human resourcc development.* New York: Jossey-Bass.

Nonaka, I. (1991). The knowledge-creating company. Harvard Business Review, November-December: 96-104.

———— (1994). A dynamic theory of organisational knowledge creation. *Organisation Science,* Vol.5: 14-37.

———— and Takeuchi, H. (1995). *The knowledge-creating company.* New York. Oxford University Press.

Ouchi, W.G. (1981). *Theory Z: How American business can meet the Japanese challenge.* Reading, MA: Addison-Wesley.

Peters, T. and Waterman, R. (1982). *In search of excellence.* New York: Harper & Row.

Phatak, A.V. (1992). *International dimensions of management*. Boston: PWS-Kent.

Porter, M.E. (1980). *Competitive strategy*. New York: Free Press.

——————(1985), *Competitive advantage: Creating and sustaining superior performance*. New York: Free Press.

——————(1990). *The competitive advantage of nations*. London: Macmillan.

Powell, G.N., and Butterfield, D.A. (1994). Investigating the "glass ceiling" phenomenon: An empirical study of actual promotions to top management. *Academy of Management Journal*, 37: 68-96.

Reid, M.A. and Barrington, H. (1997). *Training interventions: Managing employee development*. 5th edition. London: Institute of Personnel and Development.

Rothwell, W.J and Kasanas, H.C. (1989a). *Strategic human resource development*, Englewood Cliffs, NJ: Prentice Hall.

—————— and——————(1989b). *Human resource development: A strategic approach*. Revised edition. Amherst, MA: HRD Press.

——————and——————(1991), *Strategic human resource planning and management*. Englewood Cliffs, NJ: Prentice Hall.

Saari, L.M., Johnson, T.R., McLaughlin, S.D., and Zimmerle, D.M. (1988). A survey of management training and education practices in US companies. *Personnel Psychology*, 41: 731-43.

Scarbrough, H., Swan, J and Preston, J. (1999). *Knowledge management: A literature review*. London: Institute of Personnel and Development.

Schein, E.H. (1978). *Career dynamics: Matching individual and organisational needs*. Reading, MA: Addison-Wesley.

Schuler, R.S., and Macmillan, I.C. (1984). Gaining competitive advantage through HR management practices. *Human Resource Management*, 23: 241-55.

Scott, W.R. (1987). The adolescence of institutional theory. *Administrative Science Quarterly*, 32: 493-511.

Senge, P. (1990). *The fifth discipline: The art and practice of the learning organisation*. London: Century Business.

Simon, R.J and Streumer, J. (2001). Position statement on HRD. *Second international conference on HRD research and practice across Europe:2001*, The Netherlands: University of Twente.

Stead, V and Lee, M. (1996). Inter-cultural perspectives on HRD. In:

J.Stewart and J.McGoldrick. Eds. *Human resource development: Perspectives, strategies and practice.* London: Pitman, 47-70.

Stewart, J. and McGoldrick, J. Eds. (1996). *Human resource development: Perspectives, strategies, and practice.* London: Financial Times/ Pitman publishing.

Stewart, J. and Tansley, C. (2002). *Training in the knowledge based economy.* London: CIPD.

Stewart, J. (1996). *Managing change through training and development.* 2nd edition. London: Kogan Page.

——————(1999). *Employee development practice.* London: Financial Times/Pitman Publishing.

Streeck, W. (1989). Skills and the limits of neo-liberalism: The enterprise of the future as a place of learning. *Work, Employment and Society*, 3(1): 90-104.

Swanson, R.A. (1995). Human resource development: Performance is the key. *Human Resource Development Quarterly*, 6(2): 207-213.

——————(1999). HRD theory, real or imagined?. *Human Resource Development International*, 2(1): 2-5.

——————(2001). Human resource development and its underlying theory. *Human Resource Development International*, 4(3): 299-312.

Taylor, F.W. (1911). *Principles of scientific management.* New York: Harper.

Thomson, R. and Mabey, C. (1994). *Developing human resources.* London: Butterworth-Heinemann.

Tiepkerna, S., J.Stewart, et al. Eds. (2002). *HRD and learning organisations in Europe.* HRD Research Monograph Series. London: Routledge.

Triandis, H.C., Dunnette, M.D., and Hough, L.M. Eds. (1994). *Handbook of industrial and organisational psychology.* Vol.4, 2nd edition. Palo Alto, CA: Consulting Psychologist.

Trist, E and Bamforth, K. (1951). Some social and psychological consequences of the longwall method of coal-getting. *Human Relations*, 4: 3-38.

Trussler, S. (1998). The rules of the game. *Journal of Business Strategy*, 19(1): 16-19.

University Forum for Human Resource Development (1995). *Emerging concept of HRD – A position statement.* London: UFHRD.

Valkeavaara, T. (1998). Human resource development roles and competencies in five European countries. *International Journal of Training and Development*, 2(3): 171-89.

Viney, C., Adamson, S.J. and Doherty, N. (1995). Organisations' expectations and career management of fast track recruits. *Paper to the new deal in employment conference*, December, City University Business School.

Von Bertalanffy, L. (1950). The theory of open systems in Physics and Biology. *Science*, 111: 23-29.

Walton, J. (1999). *Strategic human resource development*. Essex: Financial Times/Prentice Hall.

____________(2001). *UFHRD chairman's report Spring 2001. Annual Report for 2001-2002.* Oxon: University Forum for Human Resource Development.

Watson, T.J., and Harris, P. (1999). *The emergent manager*. London: Sage.

Weinberger, L.A. (1998). Commonly held theories of human resource development. *Human Resource Development International*, 1(1): 75-93.

Wenger, E. and Snyder, W.M. (2000). Communities of practice: The organisational frontier. *Harvard Business Review*, January-February: 33-41.

Wick, C.W. and Leon, L.S. (1995). Creating a learning organisation: From ideas to action. *Human Resource Management*, Summer: 299-311.

Wilson, J. Ed. (1999). *Human resource development*. London: Kogan Page.

Willis, V.J. (1997). HRD as evolutionary system: From pyramid building to space walking and beyond. *Proceedings of the Academy of HRD*, Atlanta.

Wright, P.M. and Snell, S.A. (1991). Toward an integrative view of strategic human resource management. *Human Resource Management Review*, 1: 203-25.

Yadapadithaya, P.S. (1998). Strategic human resource development (SHRD): A key to competitive advantage. *The Indian Journal of Commerce*, 51(4), October-December: 195-203.

__________________(2000). Training and development in India. *International Journal of Training and Development*, International Briefing 5, 4(1): 79-89.

——————————(2001). Evaluating corporate training and development: An Indian experience. *International Journal of Training and Development*, 5(4): 261-74.

Zenger, J. (1985). Training for organisational excellence. Journal of European Industrial Training, 9(7): 3-8.

—————— and Hurgis, K. (1982). Assessing training results: It's time to take the plunge. *Training and Development*, Vol.20, January.

Zucker, L.G. (1977). The role of institutionalisation in cultural persistence. *American Sociological Review*, 42: 726-43.

10

TRANSFORMATIVE EMPOWERMENT: A STUDY OF LEADERSHIP ROLES, STYLES, DELEGATION AND QUALITIES OF INDIAN CEOS

*Dr. T.V. Rao**
with assistance of
*Raju Rao***
*Soumya Dixit****

Introduction

Tremendous changes have taken place in the global economic environment in the last one-decade. These changes have made impact on the Indian industry. Today the world is of a different order. Today's corporate world can be characterized as highly competitive, technology and systems driven, customer centered, acting with speed, cost and quality conscious, fast changing and highly competitive. In this changed situation, to survive one has to compete with those who have technological advantages, financial advantages, systems advantages, communication advantages, and above all those with people advantages in terms of their competencies,

* Chairman, T V Rao Learning Systems Pvt. Ltd., Ahmedabad, India.
** Director, T V Rao Learning Systems Pvt. Ltd., Ahmedabad, India.
*** Research Associate, T V Rao Learning Systems Pvt. Ltd., Ahmedabad, India.

attitudes and work culture. In such a situation, Indian companies need to have a highly competent top-level managers to lead them. The top team of each company becomes important. They need to perform leadership and institution building roles very effectively. They need to balance short-term targets with long-term organization building concerns. They need to inspire and develop their staff. They need to be customer driven and quality driven. Each of the individual managers plays a critical role in the company. The managers can be a good change agent by constantly improving themselves in relation to the roles they are playing, styles with which they are playing, delegating and making the right impact on others through their behavior. In this chapter, we highlight how the development style of the Indian CEOs is oriented towards transformative empowerment of their subordinates, where the subordinates are encouraged to learn from their own experiences.

Literature Review

Leadership has been defined in so many ways and by different authors and experts.

Noel Tichy and Cohen (1997) the authors of "Leadership Engine" points out:

" The scarcest resource in the world today is the leadership talent capable of continuously transforming organizations to win in tomorrow's world. The individuals and organizations that build Leadership Engines and invest in leaders developing other leaders have a sustainable competitive advantage." (p.8)

According to Tichy and Cohen:

- Winning leaders with a proven record take direct responsibility for developing other leaders
- Winning leaders can articulate and teach to others about

how to make the organization successful. They tell stories about their past and explain their learning experiences and beliefs

- They have well-developed methodologies for teaching others.
- Leadership talent can be nurtured and it is never too late or early to develop one own leadership abilities and talent of others.
- Leaders are normally viewed as those people who motivate one or more people to do a specific thing.

Warren Bennis says that the basis of the leadership is the capacity to change the mindset or framework of the other person. (Tichy, and Cohen, 1997)

Briane Lee (1997) of Franklin Covey after reviewing a number of studies on leadership states after a review of modern definitions of leadership that leadership is

" An intensely human enterprise, and does not fit neatly into definitions and boxes. Leaders have all the spontaneity, unpredictability, frailty, vulnerability and potential that is possible in the human race. If we are to lead with honor, we must start with the premise that flexibility, adaptability, and wisdom are possible, that we have seeds of greatness in us, and if we care deeply about the lives of others, we can work together to accomplish worthwhile things." (P265).

Tom Peters (1997) quoting Warren Bennis points out that one thing in common to most leaders is that they all make mistakes but bounce back from them. They use failures as building blocks.

The ability to spend more time framing contexts and less time defining the content more through coaching and supporting rather than directing and controlling becomes the model for middle managers (Ghosal and Bartlet, 1997)

Hessebbein and Cohen (1998) of the Drucker Foundation say that leaders exist at all levels of the organization. They identified the following traits of leaders:

- They excel seeing things from fresh eyes and they challenge status quo
- They are energetic and seem to be able to run through obstacles
- They are deeply interested in a cause or discipline related to their professional arena
- They can tap convictions of others and connect them to the organizational arena
- They help every one see what their everyday work means to larger purpose They have a high quest for learning
- They are open to people and their ideas
- They are driven by goals or ideals that are bigger than what an individual can accomplish
- They are willing to push themselves from comfort zones even after they have achieved success

Smart (1998) in his book on "Top Grading" lists 50 critical competencies for top graders. Some of these include: Intelligence; Analytical skills; Judgement and decision making; Conceptual ability; Creativity; Strategic skills; Pragmatism; Risk taking; Integrity; Initiative; Excellence; Self awareness; Adaptability; Listening; Team Player; Assertiveness; Communications; Political savvy; Running meetings; Vision; Change management; Conflict management; Energy; Ambition; Enthusiasm; Tenacity; and Balance in life.

Daniel Goleman (1998) considers Emotional Intelligence as central to leadership. In his chapter on the competencies of stars Goleman identifies personal and social competencies as constituting the emotional competence. The following characteristics have been included in his framework:

• Personal competencies determine how we manage ourselves. These include:

1. Self-awareness (knowing one's internal states, resources, and intuitions). This includes emotional awareness, accurate self-assessment, and self-confidence.

2. Self-regulation including managing one's internal states, impulses and resources. These include self-control, Trustworthiness, Conscientiousness, Adaptability, and Innovation

3. Motivation, including the tendencies that guide or facilitate reaching goals. These include Achievement drive, Commitment, Initiative, and optimism.

• Social Competencies that determine how we handle relationships. These include:

1. Empathy or awareness of others' feelings needs and concerns. These include understanding others, developing others, Service orientation, Leveraging Diversity, and political awareness.

2. Social skills dealing with adeptness at inducing desirable response. These include

Influence, Communication, Conflict management, Leadership, Change Catalyst, Building bonds, Collaboration and Cooperation and building team capabilities.

Goleman observes " Emotional, a role whose essence is getting others to do their jobs more effectively. Interpersonal ineptitude in leaders lowers everyone's performance: It wastes time, creates acrimony, corrodes motivation and commitment, and builds hostility and apathy. A leader's strengths or weaknesses in emotional competence can be measured in the gain or loss to the organization of the fullest talents of those they manage." (P32).

Goleman indicates that the traits of outstanding leaders transcend cultural and national boundaries. The most effective CEOs have been found to have three main clusters of competencies. The first two fall under emotional intelligence. They include: personal competencies like achievement, self-confidence, and commitment and the second consists of social competence like influence, political awareness and empathy. The third clusters of competencies are cognitive: they think strategically, seeking out information with a broad scan, and apply strong conceptual thinking. They blend all these into an inspired vision and influence the thinking of others.

Jefery Peffer (1998) observes three qualities of most successful transformations:

- Build trust
- Encourage change
- Measure the right things and align the incentive system to new practices

Peffer argues that a people centered approach can increase profits and give competitive advantage to itself.

Implications for Organizations

The various studies and points of view from researches reviewed above indicate the following:

- Leadership is critical for Business development or for any form of development
- Leadership is not anymore limited to a few.
- Every one's leadership competencies can be developed.
- They need to be developed and multiplied for growth and survival.

- It is imperative for managers to explore their talent and develop their leadership competencies for their own good and the good of their organizations.
- Self awareness is very critical first step in developing their leadership talent
- Organizational programs and plans are required to develop leadership talent and leadership development programs do help developing the same.

If leadership is so critical and the future of corporations depends upon having as many leaders as possible it is critical for corporations to develop more and more of leadership talent.

Many leadership programs focus on specific traits rather than any comprehensive qualities. This is because it is difficult to have any one quality focussed. Team building exercises help develop team building skills. It is for this reason many organizations have attempted in the last one-decade to use the 360-degree feedback as Leadership development tool. In India also it is becoming popular.

RSDQ Model of 360-Degree Feedback

TVRLS (a consulting company based in India) has developed a model for Indian Top and Senior Management in terms of managerial and leadership competencies needed which is termed as the RSDQ model (Roles, Styles, Delegation and Qualities). This model of leadership and managerial effectiveness views effective management and leadership as a combination of four sets of variables. These are:

Roles: The extent to which the individual plays various leadership and managerial roles and activities. There are a number of roles, which have to be played by every manager in order to be effective as managers. These are both transformation roles (leadership roles) and transactional roles (managerial) some of these are:

- Articulating and communicating vision and values
- Formulating long term policies and strategies
- Introducing and managing new technology and systems
- Inspiring, developing and motivating juniors
- Managing juniors, colleagues and seniors
- Culture building
- Internal customer management
- External customer management
- Managing unions and associations.

Style: While effective managers recognize all the leadership roles and perform them well, it is not only the roles or activities that determine the effectiveness but also the way in which they are played. The model envisages that managers may play most roles well, devote time and effort but could be insensitive to the style with which they carry out these activities. Rao (1986) has classified the leadership styles, on the basis of the earlier research at the Indian Institute of Management, into the following:

- A Benevolent or Paternalistic leadership style in which the top level manager believes that all his employees should be constantly guided treated with affection like a parent treats his children, is relationship oriented, assigns tasks on the basis of his own likes and dislikes, constantly guides them and protects them, understands their needs, salvages the situations of crisis by active involvement of himself, distributes rewards to those who are loyal and obedient, shares information with those who are close to him, etc.

- A Critical leadership style is characterized as closer to Theory X belief pattern where the manager believes that employees should be closely and constantly supervised, directed and reminded of their duties and responsibilities, is short term goal oriented, cannot tolerate mistakes or conflicts among employees, personal power dominated, keeps all information to himself, works strictly according to norms and rules and regulations and is highly discipline oriented.
- A Developmental leadership style is characterized as an empowering style, where the top manager believes in developing the competencies of his staff, treats them as mature adults, leaves them on their own most of the times, is long term goal oriented, shares information with all to build their competencies, facilitates the resolution of conflicts and mistakes by the employees themselves with minimal involvement from him.

Developmental style by nature seems to be the most desired organization building style. However some individuals and some situations require at times benevolent and critical styles. Some managers are not aware of the predominant style they tend to use and the effects their style is producing on their employees.

Delegation: The RSDQ model considers level of delegation as an important part of a senior executive's effectiveness. This dimension has been included because most senior managers seem to have difficulties delegating, especially those effective managers who get promotions fast in their career. In view of these experiences, delegation has been isolated as an important variable of leadership. Those who delegate release their time to perform higher-level tasks and those who don't continue to do lower level tasks and suppress their leadership qualities and managerial effectiveness.

Qualities: The model envisages that managers should exhibit qualities of leaders and world-class managers (e.g. proaction, listening, communication, positive approach, participative nature, quality orientation etc.). Such qualities not only affect effectiveness with which top-level managers perform various roles but also have an impact on the leadership style and hence are very critical.

Research Design

This study aims at answering the following questions:

1. What roles are the Indian CEOs good at performing extraordinarily well?
2. What Roles are they weak at performing?
3. What are their predominant styles of leadership and supervision?
4. What impact do they have on their subordinates?
5. What are their patterns of delegation?
6. What are the qualities they exhibit and what do they lack?
7. How do they delegate?

The Instruments

These issues were studied using the results from 360 Degree feedback on an instrument based on RSDQ model of TVRLS. The questionnaire had five parts: the first part dealt with Leadership and managerial roles and an assessment of how well he performs these various roles. The questionnaire measuring these consists of 75 items grouped under the various leadership and managerial roles explained earlier. Each CEO was assessed on a six point scale where a score of 6 represented that the CEO performs that activity or role extraordinarily well (percentage score of 100), 5 represents that he performs that role or activity very well (80% score); 4 represents that he performs that role reasonable well (60% score); 3 represents that he performs that role satisfactorily (40% score); 2 represents that he performs that role not so well and rather unsatisfactorily (20% score) and 1 represents that he performs that role very poorly or very inadequately (0% score).

The second part consisted of a Leadership styles questionnaire that assessed the style of dealing with 12 different situations like managing rewards, managing conflicts, managing mistakes, assignment of tasks, communication etc. For each situation three alternative styles that are supposed to most characteristic of Indian Managers (on the basis of previous research) were presented and the assessor was asked to indicate which of the extent to which each of the styles characterize the individual. The respondent is expected it distribute six points between the three styles using six points. The points were later converted into a percentage score. The style average was calculated using the average score obtained by each candidate on the style item.

Delegation was measured using a 10-item scale that measured various symptoms of delegation or non-delegation. These include:

- Not assigning even routine operations as well as decisions to the lower levels
- Not allowing subordinates to take minor risks
- Not giving authority and resources required to enable lower levels to perform tasks
- Not allowing subordinates to take even minor decisions in absence
- Keep others waiting for decisions, for example when on tour
- Piling up of papers

- Getting involved in everything juniors do
- All the time rushing to meet deadlines

The extent to which the candidate exhibits each of these symptoms was assessed by the percentage of assessors checking the items.

The fourth part of the questionnaires consisted of assessment of the extent to which the candidates each of the 25 qualities of leaders. A seven point semantic differential scale was used where "+3" score that the quality is extremely characteristic of him (100%) score, "+2" indicated that the quality is somewhat characteristic of him (84%), +1 indicated that it is a little characteristic of him (67%); "0" indicated that the quality is as much a characteristic of him as the negative part of it, "-1 " indicated that the negative side of that quality is more characteristic of him than the positive side (33%), "-2" indicated that the negative side of it is more characteristic of him (17%); and "- 3 " indicated that the quality is not at all characteristic and the opposite of it is most characteristic of him (0%).

The Sample

The sample consisted of 26 CEOs from Indian organizations. These are all different organizations consisting of manufacturing sector, services, information technology, consumer electronics, financial services etc. The organizations are located in different parts of the country. The CEOs are all those responding to the 360 Degree Initiatives. They all belonged to organizations that are interested in using 360-Degree feedback as a development tool. Each of these CEOs was assessed by their colleagues, subordinates and their seniors (other Board members etc.). In all these 26 CEOs were assessed by 373 Assessors. The number of assessors ranged from 2 in one case to 38 assessors in another case. The assessment of others was only taken into consideration for the purposes of this paper. Self-assessment was not taken into consideration. It was assumed that the combined assessment of other persons is representative of the actual performance of the individual CEO.

Limitations

The study is based on 360-Degree feedback and is only indicative of perceptions of the assessors. An actual observational study may indicate the actual roles performed, time devoted the impact etc. This study at best could be limited by the perceptions of the assessors and suffers the usual limitations of 360-Degree feedback studies.

Results

Tables 1 and 2 present the five best performed and five least well performed roles by Indian CEOs. The group as a

TABLE 1

The Five Most Well Performed Roles of CEOs in Indian Corporate Sector

S. No	*Item content*	*Average Percentage score*	*Lowest score*	*Highest score*
1	Communicating effectively with the boss, keeping him informed and maintaining good interpersonal relations	82	66	100
2.	Understanding The expectations of the boss and the top management and trying to meet them	81	65	100
3.	Influencing the thinking of the boss and getting his support and resources	76	53	91
4.	Taking guidance and learning from the experiences of the boss	76	61	92
5.	Liaison with top functionaries and the top management to keep them informed of developments	75	48	92

whole scored the highest and lowest respectively on these items. The tables also present the range of scores among the 26 CEOs studied.

The top five of the well performed activities in Table 1 indicates that the Indian CEOs are good at managing their seniors. They communicate and liaise well with them, understand their expectations, take guidance and also influence their thinking. Most of the seniors for these CEOs include their Chairman, Board Members, and other full time Directors. The Indian CEOs are weak in managing their unions and also in providing periodic feedback to their juniors. Three of the five least well performed roles deal with managing their junior employees.

TABLE 2

The Least Effectively Performed Roles of the CEOs

S. No	*Item content*	*Average Percentage score*	*Lowest score*	*Highest score*
1	Working with the unions and office bearers to control sloppiness, incompetence and indiscipline	56	40	80
2.	Carrying the unions along to contribute to the organizational goals and standards	58	33	90
3.	Monitoring to ensure that all the organizational values are followed by the staff	60	44	77
4.	Motivating the union representatives to have positive influence on the staff to maintain the image of the organization	60	38	100
5.	Providing periodic feedback to his juniors and other staff.	61	43	80

A further analysis of the data (see appendix 1 for details) revealed that culture building, inspiring and developing staff by investing time and effort on their development are assessed as the least well performed activities. It seems from the 360 degree Feedback data that the top management are still busy impressing their seniors than juniors. If they have to be good leaders, they need to shift their focus to competence building of their juniors.

TABLE 3

How Indian CEOs Fare on Transformational Leadership Roles?

S. No	*Item content*	*Average Percentage score*	*Lowest score*	*Highest score*
1	Inspiring staff with vision and values	64	39	91
2	Learning from Colleagues and benefiting from their experience	66	51	86
3	Policy formulation for the unit in relation to various issues like business development and staff management	66	43	92
4	Introducing new systems of management to manage various activities and operations effectively	67	36	86
5	Articulating the culture that should characterize the unit	67	45	94
6	Setting long term goals and objectives	68	43	88
7	Evolving strategies to improve customer satisfaction	68	44	87
8	Understanding business environment and opportunities to make an impact	75	44	96
9	Setting personal example in terms of following vision and values	72	43	97
10	Articulating vision for the unit	70	43	90

Table 3 presents data on 10 transformational roles performed by the Indian CEOs. The data indicate that Indian CEOs perform transformational roles much less effectively than transactional roles. All the roles they perform well as is evident from Table 1 are transactional roles. Even the well-performed transactional roles are limited to effective management of boss and seniors. Transactional roles with the unions and staff seem to be relatively poor.

Leadership Styles

The leadership styles were assessed on 12 style dimensions and the impact measured on five dimensions. Items 1 to 12 in Appendix 2 give details of the styles and items 13 to 17 the impact. In items 1 to 12 in Appendix 2 below all those marked as "a" are reflective of "Benevolent Style"; items marked as "b" are reflective of critical style; and those marked as "c" are reflective of "Developmental Style".

The analysis of the Leadership Styles indicated that the Indian CEOs are predominantly developmental in their style for example: when mistakes are made they tend to encourage people to learn from their mistakes (53% score) rather than protecting the subordinates and salvaging the situations themselves (34% score) or getting emotional even for minor mistakes (13%). When conflict arise they encourage people to solve their problems in such a way that they develop capability to resolve conflicts in future (58% score) rather than giving their judgment and making the employees dependent on them (30% score) or reprimanding the erring side (12% score). The development style was indicated in the way they take decisions, the way they assign the tasks, the way they communicate and the way they treat the juniors in other matters. In all this areas their benevolent or paternalistic style was about 30% as compared to 60% developmental style and 10% critical style.

As a result of this developmental style they seem to be creating certain amount of empowerment. The data also indicated that even the 30% of paternalistic style which is characterized by value for relationships and a tendency to favor few of their subordinates leads to a substantial degree of dependence. About 30% of their subordinates perceived them as favoring a few. This is a high percentage. The Indian CEO is in transition. Most organizations in the past used to be managed with a paternalistic style. This style seems to create dependence while it also gets loyalty and hard work. Juniors of the CEOs who predominantly use paternalistic style were found to have high degree of dependency and at the same time admiration for the CEO. However, only some of their juniors reported learning from them. They seem to work in order to maintain relationship and out of admiration for the boss rather than out of enjoyment of the work.

While developmental style was the most predominant style for all the CEOs. There were a few CEOs who scored high on critical style. These CEOs were found create resentment among their subordinates and some of them felt that they are unable to learn much while working with such CEOs. Such CEOs found the 360 degree feedback very helpful and prepared plans to change their styles.

Delegation

The extent to which the symptoms of delegation or non-delegation are exhibited by the CEOs is presented in Table 4. The table indicates that the Indian CEOs in general are delegating type. The table indicates that in general the Indian CEOs are perceived as delegating about 74% of the time. They generally prefer their subordinates to check with them when problems arise. On all the other areas the delegation seems to be reasonable good. There is however a great degree of variation among the CEOs on the extent to which they delegate.

TABLE 4

Delegation/Non-delegation Symptoms Exhibited by the Indian CEOs (Higher the Percentage Less the Delegation)

S. No	*Indicator of delegation*	*Average % score*	*Lowest % score*	*Highest % score*
1	He generally prefers his juniors to wait for his return rather than take decisions in his absence.	19	98	0
2	He does not leave routine decisions entirely to the lower levels.	24	100	0
3	Generally his in-tray piles up quite full with files and papers when he goes away on tour.	22	95	0
4	He is cautious and does not let his subordinates take even minor risks.	17	95	0
5	He spends time on activities and problems that he was handling before his last promotion/or his previous job.	18	70	0
6	He prefers his subordinates to check with him whenever a problem arises in an on-going project or assignment	55	100	0
7	He likes to keep himself fully involved in everything being handled by his subordinates.	32	80	0
8	He likes to be consulted even on matters where a rule or precedent already exists.	24	95	0
9	We often wish he would not spend time doing work which we can easily handle.	17	81	0
10	He is often rushing to meet deadlines.	29	58	0
	Overall	26	62	8

Behavioral Qualities

The assessment of the 26 CEOs on 25 behavior Qualities is presented in Table 5.

The CEOs in general are rated very high on almost all the 25 behavioral qualities. However they scored high on the following qualities. The percentage scores are given in brackets. A score around 80% can be treated as a high exhibition of that quality (the opposite of it is only 20%).

TABLE 5

Top 5 High Scoring Behavior Qualities of the 26 CEOs

S. No	*Behavior dimensions*	*Average % score*	*Lowest % score*	*Highest % score*
1	Clear and persuasive communication rather than unclear and long winded communication (85% score)	85	68	100
2	Active rather than passive (85% score)	85	57	100
3	Takes positive approach rather than negative approach (84% score)	84	70	95
4	Change oriented rather than status quo oriented (83%)	83	63	97
5	Encouraging rather than discouraging (83%)	83	70	97

The five qualities on which they scored relatively lower are presented in Table 6. (Percentage scores given in brackets).

TABLE 6

The Lowest Scoring Five Behavior Qualities of the 26 CEOs

S. No	*Behavior dimensions*	*Average % score*	*Lowest % score*	*Highest % score*
1	Empathetic rather than corrective (68% score indicating that they could be 32% corrective)	68	46	87
2	Participative rather than authoritarian	69	36	92
3	Calm and composed rather than irritable	71	33	100
4	Patient and accepting rather than impatient and intolerable	71	48	100
5	Proactive rather than reactive	71	43	90

Conclusions and Recommendations

In terms of Tichy and Cohen (1997) Indian CEOs have a long way to go for the following reasons as evident from their 360 degree feedback:

- There is a great degree of variation in the effective performance of roles, styles, delegation and qualities. This indicates the need for 360 Degree feedback as tool to create more self awareness.
- They are not yet taking direct responsibility for developing others as leaders. They seem to do little to inspire and develop their juniors.
- While they are good at articulating their vision, and communicating the same to their juniors, the impact of this gets limited and they are not able to teach others about how to make the organization successful. They are still operating at conceptual level and are reluctant to share their past and explain their learning experiences and beliefs
- They are not spending adequate time and effort to develop their own leadership abilities and talent of others. Their investment in the 360 degree feedback is just a beginning.

In sum, Indian CEOs seem to be good at boss management and weak at managing Unions and also on transformational roles. They seem to perform less effectively the transformational roles. Among the transformational roles their strengths lie in articulating vision for the unit and influencing the thinking of their seniors. On a large number of other areas like culture building, inspiring and developing staff they need to develop a lot more. Future leadership programs should focus on their change management skills. Their styles are predominantly developmental. They seem to delegate a good deal. High activity level, positive thinking, communications, and change orientation are some of the notable strengths. Proactivity, cool and composed nature, empathy, patience and participative nature could be developed more to make an impact. Some of these roles and qualities could be developed to make an impact.

REFERENCES

Ghosal. Sumantra and Bartlett, C.A. *The Individualized Corporation*. Harper Business Book, NY 1997

Goleman, Daniel. *Working with Emotional Intelligence*, Bantam Books, New York, 1998.

Hesselbein, Frances and Cohen, Paul, M. *Leader to Leader*. Jossey bass, San Francisco, 1999

Lee, Briane, *The Power Principle: Influence with Honour*. Franklin Covey Co, , Fireside, NY, 1997

Peters, Tom. *The Circle of innovation: you can't shirk your way to Greatness*, Hodder & Sloughton, London, 1997

Pfeffer, Jeferey. *The Human Equation*. Harvard business School Press, 1998

Smart, Bradford D. Top Grading: How leading companies win by hiring, coaching and keeping the best people, Prentice Hall, New York, 1999

Rao, T. V. The supervisory and leadership beliefs questionnaire, in J.W. Pfeiffer and L.D. Goodstein. (Eds) *The 1986 Annual: Developing Human Resources*, San Diego, California: University Associates, 111-116

Rao, T. V. and Vijayalakshmi, M. RSDQ Model of 360 Degree feedback. In "Rao, T. V., Vijayalakshmi, M and Rao, Raju. (Editors) *360 Degree Feedback and Performance management Systems*, New Delhi, Excel Publications, 2000

Tichy, Noel M. and Cohen, Eli. *The Leadership Engine: How winning companies build Leaders at Every Level*, Harper Business, 1997, NY

APPENDIX 1

Average Percentage of Effectively Performance of Various Activities by CEOs

Average % score	*Item number*	*Item content*
56	40	Working with the Unions and office bearers to control sloppiness, incompetence and indiscipline
58	38	Carrying the unions along to contribute to the organizational goals and standards
60	8	Monitoring to ensure that the values are followed by all staff in the unit
60	37	Motivating union-representatives to have a positive influence on the staff to maintain the image of the organization and contribute to its growth
61	24	Providing periodic feedback to his juniors and other staff and helping them to review their performance
61	35	Instituting organizational processes and mechanisms to build the desired culture
61	34	Monitoring development of the desired organizational culture
61	11	Investing time and effort in the growth and development of the juniors and other staff
62	29	Consistency and objectivity in relation to staff decisions
62	18	Helping staff to recognize their own contributions to the achievement of the goals and growth of the organization
63	36	Maintaining good relations with office-bearers of unions and associations
63	27	Resolving conflicts or helping staff to resolve conflicts

Average % score	*Item number*	*Item content*
63	13	Providing proper guidance and counseling to his/her staff
63	22	Providing guidance to staff to perform their tasks well
63	28	Handling staff grievances
64	16	Taking time to explain to his juniors and other staff on how to do things
64	70	Monitoring the effective implementation and utilization of systems and technology
64	9	Inspiring the staff with the vision and values
65	20	Setting and communicating clear-cut norms, values discipline and other standards of excellence to be followed by staff
65	43	Managing different view points among staff members to build collaborative culture
66	23	Monitoring staff performance
66	44	Providing information and assistance required by other colleagues in the unit to help them work with high team spirit
66	73	Anticipating crisis situations (internal and external) and diffusing them quickly
66	50	Learning from colleagues and benefiting from them experience
66	3	Creating opportunities for the employees to make an impact
66	64	Fair allocation of work to staff in the unit
66	21	Providing information and other

Average % score	*Item number*	*Item content*
		resources necessary for the staff to perform their tasks well
66	65	Policy formulation for the unit in relation to various issues like business development, staff management, quality, costs, recoveries etc.
66	75	Responding to the needs of the local communities and region whenever crises, calamities etc. arises
67	42	Creating a feeling of oneness (we feeling) and team spirit among the employees of the unit
67	69	Introducing new systems of management to manage various activities and operations effectively
67	60	Seeing suggestions from customers in order to improve services provided by the unit and taking the seriously
67	32	Reminding the members about the culture of the organization/ unit
67	48	Helping other employees and colleagues in the organization wherever possible
67	12	Motivating and inspiring juniors and other staff to be excellent performers
67	14	Giving proper public recognition to outstanding work done by any junior member in his/her unit
67	31	Articulating the culture (norms, values and organizational processes) that should characterize the unit
67	47	Understanding the needs, expectations and requirements of the colleagues
67	45	Recognizing and praising the contributions of every member in the team

Average % score	*Item number*	*Item content*
67	4	Communicating or sharing his/her vision with the staff
67	67	Building technological competence of staff through training etc.
67	6	Developing new activities and schemes for the unit to achieve the vision and make impact
68	62	Setting of long term goals and objectives for the unit
68	19	Setting clear cut performance goals for his juniors as well as the others in the unit and helping them to set clear cut goals
68	57	Evolving strategies to improve customer satisfaction
68	30	Encouraging innovativeness among the staff
68	74	Securing and understanding of the unit's stake holders, competitors and vendors
68	26	Listening to problems and difficulties of employees/staff
68	41	Fostering a spirit of team work and collaboration among the staff in the unit
69	25	Recognizing, rewarding and encouraging good performance of employees
69	66	Introducing new technologies for facilitating good products and services and work efficiency
69	39	Showing a high concern for staff welfare and helping staff to have a good quality of work life
69	59	Understanding the difficulties and solving problems of customers

Average % score	*Item number*	*Item content*
69	17	Providing a sense of ownership and significance to the employees and staff
70	61	Securing the critical information required for strategy formulation and planning performance improvements of the unit
70	72	Representing the unit in functions and other ceremonies and performing ceremonial roles
70	15	Acting as a role model for juniors/staff to emulate by high standards of personal example
70	58	Communicating to other staff about customer requirements and concerns
70	56	Meeting customers (internal/external) frequently and getting to know them better
70	1	Articulating his/her own vision for the unit
71	33	Setting personal example in terms of following the norms and values
71	68	Keeping in touch with the technological developments in the related industry and/or function in India and abroad
71	49	Getting the cooperation of colleagues in furthering the objectives and goals of the units
71	7	Clearly stating the values of the unit/organization e.g. Customer Service, Service quality, Punctuality, Cost-effectiveness etc.
71	71	Maintaining good relations with various government, media and other public agencies
72	10	Setting personal example in following the values and vision

Average % score	*Item number*	*Item content*
72	63	Setting short term tasks and targets for the unit in various areas of operation
72	5	Understanding the top management's vision for the organization and communicating the same to the staff
75	2	Understanding the business environment and opportunities for the unit to make an impact
75	46	Development of good working relationships with colleagues - be interacting with them; showing them respect; using tact and being frank
75	55	Liaison with other functionaries and the top management to keep them informed of various developments and to get support needed by the region
76	54	Taking guidance and learning from the experiences of the boss and other seniors
76	53	Influencing the thinking of the boss and getting his support and resources
81	52	Understanding the expectations of the boss and the top management and trying to meet them
82	51	Communicating effectively with the boss; keeping him informed, maintaining good interpersonal relationships and interactions

APPENDIX 2

Leadership Styles of Indian CEOs and Their Impact on the Subordinates

(Items 1 to 12 are Style Items and 13 to 17 Impact Items)

S. No	*Behavior dimensions*	*Average % score*	*Lowest score*	*Highest score*
1	**BELIEFS ABOUT SUBORDINATES**			
A	Seems to believe that subordinates should be treated affectionately and constantly guided and helped. Therefore, he tends to give instructions regularly.	28	10	58
B	Seems to believe that his subordinates tend to avoid work unless they are closely supervised. Therefore he tends to keep a close watch on them.	13	3	27
C	Seems to believe that his subordinates are capable of working on their own. Therefore he leaves them to work on their own most of the time, providing support only if needed.	59	33	87
2	**ORGANIZATIONAL AND PERSONAL GOALS**			
A	Shows concern for the individual needs and personal goals of employees who work with him. He takes trouble to help them achieve their personal goals.	32	15	46
B	Seems to be excessively concerned with immediate tasks and organizational goals. Has no concern for individual needs an goals	29	0	73
C	Is readily willing to sacrifice personal goals for organizational goals and sets an example for others. Helps employees see the linkage between personal and organizational goals.	39	10	73
3	**VISION CONSTITUTION**			
A	Thinks only in terms of his people and protecting them. Makes efforts to gain	15	3	42

S. No	Behavior dimensions	Average % score	Lowest score	Highest score
	the personal loyalty of subordinate by satisfying them			
B	Thinks only in terms of immediate tasks or short them goals. Does not mind dissatisfying a few employees if immediate tasks are not accomplished.	30	6	68
C	Thinks in terms of the long-term goals and interests of the organization. Is a visionary? Invests time in developing juniors for future of the organization.	55	25	87
4	**PROVIDING SUPPORT TO SUBORDINATES**			
A	Expects subordinates to come to him whenever they are in difficulty and solves their problems	29	10	47
B	Treats subordinate as problem for him and grudgingly provides help whenever they ask.	5	0	19
C	Expects subordinates to develop competencies by working through their difficulties and by learning to solve their own problems. But readily provides support when they need.	67	40	90
5	**MANAGING MISTAKES**			
A	Tolerates mistakes and salvages the situation. Protects the subordinates as far as possible	34	17	58
B	Cannot tolerate mistakes. Gets emotional at times even for minor mistakes	13	0	38
C	Encourages subordinates to use mistakes as learning opportunities. Discusses with them, educates them and makes them more competent.	53	31	83
6	**CONFLICTS**			
A	When conflicts arise, he gives a judgement on who is right and who is wrong and employees normally look up to him for his decision.	30	6	53

S. No	*Behavior dimensions*	*Average % score*	*Lowest score*	*Highest score*
B	When conflicts arise he complains to others or takes action to pull up the erring side.	12	0	26
C	When conflicts arise, he calls the parties together and tries to help them solve problems in a manner that understanding between them is increased and their own competency for resolving conflicts is built up.	58	30	87
7	**DECISION MAKING**			
A	Prefers to take most decisions himself and informs only those who are loyal or close to him. Prefers that subordinates consult him before they take any decision themselves.	27	5	50
B	Takes all decisions by himself, as he does not seem to believe that his subordinates are capable of decision-making.	9	0	31
C	Prefers his subordinates to take most decisions on their own. However, he consults people in critical decisions and keeps them informed to give them a sense of involvement and identification with the organization.	64	20	88
8	**ASSIGNMENT OF TASKS**			
A	Tends to assign tasks on the basis of his personal preferences.	22	0	46
B	Tends to assign tasks purely according to organizational norms without any flexibility or concern for people.	17	4	37
C	Tends to assign tasks in such a way that they match the competencies of the subordinates and at the same time provide opportunities for developing them.	61	38	90

S. No	Behavior dimensions	Average % score	Lowest score	Highest score
9	**PROVIDING SIGNIFICANCE TO OTHERS**			
A	He likes others to treat him with respect, admiration and personal loyalty. He can always be counted upon to protect the interests of those loyal to him.	31	15	56
B	He tends to treat other employees or his subordinates as less important or significant people. Prefers to go by designation and status.	9	0	21
C	Tends to treat other employees and subordinates with respect. He seems to believe that he can become significant or powerful only by making all those who work with him significant and powerful.	60	32	85
10	**COMMUNICATION**			
A	Shares information about company policies, environmental changes, technology, and strategies etc.selectively with those close to him or whom he considers dependable.	31	11	58
B	Keeps all information to himself and uses it to control people. Uses information as a source of power.	7	0	33
C	Takes subordinates into confidence and keeps all of them informed of company plans, policies and changes in environment, technology strategies etc. with a view to get them involved or preparing them for future challenges.	63	40	86
11	**INSPIRING OTHERS**			
A	He is interested in maintaining good relationships. Highly relationship oriented.	29	11	63
B	He is quite task-oriented and cannot tolerate any delays or deviation. He has no concern for people and their difficulties.	18	0	36
C	He inspires people to give their best to	53	28	73

S. No	*Behavior dimensions*	*Average % score*	*Lowest score*	*Highest score*
	the organization. He creates conditions to help people enjoy their work			
12	**INITIATIVE**			
A	He gives freedom and opportunity for employees to take initiative. He encourages a few who are close and loyal to him to take initiative.	29	11	48
B	He prefers employees/subordinates to conform strictly to rules, regulations, procedures and norms and tends to enforce them even with some coercion.	14	3	28
C	He encourages all his employees to take initiative. He believes that employees cannot develop unless they have some freedom to take initiative and experience personal worth.	57	31	80
13	**IMPACT ON FEELINGS**			
A	His subordinates seem to like him and admire him. Some of them may even be missing him when he is away.	33	20	50
B	His subordinates seem to feel that they could grow better under a different leader. They seem to resent his style. They feel good when he is away.	11	0	36
C	There is quite a bit of "we" feeling and team spirit among the people who work with him. They continue to work hard even when he is away.	56	34	71
14	**JOB SATISFACTION**			
A	People who work with him have high level of satisfaction as they enjoy their closeness and personal relationship with him more than their work.	30	10	42
B	People who work with him do not enjoy their job and tend to look for a change of him or their job.	9	0	29

S. No	Behavior dimensions	Average % score	Lowest score	Highest score
C	People who work with him enjoy their jobs.	61	37	87
15	**WORK COMMITMENT**			
A	He tends to make people admire him rather than getting them to enjoy their work	18	3	43
B	He tends to make people develop avoidance or negative attitudes to work.	7	0	15
C	He inspires people to identify themselves with their work and the organization.	75	46	93
16	**DEVELOPMENT**			
A	One can learn something by working with him.	30	7	60
B	One learns little while working with him.	6	0	32
C	One learns a lot while working with him.	64	31	93
17	**MORALE**			
A	People in his department (i.e. those who work with him) exhibit morale in his presence or when he is around.	29	10	42
B	People in his department have a low morale.	8	0	27
C	People in his department have a high 'morale' (togetherness, we feeling and happiness).	64	39	90

11

OPINION: INTEGRATING HRD WITH APPLIED BEHAVIOURAL SCIENCE.CHALLENGE FOR HRD—WHEN DREAMS DIE.THE EKLAVVA SYNDROME

*Harsh Rai Puri**

INTEGRATING HRD WITH APPLIED BEHAVIOURAL SCIENCE

The adage of *Vasudhaiva Kutumbkum* is very evident *and live* in this millennium. The major developments impacting the world are:

(a) Companies are global in their operations

(b) Breakthrough in Information Technology (IT)

(c) Delayering of organisations would curtail the role of the middle manager

(d) Total focus on the customer (with effective and creative usage of IT as the driver of the process)

(e) Knowledge—not currency—shall be the capital of tomorrow's enterprises

Continuous learning is the key to responding to the

*Sr DGM, BHEL, Bhopal.

above developments. Both corporations and individuals will have to constantly reinvent themselves.

Surviving this frenetic pace has made learning to cope with the resultant stress a top priority on organisational as well as individual charters. One has to be ready and willing to examine—on a continued basis—the process of adjustments in facing these continuous upheavals.

This brings the role of Human Resource Development into sharper focus. HRD is undergoing a metamorphosis in terms of:

- — Coming out of the shadow of Personnel Management and claiming its rightful place
- — Becoming a multi-faceted function embracing a wider range & repertoire of approaches, skills and activities rather than being narrowly focussed on conventional training activities alone
- — Moving from mechanistic to humanistic thrust with concern being exhibited for social and ecological issues also *(propagation of a holistic orientation)*
- — Each Line Manager is viewed as an interdependent resource person for HRD

Applied Behavioural Science with its process orientation facilitates the above transformation of HRD through interventions designed at individual and organisational levels covering:

(i) Evaluation & integration of Experience

(ii) Unleashing & unblocking of creative human potential

(iii) Action orientation leading to transfer of learning to one's workplace

(iv) Encouragement of exploration & extension of personal space and introspective approaches (lesser compartmentalisation of work & cutting across hierarchy – induced partly through *delayering*- role boundaries under constant upheaval)

(v) Thrust on wholeness and mutuality (leading to integration of the individual and the organisation) and realised through self-managing and self-determining multi-disciplinary teams. The individual is encouraged to be a member of more than one team (each with a finite life), leading to exposure to wider & constantly changing roles.

The underlying thrust is on understanding the prevalent organisational culture. Edgar Schien defines Organisational Culture as "A pattern of basic assumptions -invented, discovered or developed by a given group as it learns to cope with its problems of EXTERNAL ADAPTATION & INTERNAL INTEGRATION- that has worked well enough to be taught to new members as the correct way to perceive, think & feel in relation to those problems".

If we take the analogy of an organisation as a patch of land then HRD focus is on preparing soil for utilisation ensuring (1) optimal use of resources; and (2) maximising output over both short & long -term.

Applied Behavioural Science (ABS) enables HRD to ensure:

(i) Resources are deployed optimally

(ii) Impact of conversion or transformation process balances short/long term impact without denuding land and resources causing an early burnout

(iii) Heightened awareness of and sensitivity to changes within and outside the defined boundaries through experience—by undergoing introspective processes (at both individual & group levels)

The Role of HRD that emerges from this application of ABS:

(A) Provide Performance Support to the organisation

(B) Promote "Shared Values" as the glue that holds the organisation together

(C) The thrust areas of HRD efforts:

- multi-tasking abilities
- promote coaching & risk-taking abilities

(D) Continuous education of those at the higher echelons

(E) Initiate networking processes with the inherent assumption that learning emerges through respect, cooperation and dialogue

To make this happen HRD would have to stop cribbing that

— if only we were invited to management meetings...

— if only we were asked for our opinion...

— if only we had more status and credibility...

HRD needs to align itself to the REAL needs of the organisation, redefine its customers/clientele, constantly learn and adapt, and harness support treating EACH individual as a resource. The training & development is not confined to the classroom situation alone, and is an activity being performed continuously in the workplace.

The role of HRD would be akin to that of the Genome in living organisms. The Genome denotes the complete set of genes forming a vast inter-woven self-organising network, rich in feedback loops, in which genes directly or indirectly regulate each other's activities. The focus is shifting from evolution to CO-EVOLUTION -an ongoing process that moves through networking & is a subtle interplay of competition & collaboration, creation & mutual adaptation.

POSTSCRIPT:_What does the above mean to an MBA student?

(i) Impact of changing roles in the Industrial scenario:

* Your competitor in one contract may be your collaborator in another

* The ethical facets of business are increasingly coming into play (especially in the context of the global market)

(ii) It is important to build bridges in the form of relationship networking *and maintain these linkages*

(iii There is a need to specialise "but not at the cost of knowing more and more about less and less". Continuously strive to broaden repertoire of skills.

(iv) Learn to postpone gratification (many a times the need for instant gratification leads one astray)

(v) It helps to have a small support group of a few individuals to help tide over (& learn from) difficult experiences

(vi) Sharpen your observational skills (utilise every opportunity to observe "process" or "behaviour in motion") and jot emerging hypotheses

(vii) Keep yourself updated (READ, READ, READ & just magazine reading *not* enough – *sole thrust on extensive browsing the internet may overload your circuits*)

(viii) Maintain a journal – to document your journey and its *ups* and *downs* – this could be a potential source of recharging your batteries.

* * * *

CHALLENGE FOR HRD—WHEN DREAMS DIE

There is a dreamer hidden in each one of us. Lucky are those people who are able to sustain their dreams as well as their dreaming. Usually in our journey called life we are prone to getting caught in the nitty-gritty of day-to-day life which snaps the fragile link that we have with our dreams.

What are the nature of our dreams? Most often they are of the ordinary type—in which we visualise a limited-hassle style of living: we are able to manage the daily tribulations that we face, we are able to provide for our loved & dear ones the kind of relationships and things they are aspiring for; that we are able to ensure that our progeny is endowed with the basic qualities that not only he/she is able to stand up on one's own with pride at being a human being without losing touch with the innate spirituality that we are all blessed with. The magic of the little infant curling up in our arms with the security that could reflect a continuity of what was experienced in the mother's womb; which is cathartic in our own reliving our own attachment to our parents. The joy and the pain of the growing-up pangs culminating in the flying away to their own pasture and field to set up their own homes. The pain of parting and the pleasure of meeting go hand in hand.

In the *organisational* setting too we have our dreams: at one end we seek growth and advancement in our chosen field; at the other we seek nourishing relationships that supplement our social & personal needs —providing us an anchor of belongingness, of being moored at a certain fixed space. Its like dreaming of a home-nest that one takes off from with the security that "there is someone waiting for you" (the phrase painted on many boards as well as behind trucks) and one may wander & explore yet there is some place for you to come back to.

The home and the workplace complement each other. Yet there is a difference. The dreams at the workplace help realise many dreams of the home front. Vacuum in one area creates ripples in the other, some kind of an imbalance. At home there are lesser problems of acceptance (and even if there are over a period of time these quirks & eccentricities are tolerated) but a TOTAL *LACK* OF CONCERN FOR THE PERSON is often experienced on the workfront.

It is the frequent experience that Bosses find it easier to eloquently eulogise a subordinate at his funeral—as they are assured that this is the last contact with the individual. The family is left to fend for itself, as the organisation owns responsibility only to the living employee—no matter if only to ignore his/her existence altogether.

In an atmosphere like this when nobody is really interested in making any kind of improvement whatsoever in terms of working relationships, someone raising a dissenting voice is seen as a crackpot, one who should be taken to the nearest public square and publicly hanged. The organisation does do this -if only in figurative terms: it hangs him/her EVERY day of his worklife by CHOOSING to ignore his very existence; and when there are suicides and accidents everyone goes into their respective shell thanking God that it wasn't "me". No one stops to look around whether the idea of self-flagellation and hara-kiri has taken anyone else into its fold.

It is NOT the concern of any organisation, of any Boss, of any Senior, of any Colleague as to whether they are in touch with those persons who may be harbouring deep thoughts of disillusionment and despair within themselves; of how many times they have come to the brink and then gone back. What if the next time there is such a temptation there is no counter-force pulling them back and telling them what would happen if they took the extreme step?

Why do dreams die? When there is no hope of any change, rather the feeling experienced is of NO HOPE; period!

What is a person asking for: some attention, some support, some guidance, some meaningful work, a social anchor & some affection. It is a Catch-22 situation: as I am aware that I am lacking something and I am struggling to keep my emotional balance hence how could I be on the verge of lapsing into insanity—temporary or permanent? The appeals for help go unresponded as it is seen as a game being played by this individual to "shun any real work", "to attract attention", etc etc. These rationalisations are also needed to reject any feeling of responsibility towards that person, even though he may have been crying on your shoulder pouring out his troubles to you and sharing that he needs help to get out of this vicious cycle & is not sure whether he would be able to control himself or not next time a fatal wave of despair deluges him.

Will *someone* lose sleep over these dreams that are dying around us everyday? So much so that individuals are becoming automatons who have cut off those parts of themselves that are painful to handle, & whose probing questions to their conscience they do not have the answers to. This malaise is spreading and we are bound to see a spate of such self-victimising activities due to the total lack of any formal support system at the organisational level.

There are also dreams of *another* kind—wherein the individual tries to see oneself as a part of a *higher* order of things: at the family, at the organisational & at societal levels.

Definitely visionaries are NOT the flavour of the day and they face the immense challenge of being annihilated altogether in spirit. The pressure to conform is so strong that unless the individual has the backing of a formal/informal support group he/she would *have* to relent. There is also the risk of their being manipulated by "special-interest groups" who would use and discard them at their will and convenience. The Organisational setting is a graveyard of many such "Dreamers" —the epitaph inscribed over their graves would be *"Here lie a very skilled & aware person whom we did not know **how** to utilise"*. This tacitly acknowledges the organisational confession that these persons could have contributed "something" that we were knowing about but were afraid to risk experimenting with.

Any process of change has to have two essential components: a dream for the future or "where/what we want to reach/achieve"; and an introspective diagnosis of the "present" that embodies our history & values. The dreamer is a potential -and fragile- seed for crystallising such a vision in the organisational setting. These persons can be ignored in favour of the status quo or the organisation (or rather those who matter in it) can undertake some risk in exploring alternative creative options.

The message is clear: *If a dream dies, closely following in its path is the dreamer*. A person devoid of dreams is just a shell, and its does not matter as to what label in terms of "kind of human resource" we place on it as the spirit is not kindled enough to spread the light.

The challenge for the Human Resource Development professionals is to *not* dismiss them off as vain, arrogant and narcissistic folk in love with their own self, whose attempts to integrate themselves in the organisational setting only led to their experiencing problems of maladjustment, low self-esteem & self-confidence, feeling isolated & insulated, etc.

Special endeavour is needed to keep the dreamer alive as

a *vital* organisational resource- one who is beneficial to the community as well as the world at large. Only then would there be collective enunciation of organisational dreams that would endure the litmus test of time, come to life and be realised.

* * * *

THE EKLAVVA SYNDROME

PREAMBLE

We are all aware of the story of Eklavya, the tribal boy, whose attempts to seek discipleship of Guru Dronacharya were foiled by the Guru's attitude of non-acceptance. However, Eklavya persevered in his attempts to be an expert in archery and paid obeisance to his perceived Guru in the form of a clay image. His determination and resolve led him to master the art — even surpassing the skill level of Arjun, Drona's favourite & most-favoured pupil. Drona's discovery of this single-mindedly devoted disciple led to the most quaint guru-dakshina a shishya could make: cutting off his right thumb as a tribute & gift offered at the lotus feet of the Guru; immaterial that it was most central to the developed skill. Loyalty & devotion to the Guru took its toll ensuring Eklavya a permanent place in the annals of history.

The author proposes that The Eklavya Syndrome is relevant in terms of understanding certain personal relationships that evolve in the workplace. Some organisations have institutionalised formal mentor-protegee linkages, whereas some have these in place in an informal manner. Working closely with a senior leads to the development of a relationship that undergoes the classical four-step evolution from stages of "Dependence", "Counter-dependence", "Independence" & to "Inter-dependence or Mutuality". The elements are detailed below:

(1) In the stage of ``Dependence", the Mentor/Guru gets the opportunity to groom his junior. This process entails getting to know the potential of the junior, facilitating the process of adjustment in the set-up, familiarising

with the prevalent systems & procedures, induction into the relationship- cum-human network involved in performing the tasks/functions assigned to the group/ department.

(2) In the stage of ``Counter-dependence'', the junior makes attempts to break away the perceived shackles that apparently are preventing him from performing the assigned tasks on his own. This is akin to the ``Look-Ma-No-Hands'' attitude of a person who has just learnt to ride a bicycle! The need to exhibit one's readiness to ``perform'' predominates; one is likely to stub many toes. In fact many directives (do's and don'ts(are flouted in this mode of working. This often leads to many conflicts with the seniors; further inflamed and intensified if the senior has a strong need to control & dictate to his juniors.

(3) In the stage of "Independence" the disciple is ready to discharge most of his responsibilities on his own. This is also the time when efforts usually focus on practising what one has learnt and experimenting with alternate/better ways of doing things. The pleasure of performing can lead to the individual becoming a workaholic—setting very rigid standards of work-performance for himself (and others); the tendency to share relevant information, give and receive feedback (both task-related as well as at a personal level) remain at a low level.

(4) In the stage of "Inter-dependence or Mutuality" the worth of working together is realised and understood. Tasks are jointly discussed and both understand that the resources of the other person(s) are available and can be tapped. There is respect for the skill and abilities of others with the understanding that individual shortcomings can be appropriately managed.

The Eklavya Syndrome Surfaces in Many Forms

The first manifestation is in the form of extreme adulation by the protegee so much so that the entire behavioural patterns of the senior are perfectly mimicked. It is as if the personality of one has been totally submerged into the other's. This happens if the person gets stuck in the Dependence Stage. The senior's sayings become the gospel truth, to be defended at all costs.

As the personal relationship matures further there is a shift from the earlier "Senior-on-a-pedestal" mode to confronting the human face of Guru-as-a-person. In other words from an omni-potent person, the perspective changes to one in which the "Guru" is seen as a down-to-earth human being with frailities & weaknesses, one who does not have answers to all your questions, and so on. The junior at times feels exasperated with the old-fashioned and self-preserving approaches of his Guru, feels let down, and attempts to severe linkages. The irony is that neither can he get away nor does he feel confident enough to detach the emotional umbilical cord. The wavering between dependence and counter-dependence makes him a Trishanku; and a lot of energy is used up in cyclically confronting his Guru over a variety of issues (many would be trivial but blown-up to abominable proportions due to the mental turbulence) and then apologising and making up!

When the relationship has matured sufficiently it does not need to be publicly exhibited & acknowledged to support/ supplement the powers delegated/ascribed to the junior. This indicates completion of the process of grooming of the shishya for performing his assigned role. At this stage often the guidance received is perceived as nominal & sketchy, and could even be in absentia — with brief notings on formal papers, and public & personal utterances could be in terms of indirect analogies in lieu of 100% dictation of direction. However, the shishya may not be fully at peace with his well-earned "independence" and may occasionally regress to stages of dependence. The Eklavya Syndrome arises when there is a need felt by the junior to interact with his "boss" who does not reciprocate in kind (as he feels that the junior is well-equipped to handle the conflicting situation faced!). In other words the appeal for help/support is often seen as a wolf-wolf call. However, if this is not resolved the junior could regress to the dependence mode, create an uproar so that perforce the Guru has to come to his aid.

After going through the above rigamarole, almost like the proverbial game of snakes-and-ladders, with each successive interaction the Guru-Shishya relationship reaches its pinnacle: one where there is near-perfect understanding of each other's expectations and needs. It is here that the synergestic application takes place and together they contribute a lot towards fulfilling their own as well as the organisational objectives.

In the context of the organisation there would be constant pressure to internally-integrate-and-conform and simultaneously to externally-adapt (within and outside the organisation). The evolved relationship could have either of two forms: an organisationally-sponsored-one with an hierarchical linkage or as an extension of a personalised linkage cutting across organisational ramifications. There would be experienced various organisational pressures that would dictate that the contribution be limited to the formal structured role.

The dilemmas would be: "Does having an strong emotional linkage strengthen the freedom and autonomy to extend one's role addressing *as-yet* unspoken or unverbalised needs?" *And* "In anticipating and responding to needs without their being abjectly expressed am I encroaching upon the personal space of the Guru-like persona I have attached to my mentor?" *And* "The senior may have done his duty towards me, but how do I reciprocate and acknowledge whatever has been learnt by me? And what if these attempts of mine are met with reluctantly and in a silent manner, have I kind of devalued our relationship?" etc.

This is the point at which the Eklavya Syndrome makes its most potent and poignant entry: The Guru -not unlike Dronacharya- may feel inclined to flow with the organisational tidal movements & ask for the supreme sacrifice as his dakshina: "Do NOT utilise your potential at your own initiative" (this gets done in a very tacit manner- by cutting down on opportunities with potential for your participation through usage of your unique skills he himself has been instrumental in bringing to the fore). Since there is no way in which you can be utilised in an optimum manner, or he does not project your special skills as he is afraid of losing you for alternative placement in another Group, or he has another favourite candidate & is unwilling to part with neither you *nor* him! So "loyalty" has claimed yet another victim in the corporate rat race.

The individual's faith in the Guru—who may have been adorning that role in a very reluctant mode or may have had that role thrust upon him!- is akin to the icon-like status given by Eklavya to Drona's clay image. A very physically vulnerable one -yet one that is enough to consistently support Eklavya's determination to attain outstanding skill levels in terms of self-development. The ultimate sacrifice (usually implicit in the organisational setting) is all this conscious & innovative effort coming to naught through its being kept dormant by those very persons instrumental in these special skills being developed by an individual!

The individual is often used as a pawn on the organisational chequerboard; there are latent intentions in developing a person akin to the guru-dakshina asked for by Dronacharya from the Pandava brothers which was sheer vendetta, sans any camouflaging whatsoever!

The author has no specific all-pervasive solutions to offer to counter this setting in and taking root of the Eklavya Syndrome. He can only offer the cryptic allegory of the Panchatantra fable of the captivated birds collectively flying off with the hunter's net. The net symbolises "the system", "the steel-frame", "the status quo", "the weight of past & prevailing practices" et al which need to be swept off with collective efforts towards an unbiased harnessing of human resources for progress of the organisation and society at large. Empowerment of the individual -through various integrated value-based approaches without personal prejudice- leading to an effective human network is the need of the hour.

12

HUMAN RESOURCE IN IT INDUSTRY: REDEFINING STRATEGIC PARTNERSHIP

*Piyali Ghosh**

> *The only resources capable of enlargement are the human resources.... All other resources can be better utilised or worse utilised, but they can never have an output better than the sum of inputs.... Man alone, of all the resources, can grow and develop.*
>
> —Kumar and Mishra, 2001

Creation of wealth of any nation or its agenda of economic development rests on all forms of capital- natural, physical, human and social. A nation that ignores or fails to upgrade and invest in any of these areas faces the risk of jeopardising the long term health of its economy.

Of the different forms of capital, human capital enables a nation to enhance its wealth generating capability in a significant manner. Conventionally, economic growth can be attributed to three main factors of production- land, labour and capital. The pace of economic growth of any nation depends primarily on capital accumulation of the nation. Such accumulation is possible not only by growth of physical capital, but also by investment in human capital, which in turn, determines the quality of labour force and productivity.

* Research Scholar, School of Management Studies, Motilal Nehru National Institute of Technology (Deemed Univesity) Allahabad.

In other words, economic growth of a nation is contingent not only on its natural resource advantage, but also on its ability to exploit industrial resources for maximum advantage. Hence is the relevance of human resource in the economic development process. This would imply an effective utilisation of capital stock and the capacity to organise, educate and develop the skill and competence of the workforce. In fact, productivity and its management are largely dependent on human resources to make it an important sector that builds competitiveness in the marketplace (Ahuja, 2002). Singh (1998) has stressed that any organisation needs to manage three kinds of resources. Financial resources are short term; technical resources are more medium term and human resources a long term strength of a company, in particular in the new millennium. High performing organisations, in order to keep performing and staying ahead of competitors on a continuous basis, must treat their human capital as their most important and valuable asset. The higher the investment in human capital, it is argued, the greater would be the efficiency of work force per unit of output, resulting in wealth generation in the productive segments of the economy. Hence greater investment in human resource development is a pre-requisite for building a vibrant and resurgent industrial sector and the economy (Ahuja, 2002).

Propounders of Resource- Based View of the firm suggest that resources are valuable when they enable a firm to enact strategies that improve efficiency and effectiveness, exploit market opportunities, and or neutralize potential threats (Barney, '91; Porter, '85, Ulrich and Lake, '91; Wright and McMahan, '92).Thus, the value of human capital is inherently dependent upon its potential to contribute to the competitive advantage or core competence of the firm. The degree to which an asset is unique directly influences its potential to serve as a source of competitive advantage. If an asset or skill of a firm can not be duplicated or imitated by another firm, it provides a potential source of competitive advantage to the firm (Barney, '91).

Human expertise, according to Ahuja (2002), has the distinction of leveraging profits for the company, due to the following advantages:

- It provides a company with a product, which is non-replicable, unique and non-substitutable.
- It propels innovation and value addition.
- It helps generate productivity out of fewer assets.

Thus, as human capital becomes more idiosyncratic to a particular firm, it helps the firm in attaining core competence and an edge over competitors.

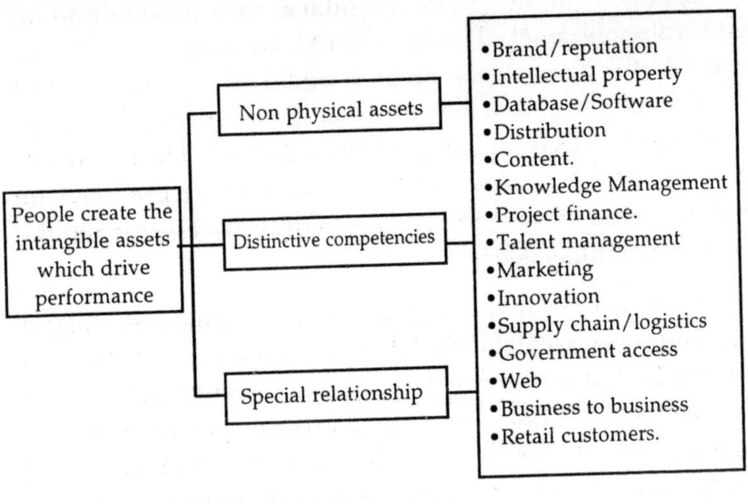

Figure 1: The Intangible Advantage
Source: McKinsey and Co.

Human Resource for Competitive Advantage: The Indian Experience

India's potentially major resource endowment is its huge reservoir of human resource. Unfortunately a large mass of this resource is under utilised and deprived in terms of human development. Enterprises in the developed nations have been able to enhance productivity substantially and reduce labour costs significantly by creative application of technology to manufacturing and product design. On the contrary, corporate India has yet to invest commendably in its intangible assets. As an obvious implication of this, value added to the Indian economy continues to be quite low and the nation is entrapped at the lower end of the value chain.

During Independence, India was largely an agrarian country, with her industry in its infancy. The 1950s and 1960s saw managerial objectives governed by the notion that *"bigger organisations are better organisations"*. According to Monappa (1997, 1-3), the evolution of Human Resource Management in Indian context can be traced to three distinct phases- the initial phase, which involved more of an approach towards labour welfare; the fire-fighting phase, where the emphasis was on keeping the wheels of the production factories running; and the evolution phase, where the human resource function actually begun to evolve due to a variety of factors, including of increasing cost of human resource due to the increased number of benefits, increased cost of living, higher expectations and higher costs of skilled manpower, etc. Thus a reactive, maintenance-oriented Personnel Management and Industrial Relations function has gradually been transformed to an initiative-oriented, proactive Human Resource Management role.

The last twenty years have seen radical changes taking place in the functional area of human resource in India (Rao, '99, Rao et. al, 2001). The spate of economic reforms initiated by the Rao Government in mid-1991, have transformed the entire backdrop of Indian economy. The opening up of the economy and uniting the domestic market with the global village has now exposed Indian organisations to fierce competition, not only from multi- nationals, but also from newly emerging domestic rivals. Indian companies, observe Singh and Singh ('95), must now move from complacency to competition, from internal orientation to international standards of quality, from low customer orientation to total customer orientation, from soft work ethics to total work commitment and from traditional management practices to pioneering innovative management policies. With enhanced competition, companies are facing immense pressure to render cost- effective products and services with care and concern for employee needs. Moreover liberalisation of the economy has resulted in demographic changes in the employee profile, retaining and re-deployment of work force, focus on performance appraisal and performance- based incentive systems and rightsizing (Budhwar and Sparrow, '97; Som, 2002). It is suggested that larger organisations should adopt more sophisticated and socially responsive human resource management activities, because these more visible organisations are under more pressure to gain legitimacy (Jackson and Schuler, '95: 245-6). Thus human resource of any organisation has emerged as the most vital asset for the organisation, as it can render competitive advantage to that organisation. The change from a regulated environment to a free market environment has put Human Resource specialists and Human Resource departments under severe pressure to inculcate large scale professionalised changes in their organisations, in order to cope with the changes brought about with the waves of LPG (Liberalisation, Privatisation and Globalisation). Thus there has been renewed focus on recruitment of professional personnel, performance- based management system, performance appraisal, evaluation of training, retraining and redeployment and a new emphasis on communication, organisational development, the role of HR personnel and the HR department (Som, 2002). This has led the growth of Human Resource Management into the fourth phase-Strategic Human Resource Management. Organisations are thus considering their human resources as a basic source of quality and productivity improvement and have started valuing their views and suggestions. In this new philosophy, people are a strategic resource (Ahuja, 2002). Strategies and commitments to gear human resource are accordingly being designed by Indian corporates, with the perspective of achieving organisational as well as individual goals.

Relevance of HR in IT Industry

In a knowledge-based economy, intellectual capital, especially the power and product of human mind, is considered to be the supreme source of core competence. Stewart ('97) has defined intellectual capital as the sum of everything the people of the organisation know, which gives the organisation a competitive advantage in the market. Such intellectual capital is made up of human capital and knowledge capital. Maximising productivity would necessitate effective interaction of these two kinds of capital. Human capital is capable of generating differential levels of economic returns for an organisation. On the other hand, according to the knowledge-based view of the firm (Kogut and Zander, '92, Grant, '96), knowledge is seen as a critical organisational resource, enabling effective deployment and transformation of other resources such as money or physical plants and equipments. The rapid diffusion of technological innovation all over the globe has dramatically accelerated competition. As competition among technology- based firms has increased, the source of competitive advantage in firms has shifted focus from tangible resources to knowledge.

Modern organisations face a rapidly changing environment in which technologies change every day and obsolescence is an inevitable phenomenon. An era of new competition and new customers, with an altogether new value system has now become a reality facing companies. Economic reforms brought about by globalisation have brought twin advantages to both marketers and consumers. While marketers benefit from new market openings and new technologies, consumers benefit from a wide range of products from the global market. According to Saxena ('99), only those firms are going to survive in such competitive global environment, which provide greatest utilities to their consumers in the form of product and service utility, possession utility, time utility and place utility. The waves of globalisation have thus impelled firms to introduce structural changes and new forms of work, which would impinge on their human resource. Any futuristic firm that has long term vision would thus focus on accumulation of knowledge and talent. The tool which has emerged as the solution to creating costumer value at a competitive advantage at this hour is "Information Technology" (IT). The term information technology is used in a broad sense, to indicate a set of technologies ranging from computers, telecom- based networks and smart chips. It is IT which can leverage the twin components of intellectual capital- human capital and knowledge capital. IT industry is significant for creating high value jobs, enhancing business efficiency and earning much-needed export revenues. Besides, it provides support to the development of other industries. The major challenge before policy makers thus, is to formulate constructive policies in areas of capital formation, human resources, technology and trade. Such polices should also have a strategic orientation, thus aiming at creation of value for customers through products and services, over and above the value created by competitors.

As suggested by Alvin Toffler, we are currently in the Third Wave-the Information Age, creating the knowledge economy. This has been preceded by the First Wave or Agrarian Revolution and the Second Wave or Industrial Revolution. Information Revolution is not only about technology- but it is also about how to focus on knowledge and impacts of information on culture and civilisations.

A number of special features distinguish the IT industry from other industries—the most important of them being human resource as its key asset. Unlike manufacturing and some other service industries, this industry does not require voluminous investments in equipments, plant, machinery and/or real estate. Revenue generation of IT industry is primarily contingent upon the number and quality of its technical staff. There is growing recognition that comparative advantage for achieving higher growth not only lies in factor endowments, but also in human capital on information technology, particularly in the context of paradigm shift to market- oriented growth process (Kamesam, 2003). IT is one of those sectors that need a strong, educated and trained manpower base. This sector needs professionals who can learn continuously and are also able to create intellectual assets from their experience. The emergence of the "knowledge worker" in the IT industry has brought a paradigm shift in Human Resource Management and employment relations. While a traditional industry banks on a homogenous work force, competitiveness in Information and Communication Technology (ICT) sector is contingent on heterogeneous workforce for creativity and innovation (Bhaskar, et. al, 2003). Thus, in an industry in which strategic management of intellectual capital as the sum of human and knowledge capital requires harnessing and leveraging the knowledge, experience and expertise of employees, human resource enjoys a crucial position.

As IT industry as a whole, has emerged as a strategic tool for attaining success and continuous growth, human resource, which is difficult to imitate, has also started being considered as one of the key ways of gaining competitive advantage (Grundy, '97). IT industry has initiated flat, non-hierarchical structures with a culture that encourages ideas to come from every organisational member. In traditional manufacturing sector, if the focus is now on aligning human resources with business strategy, in software the focus is on aligning personal goals of the employees with that of the organisation (Bhaskar, et. al, 2003).

In the current context of cost pressure of organisations, driven by lower cost structures of the new economy, human resource finds a new challenge in adding business value to the organisation and in deriving synergistic benefits accruing from such a relatively young industry. Human resource function in IT companies is thus moving beyond head- hunting to virtual hiring, induction and virtual integration, performance appraisal and employee development.

In this virtual world, human resource thus needs to ensure speed of service, rapid implementation of policies and benefits and e-enablement of communication strategies, in order to reach out to employees in the IT sector.

REFERENCES

Ahuja, Shobha (2002) Creating Corporate Advantage through Human Resource Development. *Vision: The Journal of Business Perspective.* Jan.-June 2002, pp. 73-86.

Barney, J.(1991) Firm Resources and Sustained Competitive Advantage. *Journal of Management*, 17: 99-129.

Bhaskar, A.U., Ratnam, C.S.V. and Bhal, K.T. (2003) Employment Relations in a Global Economy: A Paradigm Shift.

Grant, R.M.(1996) Prospering in Dynamically Competitive Environments: Organizational Capability as Knowledge Creation. *Organization Science*, 7: 375-387.

Grundy, T.(1997) Human Resource Management- A Strategic Approach. *Long Range Planning*, Vol. 30, 4: 507-519.

Jackson, S.E. and Schuler, R.S. (1995)Understanding Human Resource in the context of Organizations and their Environments. *Annual Review of Psychology*, 46: 237-264.

Kamesam, Vepa (2003)The role of Quality Human Resource in Target Setting for Economic Growth. Address at a meeting organised by the Technology Information, Forecasting and Assessment (TIFAC), Centre of Relevance and Excellence (CORE), New Delhi, 25 July 2003.

Kogut, B. and Zander, U. (1992)Knowledge of the Firm, Combination Capabilities, and the Replication of Technology. *Organization Science*, 3. pp. 383-397.

Kumar, Harish and Mishra, Alpana(2001) Role of IT in making HR Function Globally Competitive. People, Processes and Organisations-Emerging Realities. pp. 218-219.

Monappa, Arun (1997) Managing Human Resource. Mac Millan (India), New Delhi.

Porter, M.(1985) Competitive Advantage: Creating and Sustaining Superior Performance. New York: Free Press.

Rao, T.V. ('99)HRD Audit. Response Books, New Delhi.

Rao, T.V., Rao, R. and Yadav, T. (2001) A Study of HRD Concepts, Structure of HRD Departments and HRD Practices in India. *Vikalpa*, 26 (1): 49-63.

Saxena, R.P. ('99)Information Technology as a Strategic Tool for Attaining Success in Global Environment. Paradigm, Vol. 3, No. 2, July-Dec. '95, pp. 95-104.

Singh, Anup K. and Singh Romila (1995) Strategic Human Resource Management: A New Thrust for Indian Organisations. *MDI Management Journal*, Vol. 8, No. 1 (Jan. '95), pp. 39-52.

Singh, P.N. (1998) HRD Perspectives in the 21st Century. *The Indian Journal of Commerce*, Vol. 51, No. 4, Oct.-Dec. 1998.

Som, A.(2002) Role of Human Resource Management in Organisational Development. Unpublished Doctoral dissertation Ahmedabad: IIM.

Sparrow, P.R. and Budhwar, P. S. ('97) Competition and Change: Mapping the Indian HRM Recipe against World -Wide Patterns. *Journal of World Business*, 32 (3): 224-242.

Stewart, T.A. ('97) *Intellectual Capital: The New Wealth of Organisations.* NC Currency Doubbledey, New York.

Ulrich, D. and Lake, D. (1991) Organizational Capability: Creating Competitive Advantage. *Academy of Management Executive*, 7 (1): 77-92.

Wright, P.M. and McMahan, G.C. (1992)Theoretical Perspectives for Strategic Human Resource Management. *Journal of Management*, 18 (2): 295-320.

13

HUMAN RESOURCE DEVELOPMENT AND INFORMATION TECHNOLOGY INTERFACE: THE CASE OF JAMMU & KASHMIR BANK LTD.

*Dr. Neelu Rohmetra**

Backdrop

The characteristic feature of the present economy is that it is knowledge based, where the knowledge worker is the centrepiece of the organisation. Knowledge worker values professional freedom, innovation and integrity and exploits opportunities to learn. In knowledge organisations, people are the core around which all activities revolve. Human beings and not the machines or materials constitute the prime concern of these organisations. Clearly, these organisations cannot be managed with the traditional managerial styles and cannot have the traditional constitution in the wake of changing competitive environments characterised by technological advancements. Technological advancements, have thus, necessitated change in manpower composition and skill requirements.

The knowledge economy has opened up a whole set of

* Professor, Deparatment of Management Studies, University of Jammu, Jammu J&K State, India.

opportunities for emerging markets such as India. Dramatic changes are taking place in the ways the various sectors of economy are being managed. Change is vivid in the service sector including the banking services where Indian banks are confronted with unprecedented challenges in the form of increased competition within the industry, lower entry barriers for new players, presence of alternative forms of financial intermediation, the ever-increasing demand for skilled people and finally information technology making inroads into the organisational strategy and structures. The banking business is being automated, and the focus on electronic banking is growing. Consequently, the organisational and structural changes in the banking sector have posed several challenges namely:

- "Changes in job context where multi-skill, flexibility, initiative and good interpersonal skills are the new job requirements for bank employees.
- Change in the job content as banks reorganise their operations with the help of information technology e.g.; virtual/techno banking. There are bankers who foresee that electronic banking and off-premise banking, combined with attention to high net worth customers will represent the future of retail banking. Brick and mortar branch banking system, they feel will suffer the same fate as dinosaurs.
- Change in career prospects where prospects are good for knowledge workers while workers with inadequate or obsolete skills are at risk of losing their jobs. Managers are finding themselves in a new ambiguous situation, since customers now have direct access to much of the information formerly controlled by them."(SILS Industry Analysis Series, 1997)

Accordingly, the banking industry is under pressure to

redefine the concept of business and social responsibilities (Shah, Saiyadain and Sheth, 1984). Faced with multiple challenges it has become mandatory for the banking institutions to equip themselves with tools and mechanics that help them to respond positively, efficiently and effectively to the changing context. Thus, as Amol Maheshwari and Shweta Jhajharia (2001) put: "Since the objective of the banks in the competitive scenario is to attract, retain and expand the consumer base, it becomes imperative for banks to revamp and revitalise the entire organization culture. The change in image needs to be driven internally through the structure, culture, support systems and people within the organization. Moreover, the banks need to adapt a need-identification approach and accordingly adopt the function and the culture. The banks need to move towards a broad structure of decentralization, managing risks and opportunities, simultaneously with multiple delivery channels." Similarly, in a liberalized and competitive environment, only those banks would be effective in delivering goods, which provide excellent service quality Almost, all the banks perform same functions. Therefore, the customer takes into account the relative efficiency while choosing a particular bank. Increasingly, therefore better service quality is becoming a key variable in strategic planning. This implies that the banking industry in general and branch managers in particular have to translate corporate policies into constructive practice at the grass-root level, in matters of manpower planning, training, performance appraisal and career path planning. (Shah, Saiyadain and Sheth, 1984). Hence, there essentially lies a need for well integrated HRD policy in banks (Khandelwal, 1988), and training, the most used mechanism in human resource development in banks, needs to be evaluated time and again to verify its effectiveness (E.Abraham, 1988). Laying further stress on the need for identifying new ways of doing banking business James A. Hanson (2001) comments, "much more change in business practices is likely to be needed, including a sharp reduction in unprofitable branches, improved communication, and greater computerization." Commenting on lack of computers in Indian (public sector banking), the second Narasimham committee report said, " No area of commercial activity has been influenced more by ongoing revolution in information and communications technology than the banking and financial systems...this phenomenon has largely bypassed India" (Narasimham 1998, P40). Accordingly, computerization and the associated training of staff requires funding, again an up-front cost with uncertain returns only later. Encouragingly, the Indian banking industry has worked up to the competitive dynamics of the new market and is addressing the relevant issues to take on the multifarious challenges of globalisation. To cater to the increasing customer demands and the surge in business volumes, many public sector banks have ploughed back funds to invest heavily in technology. Banks that have employed IT solutions are perceived to be futuristic and proactive players capable of meeting the multifarious requirements of the large customer base. Further, with efficiency being the major focus, the banks have leveraged on their strengths and competencies viz. management, operational efficiency and flexibility, superior product positioning and higher employee productivity skills (www.vyapaarasia.com/india/banks.asp). The role of training and development is clearly evident in this regard. However, training should neither be a casual phenomenon nor holiday for a selected few or even all. In turn, it has to be a process of human development for the fulfillment of defined objectives (Khandelwal, 1978). Hence, the need for unusual training that will create unusual bankers, and it is only unusual bankers who can run a large, widely spread, decentralised banking industry. No training system that does not create such bankers in adequate numbers and within the time span available is worth it (Shah, 1978). However, training is a routinised ceremony with most organisations without regard to the capacity of the employees to assimilate or the organisation's ability to implement. Consequently, the training programmes conducted by these organisations are not justified. Requisite transformation in the context and mechanics of these programmes, therefore, is needed to achieve the desired results (Lynton and Pareek, 1990). Thus, in view of R. Natarajan (1999) "the numero uno position is sliding with the entry of sleeker private and foreign banks into the Indian banking scene. With the government offering an assured business, nationalized banks and State Bank of India in particular should not take a complacent view. They should evolve service-intensive products and make their employees customer-friendly. With competition from private and foreign banks knocking at the door, the banks should realize, size is no more an insurance against the onslaught of competition from sleek private and foreign banks. A revolutionary approach to privatize ownership is the need of the hour. As a hangover of the past socialistic mindset, all the nationalized banks have excess workforce. It is the semi-skilled manpower having outdated skills, which form the excess baggage. All banks must invest in re-training the manpower so that it can migrate from the areas that will be vacated by computerization."

Similarly, Verma Panel (2000) reports that there will be important preconditions to fulfill before the banks can expect to register any sizable increase in their earnings. Evaluating the status of three banks, (United Bank, Indian Bank and UCO Bank), the Panel observed that the leadership at the middle levels in these banks is seriously lacking. This is largely because of inadequacies in skills both in traditional areas of banks' operations as well as the new areas in which most banks are now moving In speacialised areas like credit, treasury operations, foreign exchange and IT, the three banks are extremely deficient in skills and are almost out of the market. Therefore, the banks clearly need considerable assistance in these regards and a longer-term training and reskilling programme will have to be undertaken by them. The Panel also reports that training facilities in these banks are inadequate to meet the needs that would arise following the restructuring efforts. Further, the banks may consider that training facilities created by more than one bank should be pooled for better utilization of the limited training skills available, which would improve consistency and quality of training. The Panel stressed that the restructuring programme will have to encompass operational, financial and systemic restructuring as a unified package and must be implemented in a time bound manner. With regards operational restructuring, the Panel suggested, "operational restructuring can be begun best with a technology change. For weak banks, which do not possess either the finances or the skills for managing such a change efficiently, it is recommended that they go in for a common networking and processing facility, an arrangement which will bring the cost down substantially and also reduce the demand for skilled people. This common facility may be outsourced from a reputed IT system and solutions providers, which will run the system for the banks. A 'Build Own Operate Transfer' (BOOT) model may be attempted."(Verma Panel, 2001) Significantly, while the piecemeal approach or a policy of pick and choose will cause more harm than good, gradualism or any delay will add to the cost of restructuring. Accordingly, a banking institution interested in achieving effectiveness has to start with the vision of what the bank is, what it ought to be, and what are the HRD strategies needed to fit that vision (Rohmetra, 1998).

In this backdrop, the present study seeks to investigate the transformative potential of Information Technology using the case of Jammu and Kashmir Bank Ltd. in India. The case highlights the perceptual response of the employees handling the computerized banking services, and identifies relevant tranformative interventions for an effective interface between IT and human resources. The work seeks to ascertain the current status of IT in Jammu and Kashmir Bank in the first place and goes on to adjudge its transformative efficacy in terms of how people feel about the technological change.

About The Jammu and Kashmir Bank Ltd.

The Jammu and Kashmir Bank Ltd incorporated on October 1,1938 commenced business on July 4, 1939. From a small beginning the bank has grown to a giant with a network of 475 branches spread over the length and breadth of the country. The vision of the bank is to be a financially sound, profitable, growth and technology oriented bank committed to building and maximizing sustainable value for all its shareholders, customers and employees. The bank in the fast growth track is now moving with time by having global approach on business, best governance practices, quality standards and continuous learning and development of its people. It is committed in its efforts for fulfilling the aspirations of all its stakeholders. The business strategy of the bank focuses on increasing visibility of the bank in the market and enhancing its market share by exploiting new markets by following a disciplined growth strategy and delivering high quality of customer service, besides integrating technology and business so as to deliver more products to more customers and to control operating costs. In its endeavour to attain the goals visualised, the bank is laying maximum emphasis on the effective system of corporate governance, with a view to improve its image, efficiency, effectiveness and satisfying the public expectations of fairness and ethical conduct.

The bank's mission is "Growth through commitment, service and trust". Bank's marketing strategy starts with identification of customer's needs and developing appropriate banking products or services to suit their needs. Keeping with this fact the bank has implemented 'Single Point Commit system' at its selected branches, wherein end-to-end service is provided to the customers at the same counter, which ensures efficiency and high speed of service to the customer. The bank for this purpose has designated 126 branches as 'All Officers Branches', which are wholly run and manned by officers (Annual Report, 2004)

Human resource policies in the bank are designed with a focus on customer service and operational efficiency. In order to enhance the knowledge and efficiency of employees, the bank imparts training to the staff from time to time to improve skills and competencies, besides changing behaviour and attitudes essential for friendly customer service. The Bank regards people as the most important resource instrumental in achieving growth, and, as such strongly advocates development of skills, attitude and knowledge of the staff. In quantitative terms, during the year 2003-04, 3901 staff members (2510 officers, 1369 clerks and 22 subordinates), were imparted training at Bank's Staff Training Colleges at Srinagar and Jammu, Bank's Technology Training Centre, Srinagar and other institutes of repute within and outside the country in various banking, economic, behaviour and IT related fields. (Annual Report, 2003-04). The Jammu and Kashmir Bank is not an ordinary Bank. It is the only bank in the country with State Government equity and it acts as a banker to the State Government. The J&K Govt. has 53.2 percent of its equity (Mitra, 2003). The bank has recently tied up with MetLife Insurance India (P) Ltd. and Bajaj Allianz General Insurance Co. Ltd. for distribution of Insurance products. The bank has launched J&K Bank Global Access Card, in collaboration with the Master Card International, which is Cirrus and Maestro enabled. The card holders of the bank are now able to purchase goods and services at all Maestro acceptance locations in India and overseas besides withdrawing cash globally through the Master Card Cirrus network of over 4700 ATMs in the country and 8 Lakh ATMs worldwide. On the technological front the bank has been swift in responding to the need of technology adaptation in meeting its commitment to the customers. To modernize bank's operations and deliver value-added services to the customers, the bank seems to be focused on application and augmentation of the Information Technology and cover more and more branches under the computerization programme. The number of computerized branches has increased to 360 at the end of March 2004 against 300 branches at the year-end 2003 covering 90% business. The bank is investing in a big way in IT and the bank has the ambitious plan of total automation of operations by the year 2005. The bank has already networked over 103 important branches at various centers to offer Anywhere Banking and the number of ATMs already installed or under process of installation has increased to 130 at the year ending March 2004. Currently, the Software Bank 2000 by INFOSYS is in use for handling computerized services With the expansion of ATM network and interconnectivity of more and more branches to offer Anywhere Banking services, the bank has as a policy issued free ATM –cum Debit Cards in all eligible Saving Bank and Current Deposit accounts. Over 50,000 ATM-cum Debit cards have been issued up to March 2004. The tele –banking facility has also been extended to more than 100 branches. The bank has set up a DATA Centre at Delhi and roll over of branches on the CBS is in progress. Besides, bank has set up an RTGS Payment Gateway at Mumbai for implementation of Real Time Gross Settlement (Annual Report, 2004)

Hypotheses

Our key hypotheses are:

H1. Computerisation has significantly improved the HRD climate in the JKB.

H2. Computerisation has significantly contributed towards productivity of the bank.

H3. Efficiency of computerized services is significantly a function of training and development in the bank.

Findings

The first step of the study was to adjudge the current state of computerisation in JKB. The study also sought to ascertain the relationship between the HRD climate and the state of information technology in the bank. The goal was to examine the transformative efficacy of the IT in relation to the development climate, including the general climate, HRD mechanisms, and Rao's (1999) concept of OCTAPAC that captures the broader cultural elements. OCTAPAC includes the values of Openness, Collaboration, Trust, Authenticity, Proactivity, Autonomy, and Confrontation.

We specifically wished to investigate the intimacy between the computerisation and the efficiency factor on the one hand and efficiency factor and training and development on the other, particularly in terms of perceptual response of the employees. For the purpose, we used two different sets of questionnaires:

1. The HRD-climate questionnaire
2. IT-perspective questionnaire

The study sought to look into development climate on the one hand and IT perspective on the other. Human resource development climate is an integral part of organisational climate. It can be defined as the perceptions that people can hold on the developmental environment of an organisation. The HRD climate represents the general climate, the HRD-mechanisms and the OCTAPAC culture, wherein; the general climate deals with the importance being given to HRD in general by the top management and the line managers.

Similarly, HRD mechanisms are the interventions initiated to develop employee competencies, which are considered as instruments to facilitate change. The OCTAPAC culture, rooted in the values of openness, confrontation, trust, authenticity, proactivity, autonomy and collaboration, is intended to facilitate HRD. The underlying assumption is that a supportive development climate facilitates human resource development. Accordingly, A forty-item HRD climate questionnaire was administered to the employees in the computerised branches of the JKB.

The IT-perspective questionnaire consisted of 33 items categorised under five main dimensions: productivity and efficiency, behavioural domain, training and development, knowledge management and collaborative culture.

The sample consisted of a total of 50 employees across ten branches in Jammu division, who were personally approached for the purpose of extracting the required response along the dimensions studied. A total of 80 employees were approached, out of which only 50 employees agreed to the interviews, making it a response rate of about 60%. The sample included both male and female employees and they belonged to both managerial and clerical cadres. Further, the response has been elicited on a 5-point scale ranging from 1 to 5 in case of the HRD climate interview and 0 to 4 in case of the IT-perspective questionnaire. For the purpose of analysis the item wise mean scores have been calculated. For HRD climate, the mean score on the responses could range from1 to 5, where 1 indicated an extremely poor climate and 5 indicated an extraordinarily good climate on that dimension. Scores around 3 indicated an average HRD climate along that dimension giving substantial scope for improvement while score around 4 indicated a good HRD climate where most employees had positive attitudes towards HRD policies and practices, and score around 2 indicated a poor HRD climate on that dimension. Similar interpretation has been extended to the percentage scores. A mean score of 1 corresponded to zero percent, 2 corresponded to 25%, 3 corresponded to 50%, 4 corresponded to 75% and 5 corresponded to hundred percent. In case of IT –perspective analysis, a mean score of 1 corresponded to 25%, 2 corresponded to 50%, 3 corresponded to 75% and 4 corresponded to hundred percent.

Findings of the study reveal that development climate in JKB is not satisfactory indicating a lot of scope for improvement (Table 1). All the three components constituting development climate, HRD mechanisms as well as the OCTAPAC value base project a low level of satisfaction among the employees along these variables. Specifically mentioning, the respondents have expressed dissatisfaction with the existing rewards systems and also believe that creativity is discouraged. Besides, secretive attitude of seniors, non- existence of the proactive culture, lack of autonomy, inadequate training and development systems, and absence of career planning provide explanation for weak development climate. However, managers in the bank believe strongly in the potential of their fellow workers who make all out efforts to improve

TABLE 1

Human Resource Development Climate Mean Scores as Obtained in JKB

Dimensions	*Mean score*
General climate	2.8
HRD mechanisms	2.5
OCTAPAC values	2.6
Overall state of development climate	**2.63 (40.75%)**
Multiple correlation	**+.90**

themselves. Similarly, people trust each other and admirable level of team spirit exists, thus suggesting considerable scope for understanding transformative initiative for furthering development culture.

The satisfaction of employees along computerization dimension has been understood in view of the impact on measures of productivity, efficiency, behavioural patterns and knowledge management besides comprehending the relationship of technology to domains of collaborative culture and training and development. Though the study reports low level of satisfaction among employees over the various issues concerning computerisation in J&K Bank, the lower satisfaction can be attributed more to the training processes and the collaborative culture variables than to the process of computerization itself. The people are happy with the introduction of the computerised services, but are dissatisfied about the management and implementation issues. The happiness derives from the fact that computerisation brings along the advantages associated with mechanised and automated services, while the key source of dissatisfaction is inadequate training and development systems (Tables 2 to 6).

A scrutiny into the results exhibits that computerisation has made the work easier and has enabled the speeding up of the delivery time. It has also helped in reduction of errors besides improving management of databases. Although in strict terms computerization may not have been of much usefulness in shifting from routine tasks to more quality time with customers for personal consultancy, it has efficiently enabled free flow of information and helped in responding to customer needs with more immediacy. Similarly, though the respondents feel that computerisation could neither reduce the chaos and confusion to a large extent nor accounted for increased interest in work in considerable measures, computerisation has contributed significantly towards reducing the work stress and enhancing the motivational level of employees besides improving the personal efficacy of the staff to a satisfactory extent.

TABLE 2

Position of Response along the Efficiency Factor

Item	*Dimension*	*Mean Score*	*Rank*	*Percentage*
Computerisation has:				
1	made work easier	3.00	I	75.00
2	helped in reducing of errors	2.47	III	61.75
3	improved personal efficiency	2.00	VIII	50.00
4	helped to make financial transactions easier to manage	2.17	V	54.25
5	enabled speeding up of delivery time	2.73	II	68.25
6	improved mgt. Of databases	2.30	IV	57.50
7	helped in checking frauds	2.13	VI	53.25
8	helped in major shift from routine tasks to more quality time	1.90	X	47.50
9	helped in customising solutions to fulfill client's requirements	1.67	XII	41.75
10	helped to respond to customer needs with more immediacy	2.00	VIII	50.00
11	enabled smoother and free flow of information	2.07	VII	51.75
12	enabled immediate availability of accurate information about custo mer feedback	1.97	IX	49.25
13	helped to provide timely and better solutions due to accuracy immediacy and richness of infor-mation	1.87	XI	46.75

TABLE 3

Position of Response along Behavioural Factor

Item	*Dimension*	*Mean Score*	*Rank*	*Percentage*
Computerisation has:				
14	helped in reducing work stress	2.17	I	54.25
15	helped in reducing chaos and confusion	1.83	III	45.75
16	increased interest in work	2.17	I	54.25
17	increased level of motivation	2.03	II	50.75
18	increased level of job satisfaction	1.80	IV	45.00

TABLE 4

Position of Response along Training and Development

Item	*Dimension*	*Mean Score*	*Rank*	*Percentage*
19	Computerisation has enhanced the skills	2.03	I	50.75
20	adequate training provided for handling computerised services	0.97	III	24.25
21	training programmes organised to match changing tech. Skills	0.87	IV	21.75
22	training, if any has increased the confidence level	1.13	II	28.25
23	effectiveness at job has increased due to training	0.87	IV	21.75

The study also reports that computerisation in JKB is suffering because of inadequate system of training and development. Although the people are handling computer machines and also offering the computerised services to the customers, the interviews reveal that no adequate advance training was provided to them for handling such services. Besides, only few training sessions are organised from time to time to equip the employees with the technological advancements in the area. Consequently, the employees feel that training being inadequate has not been able to contribute towards making their jobs effective. Similarly, training has been able to increase the confidence level only to a negligible extent. Hence, training if provided in adequate and serious terms could change people's perception of the issue in view.

TABLE 5

Position of Response along Knowledge Management Factor

Item	*Dimension*	*Mean Score*	*Rank*	*Percentage*
Computerisation has:				
24	empowered with better access to information	2.70	I	67.50
25	empowered with more control over work	2.10	II	52.50
26	magnified abilities to think and articulate thoughts	1.63	V	40.75
27	enhanced creativity	1.77	III	44.25
28	empowered to solve problems	1.63	V	40.75
29	enhanced capacity to contribute	1.70	IV	42.50
30	increased involvement in decision-making	1.70	IV	42.50

TABLE 6

Position of Response along Collaborative Culture Factor

Item	*Dimension*	*Mean Score*	*Rank*	*Percentage*
Computerisation has:				
31	helped to communicate more efficiently with peers	1.80	I	45.00
32	enhanced the collaborative culture	1.53	III	38.25
33	brought about group cohesiveness	1.60	II	40.00

Nevertheless, computerisation has enabled better access to information and more control over work. It has also enhanced creativity and capacity to work and increased involvement in decision-making significantly. However, people are still less articulate and feel less empowered to solve problems as automation of processes has not been able to promote the collaborative culture in the bank's branches. Understandably therefore, there is no visible improvement in the communication with peers and the groups are also less cohesive in their character.

Analysis and Inferences

Though computerisation of banking procedures has made the work easier to a substantial extent, yet personal efficiency due to computerisation has improved only to a small extent. Also management of databases and consequential reduction of processing time has improved only to a small extent. The irregularity may be attributed to the fact that computerisation is still in the contagion stage. The basic assumption of this stage involves a rapid proliferation of the computer resource all over the organisation. Due to this non-planned proliferation, the management information system function grows disproportionately and there is less control resulting in confusion. So where computerisation of the banking system is supposed to speed up the delivery and the processing time of services, it might sometimes show the retrograde results. The phenomenon might be existing till automation in the bank reaches its maturity. Also, the features typical to a computer i.e.; corruption of software, virus infected data etc pose a problem causing downward trend in efficiency. Since, the banking procedures have not been fully computerized in some of the branches, lot of confusion sometimes creeps into as a result of partially computerised banking system.

Further investigation revealed that, crashing of computers sometimes due to technical problems brings the total banking system to a halt. Perhaps things could be rectified through better training inputs and healthy development climate facilitating HRD initiatives in this direction. However, the study reveals that HRD climate is estimated at a meagre level of 40.75% (mean score 2.63), with general climate, HRD mechanisms and the OCTAPAC calculated at 2.8, 2.5 and 2.6 respectively. The HRD climate in the bank is unimpressive accounting for lack of orientation on the part of top and line management in respect of initiating training and development campaign so as to equip people coping with the technological change. The poor HRD climate has not been able to instill any confidence in the people who work with the computer machines. The overall satisfaction level of employees along the information technology (computerization) dimension is also estimated at impoverished level of 1.89(47.25%).

Thus, in final analysis, an unimpressive HRD climate and a weak IT perspective have not been able to contribute towards each other. A good training and development climate could possibly boost up the technological environment or a good technological environment could facilitate development of human resources. However, in case of Jammu and Kashmir Bank, computerisation has not been able to contribute significantly towards the development climate.

Moreover, essentially efficiency of computerized services is dependent on how well training and development systems are designed, planned and implemented in the organizational frame of reference, which, cater to ground modalities and address the issue of transformation and change in the wake of changing technological environment. Besides, the computerized procedures and operations in turn are seen to enhance the efficiency and productivity. However, training and development systems as understood and handled in JKB, have not been able to make any valuable contribution in promoting operational efficiency of computerized services.

Nevertheless, the study supports that even in absence of appropriate training and development opportunities, the bank has been able to respond to customer needs with more immediacy and efficiency by reducing the level of errors, speeding up of delivery time and better management of databases. Clearly, therefore, scope for improvement is indicated supported by a sound training and development policy orientation and vision. The study thus establishes that even if training and development systems in JKB are not adequate to equip employees with requisite skills and competencies to cope with changes in job context and content, as a proactive response to technological transformation, the bank has shown signs of productivity and efficiency. This is supported by the fact that despite pressures of internal environment and external volatility, the business operations of the bank have shown healthy growth in all the important areas of operation. The efficiency factor (EFB- ratio of advances to employees) for the year ending 2003 has been estimated at Rs 112.64 Lakhs as against Rs 98.90 Lakhs in 2002 and Rs 73.61 Lakhs in 2001. Besides, the bank achieved an all time high business turnover of Rs 27946.32 crore during the year 2003-04 as against Rs 22686 crore for the year 2002-03, recording a steady growth of 23.19%. The Capital and Reserves of the bank increased by RS. 351.74 crore to Rs. 1593.74 crore during the year 2003-04 from Rs. 1242 crore of the previous year, registering an impressive growth of 28.32%. Statutory and other reserves increased by 29.46% to Rs. 1545.49 crore in the year 2003-04 from Rs. 1193.79 crore of the previous year. The bank also recorded an impressive increase of 20.30% over the net profit for the year 2002-03 making it a figure of Rs. 406.33 crore for the financial year 2003-04. Further, the total income of the bank has been estimated at Rs. 1822.95 crore as on March 31st 2004,recording a growth of 6.32% over the previous year figures of Rs. 1714.56 crore. Consequently, the per branch and per employee business has increased to Rs. 6800 Lakhs and Rs. 394 Lakhs respectively and the impressive performance recorded by the bank in its operations boosted the bank's equity price in the stock market to all time high of Rs. 599.90 recently. Besides the above-cited facts, the measure of Economic Value Added (EVA) in the bank, which is a fairly reliable measure of an enterprise's effort in determining value addition, reflects consistent and positive growth of EVA. EVA for the year 2003-04 has been calculated at 23.28% as against the figures of 22.07% and 21.40% for the years 2002-03 and 2001-02 respectively (Table 7) (Annual Report 2003-04).

TABLE 7

Economic Value Added (EVA) Status in JKB

S. No.	*Financial Year*	*Post Tax Profts (Rs. in Cr)*	*Capital Employed (Rs. in Cr)*	*Cost of Capital*	*Post Tax Returns on Capital Employed*	*EVA*
1.	2003-04	406	1494	2.02%	25.50%	23.48%
2.	2002-03	337	1242	5.13%	27.19%	22.07%
	2001-02	259	937	6.33%	27.73%	21.40%

Source: 66th Annual Report The Jammu and Kashmir Bank Ltd., 2003-2004

Thus, in the light of the above, it may be inferred that though training and development contributes significantly towards efficient handling of computerized operations and services, the employees in JKB have been able to deliver good services with reasonable efficiency in spite of certain inadequacies in the system.

Conclusions and Research Implications

Over the recent years, scholars have highlighted the need for building human capital, through training and development, for successful and productive implementation of automation, computerization, and information technology (McDuffie & Krafcik, 1992). This study highlights that if the HRD climate is unimpressive, then the managers may not find investments in training and development as worthwhile. In such a scenario, investments into the information technology would be an effective way for generating the interest of workforce in training and development. When the workers are self-motivated to learn, then organizational investments into people development can be more productive. However, such IT investments must be made strategically, lest they should degenerate into power dynamics where people are just seeking to get cutting edge technology for the sake of status. The firms must respond to the positive motivations towards change using a transformative approach where the change can become a source of continuous self-learning and self-development. It is this first step of getting the organization out of a vicious circle of unimpressive HR and weak IT perspective that is the biggest challenge for crafting competitive advantage in the under-developed and emerging markets. Thence, enhanced productivity of the workforce can become a self-sustaining catalyst for a variety of investments, in sophisticated training, research, branding, relationships, and technology for further value added. To cap it all, success of any development activity depends largely on the commitment of top management to HRD systems. There stands an urgent need for articulating the human resource development philosophy with a sharp focus on developing right kind of capabilities deemed essential for successfully handling the fundamental shifts taking place in the banking business. Efforts should be made to nurture a rejuvenated development culture that promotes willingness on the part of the people to embrace change and move in with new technologies as fast as possible. To drive the technology focus of the bank, the establishment of separate 'Technological Cell' that acts, alongside the strategic cell of bank, is suggested. Further, although indicative in nature, it is hoped that the work has gone some way in providing insight into the training and development dynamics in changing technological environment. However, a major task is not simply to collect data but also to develop a robust theory, which helps to explain strategic concerns in handling such transformations. Nevertheless, the implications of the study are important, as significant observations have been made which provide the basis for further hypothesis and validation in this context.

REFERENCES

65th Annual Report, The Jammu and Kashmir bank Ltd., 2002-03

66th Annual Report The Jammu and Kashmir Bank Ltd., 2003-2004

Banks: Verma Panel Report (2000), *Business Guide to India – Indian Banks*, www.economic times.com/guide/verma8c.htm.

Bhat, Mushtaq A. (2003) *Service Quality in Service Sector Banks: An Empirical Investigation*, Business Review, Vol.9, No. 2, March.

E.Abraham, S. J. (1988) in Khandelwal, A. K. (ed.) *Human Resource Development in Banks*, Oxford and IBH Publishing Co; New Delhi.

Hanson, James A. (2001) *Indian Banking: Market Liberalization and the Pressures for Institutional and Market Framework Reform*, Working Paper No. 104, Stanford University.

Khandelwal, A. K. (ed.) (1988), *Human Resource Development in Commercial Banks*, Oxford and IBH Publishing Co: New Delhi.

Khandelwal, A.K. (1978), *Challenges in training in Banks*, Indian Journal of Training and Development, Vol. 8, No. 2, March - April, pp: 25-40.

Lynton, R and Pareek, Udai (1990), *Training for Development*, Kumarian Press: Connecticut, USA.

MacDuffie, J.P., & Krafcik, J.F. (1992). *Integrating Technology and Human Resources for High Performance Manufacturing*, in T. A. Kochan and M. Useem, eds., Transforming Organizations. New York: Oxford University Press.

Maheshwari, Amol and Jhajharia, Shweta (2001), *Private Sector Banks: Shaping Up*, Management Review, June.

Mitra, Monika,2003, *Banking on Backing*, Business Today, February, 2003 pp: 94-97

Narasimham Committee (1998), *Report of the Committee on Banking Sector Reforms*.

Natrajan, R. (1999), *Indian Banking Scenario: Need for a revolutionary approach towards privatization'*, South Asia Analysis Group Papers, www.saag.org/papers/paper75.html.

Rao, T.V. (1999), *HRD in the New Economic Environment*, Tata Mc- Graw Hill: New Delhi.

Rohmetra, Neelu (1998), *Human Resource Development in Commercial Banks in India*, ASHGATE Publishing Co., UK.

Shah, S.G. (1978), *How to make training in banking management*, CAPITAL, March, pp: 71-76.

Shah, Saiyadian and Sheth, N.R, (1984), *Human Resource Management in Banking Industry - Text and Cases*, South Asian Publishers.

SILS Industry Analysis Series (1997), *Banking Industry: Trends and Challenges*, March.

Vyapaar Asia, Asia Trade Hub (2000), *Indian Banking*, www.vyapaarasia.com/india/banks.asp

14

BARRIERS TO LEARNING: CONFLICTS THAT OCCUR BETWEEN AND WITHIN ORGANISATIONAL SYSTEMS

*Jim Grieves, Janice McMillan and Philip Wilding**

Introduction

Organizational learning (OL) is a critical component of Strategic Human Resource Development (SHRD). Without OL it would not be possible to engage with the creative faculties of individuals, teams and organizations. Consequently, it would be pointless to engage with the drive to empower individuals in order to maximize their own potential and thereby the potential to develop the organization from within. Without OL we could not seriously talk about the added value generated by intangible assets and, as a result, management would be back in the darkness of a bygone age when managers followed prescriptive formulae and workers were given blindfolds to constrain the intellect.

Despite our concern to promote OL as central to SHRD we argue that the literature is fundamentally immature, overly prescriptive and produces rhetorical clichés to the detriment

* Jim Grieves works at the Business School, University of Hull, Janice McMillan and Philip Wilding work at the Newcastle Business School, University of Northumbria at Newcastle.

of practical solutions. We argue that Organizational Learning, as the underpinning process for Strategic Human Resource Development, has not yet reached a sufficient degree of maturity. Whilst organizations desire OL in order to achieve positive outcomes and eliminate negative outcomes in performance it is equally clear that in order to create flexible employees and a learning culture capable of generating organizational effectiveness, SHRD needs to reassess the contribution of OL.

The problem is that whilst the literature is generally rich in rhetoric it is empirically doubtful. A pervasive assumption of most of the OL literature is that organizations are unitarist. In addition, it is not uncommon for accounts of behaviours to be functionalist and normative in tone by assuming that dynamics are only occasionally dysfunctional once an equilibrium is upset. Closely associated with this is the predominance of research that has tended to underplay the importance of social context, preferring instead to address issues of personal cognition. As a result, studies that do offer empirical findings rarely diagnose the organization's contextual dimensions to ascertain the meanings that lie behind the contingent political, structural and socio-cultural relationships preferring instead to limit the investigation to learning difficulties related to personal characteristics such as learning styles and techniques of facilitation and training interventions. The majority of such studies provide a value-free or neutral account reminiscent of nineteen fifties industrial psychology where the subject as individual is problemitised and where the organizational context is assumed to be rational and apolitical.

By contrast, our perspective is to suggest that managers should be capable of diagnosing organizational context not simply for learning capability but for organizational constraints that limit the actions of individuals and groups to learn effectively. In order to redress this problem we suggest that greater attention is paid to the structural, cognitive and social barriers to OL. The paper begins with a review of the literature. From this review, thematic constructs were identified in relation to systemic properties. Questions were then constructed that related directly to these systemic properties. The resulting methodology therefore comprised a survey of managers' views (36 representing 36 organisations) about the most significant obstacles to organizational learning.

Barriers to Learning: What the Literature Reveals

The concepts of organizational learning and the learning organization are constructs that have sought to build theories and demonstrate practices about systems, work practices and behaviours. Both concepts were influenced by the writing of Argyris and Schön, (1978, 1996), and, more recently by Senge (1990). Whilst Argyris and Schön sought to illustrate actions that led to organizational learning. In their early work they sought to demonstrate some of the problems of learning by discussing the ways in which error occur in organizations. More recently, Argyris (1993) identified some simple barriers to organizational learning in the form of organizational defence mechanisms. By contrast Senge (1990) applied systems theory to organizational learning and thereby sought to develop a concept for the manager interested in establishing innovative learning systems prescribing a framework for organizational and personal transformation.

Over the years we have seen a variety of prescriptive studies that pay tribute to these authors. Such studies, unfortunately, are rarely empirical and few have sought to test the underlying assumptions of organizational learning and the learning organization. Few have investigated the impact of politics on learning. This failure had occurred at a macro level (as, for example, in the case of takeovers, mergers, global capitalism) and at a micro behavioural level (examples of which include, self-interest, career progression, conflict of interests, group dynamics and so on). At an anecdotal level many managers appear to be able to provide examples of the avoidance of learning in relation to systems, practices and behaviours. This appears to be backed up by examples from the business community in which leading edge organisations have failed to practice organisational learning with the integrity and honesty that collective action clearly requires. Recent examples include Marconi, Enron, Shell. Although each case is different, they each demonstrate barriers to learning. With this in mind we sought to survey the literature on barriers to learning in order to test out these ideas empirically.

The link between ***organizational learning and efficiency*** emerged from our literature search of learning for innovation. Innovation is described as intentional change designed to improve the performance of a product or a service. Creative thinking by itself is not therefore innovation since ideas have to be implemented for innovation to occur.

The relative importance of the dimensions of innovation to organizational learning and efficiency is important. The degree to which an innovation is radical or incremental may depend on a number of factors which include organisational structure and organizational strategy. Researchers have identified various links between innovation and organizational structure, organizational determinants, organizational climate, and leadership (Gopalakrishnan and Damanpour, 1992). One consideration is whether innovation is a process or an event. Consideration of processual issues suggests that the tasks and roles of organizational participants change over time (Burgelman and Sayles, 1986) and that participants need to acquire effective communication and work relationships. In this respect, it is useful to enquire whether the internal forces of cooperation in organizations are related positively to organizational performance (Ashok, 2003).

Barriers are also identified by writers who question issues related to **ideology, philosophy and mental models.** A dominant ideology is a belief system that seeks to represent the official viewpoint of an organisation. This does not, of course, imply that an ideology is an accurate reflection of a set of ideas nor does it imply that it depicts organisational reality honestly. However, ideologies are supported through a discourse of rhetoric which sometimes takes on mythological representations (Arnopoulos, 1991; Ashley, 1984; Larrain, 1994; Rosser, 1993; Schwartz, 1993; Watson, 1993).

The relevance of this topic goes back to discussion of ideology in the work of Selznick (1953) with his investigation of the *TVA and the Grass Roots*. Selznick derived his ideas mainly from the impressions of the content of the organization's ideologies. There has since been a rise in the popular literature about organizational philosophy in the late 1970s and 1980s (Ouchi,198l; Pascale, 1990; Peters and Waterman, 1982) which links ideology to philosophy and commitment.

In relation to Ideology, philosophy and mental models Steiner (1998) has suggested that barriers to learning occur when there is a discrepancy between mental models. The biggest problem occurs when there is a significant gap between the organisation's espoused philosophy and systems of ideas held by different groups of people. When the mental models are inconsistent then an ideological discrepancy emerges. Whilst organizational learning can emerge from a healthy conflict of ideas the failure to surface subterranean dynamics will have a negative impact of the organization. A different example is suggested by Steiner when he argues that barriers to learning occur as the result of managerial efforts to implement a new ideology that is not accepted or understood by employees (Steiner 1998). Furthermore, different mental models can also be caused by different linguistic codes, insufficient levels of competence; evasion of facts, different visions of reality held by employees vis-à-vis management. Other have suggested that ideological barriers exist when there is rigidity of core beliefs, values and assumptions or when there is ineffective communication and information systems, the desire to minimize threats; cognitive narrowing and event fixation; centrality of expertise, denial and disregard of outsiders; lack of corporate responsibility; and focus upon "single-loop," or single-cause, *learning* (Elliott et al, 2000). Mitroff et al (1990) have indicated that the "core beliefs, values and assumptions of senior managers have long been considered important in incubating the potential for crises within organizations". Other writers on crisis management have argued that the core beliefs can act as powerful inhibitors to learning (Pauchant and Mitroff, 1992).

By comparison to ideology or philosophy mental models are "simplified abstractions" that may be flawed or seek knowledge that is no longer appropriate. As Chapman and Ferfolja (2001) have suggested, "The implications for organisations are many, and include threats to safety in work contexts that are known to be hazardous. The continuing high toll of deaths and injuries from industrial accidents and disasters is widely recognised" (Chapman and Ferfolja, 2001: 399; Joy, 1999). The attempt to remedy "flawed mental models" is rarely address in the literature except for Senge's descriptive statement that it is necessary to surface, test and improve theories in use (Chapman and Ferfolja, 2001: 399; Senge, 1990).

A third source of data on barriers relates to **organisational defence routines.** According to Argyris (1993), organizational defence mechanisms are barriers to organizational learning. When people in organizations employ defence mechanisms they inhibit learning. In relation to stressful situations Elliott, et al (2000) suggest that it is possible to test defensive reasoning by investigating what happens when the conditions that create defensiveness are removed. Research into situations of dynamic complexity suggest that when individuals work alone under such conditions they are more likely to display defensiveness when things go wrong (Robinson, 2001). Other examples of defensive reasoning include scapegoating, and complacency, clashes of belief systems or ideologies, holding too rigidly to core beliefs, values and assumptions, poor communication (Elliott, et al (2000).

Another direction is that taken by Pearn *et al* (1995) who focus on the blockages or barriers to learning transfer. By contrast to the work of Argyris and Schön who focused on individual interactions, the barriers described by Pearn *et al* are mostly environmentally and organizationally based (Sun & Scott, 2003).

Barriers to learning may be related to structural dynamics of the organisation or they may be related to a particular individual's biography. Since we are interested in the management of structural dynamics we are less concerned to visit the arguments related to individual behaviours. However, it is inevitable that managers must confront problems that arise from the interplay of individual behaviours through a concern with group dynamics. From a psychoanalytic perspective it is important to recognise the part that the unconscious and irrational processes play in organizational life.

These unconscious processes impact on role effectiveness, group identity, decision making and political behaviour. They also impact on external relationships clients and customers (Jaques, 1953; Menzies, 1960; Hirschhorn, 1990). Researchers from this psychoanalytical perspective are concerned to demonstrate dysfunctional behaviours and actions. Following the work of Klein (1975) barriers to learning take the form of defensive strategies often related to projection of feelings on to others, denial of aggressive feelings or thoughts, or excessive feelings of hopelessness, depression or paranoia.

A fourth source of data is related to **systems theory**. The systems approach to learning suggests that open systems are characterised by a unique type of learning. For example, creative thinking requires the discovery of new ideas. Whilst such learning may be intuitive in the sense that organisational members may have acquired a kind of craft knowledge, it is likely that negative encounters or interactions will lead to negative feedback.

An examination of chaos and instability within organizations can generate new insights into learning barriers. Such an approach is more likely to consider problems associated with single-loop and double-loop learning. Ultimately, one is therefore concerned to re-evaluate the workings of the system.

In relation to systems thinking, Senge (1990) contends that the long-term sustainable source of competitive advantage in an organization can be achieved when it learns faster than its competitors and if it is to achieve this it needs to be more effective than the sum of its parts. Systems thinking is a framework for recognising the interrelationships between component part of the organisation and its activities. In order that people can manage complexity they need to simplify by constructing a mental model of reality. If problems and solutions are seen in terms of systemic relationship among processes related to the needs and goals and the organisation then a sense of involvement in the control process is critical to this (Appelbaum & Goransson, 1997).

The ***Learning Environment*** is the fifth source of barriers. Learning environments have been transformed in recent years by electronic technology. A learning environment can now enable the learner to interact with the instructor and other learners without being in the same physical location. Will the traditional learning based on direct contact with the trainer be increasingly overtaken by a virtual classroom environment? Will contemporary learning environments with interactive activities overcome the barriers of the traditional classroom or are they likely to contain their own barriers to learning?

Learning effectiveness depends on the suitability of the environment for learning but should also include the role performance of trainers, instructors and mentors in creating, sustaining and encouraging appropriate conditions for learning. The learning environment is therefore significant to the application of technique and to the decision as to the method used in encouraging the development of the learner on a personal journey from ignorance, through to awareness, understanding, commitment, enactment and reflection (Buckler, 1996). One might argue therefore that the essential criteria for effective learning includes the *environment* to facilitate learning, the *techniques* used that enable effective learning and the methods of learning. Failure to consider these issues leads to barriers to learning. The environment may also be a limiting factor if it fails to accommodate the relevance of different cognitive styles. A learning environment must be properly supported if learning is to become part of the individual's working life. According to Mumford (1996), human resource professionals who recognize the value of organizational learning should focus on continuous development by identifying how people can work for the long term success of the organisation, know how to develop incremental improvements and ensure that successes and best practices are embedded in our work routines. For Honey and Mumford (1992), diagnosing the interactions that occur in the "learning environment" requires an examination of four managerial roles. First is the need to demonstrate enthusiasm for learning through ***role behaviours***. Second, is the *provider role* which seeks to develop opportunities for new learning. Third the *system builder role* seeks the integration of learning with other systemic processes. Finally, the *champion role* seeks to identify change agents who take initiative throughout the organisation.

Finally, barriers to learning can occur through two interrelated areas: **organisational culture** and **communication**. As Garavan (1997) points out, numerous authors who include Garvin (1993); McGill et al., (1992) and Senge, (1990) have considered the importance of culture to organisational learning. Garavan points out that although some authors have identified specific aspects of a learning organization culture and these include entrepreneurship and risk taking (Kanter, 1989; Naman and Slevin, 1993; Sykes and Block, 1989) facilitative leadership (Meen and Keough, 1992; Slater and Narver, 1995) and organic structures (Gupta and Govindarajan, 1991; Woodman et al., 1993) others (Day, 1990; Hart, 1992; Garvin, 1993, Mintzberg, 1994) have identified individual and organisational development as ends in themselves and without the need to demonstrate how they may contribute to learning activities within the organization and ultimately to enhanced organizational performance (Garavan, 1997). Although it is difficult to demonstrate how culture affects performance most authors are agreed that culture is an important determinant of organisational learning and that organisational learning affects performance.

Studies of crises have suggested that the relationship between sense-making and the development of a safety culture offers important insights into the dynamics of developing effective learning. That is, how to maintain high reliability and/or crisis preparedness. Bhopal and Chernobyl, are cited as examples of barriers to learning where managers often appear unable to deal with the emotional, informational and/ or cognitive aspects (Elliott et al, 2000). Since culture can be seen as a shared structure of meaning then it is important to identify the barriers to the learning process. Central to this is the importance of effective communication in the form of feedback for the purpose of corrective action. A useful source of investigation appears to be the distinction between simple forms of learning, involving single negative feedback and the "double-loop" learning required for complex situation.

As a result of the preceding discussion the following barriers have been identified for further investigation:

- Organizational learning focused on efficiency is related positively to organizational performance
- Ideology, philosophy and mental models
- Organisational Defence Routines
- Systems thinking
- Learning Environment
- Culture
- Communication
- Communication

Methodology

The literature search provided the themes and issues for this survey. However, because the literature into barriers to learning is largely descriptive with few known empirical studies, we highlighted the critical issues other writers considered relevant in order to test respondents' views of barriers to learning in their own organisations. The views of 36 managers with responsibility for training and development were canvassed across a range of companies (36) and sectors (private and public). The sizes of the organisations differed considerably with some regarded as small to medium and others as largely bureaucratic and performing a public service. The resulting survey is considered to be a useful starting point to identify the barriers to learning which we identified as a necessary indicator of organisational performance. Although this work is in its early stages it does, nevertheless, provide a valuable insight into what the managers define as problems in respect of learning in the workplace. At this stage the responses are constructed as a data gathering exercise in order to develop a more robust set of constructs for a wider survey at a later date. The themes and questions were derived from a detailed search of the literature. The questions resulted from a reading of key papers which had identified barriers to learning as their constructs. The response to each question asked for clarification by means of an open response to be described in the participant's own words. These open responses are important because they convey what the participants felt to be the major obstacles to performance. We therefore avoided, at this stage, a highly structured questionnaire. The survey itself was comprised of 67 questions around the themes indicated above (see figure 1).

In the analysis we have give a percentage response to each question. We have mainly expressed the responses as concerns to be addressed. We have also indicated the question in parenthesis for reference.

Analysis

We regard barriers to learning as obstacles that inhibit organisational performance. Thus, to Argyris and Schön organizational learning occurs when individuals within an organization experience a problematic situation and inquire into it on the organization's behalf (1978; 1996). The barriers to learning identified in this research indicate that whilst respondents can identify problems they do not engage in OL until they make an intervention to improve some aspect of the organisation.

Organizational Learning Focused on Efficiency is Related Positively to Organizational Performance

Organizational learning focused on efficiency is related positively to organizational performance. It was appropriate, therefore, to identify the extent to which our group of managers were able to identify their organisations as efficient and effective. Thus in response to the question "We are efficient and effective" (Q 2), 58% of respondents gave a negative response. This was felt to be an interesting starting point for the research since we could then consider other questions linking learning and innovation to how they perceived their organisations and managed performance through learning.

The measurement of innovation has been approached by asking employees about their willingness to innovate. Asking employees about their willingness to innovate results in general measures of innovation, and such information can be obtained by interviews and questionnaires although data about specific innovations can be collected by interviews, and documents. We suggest that this would inform a useful further study.

Innovation, in particular is the most important aspect of learning for performance since it reflects the intentional design for change. Responses to the question "In this organisation innovation comes from people promoting their ideas individually and in teams"(Q1) indicated that only 11% of the sample saw their activities as innovative on a regular basis. The main reason for this was largely reported to be related to **bureaucratic procedures** and comments referred to *"The decision making process for anything new is so time consuming that generally people don't bother"* and *"There is little scope for individuality in large bureaucratic organisations"*.

Organizations can innovate through the development of new systems or new technology.

Since innovation refers to intentional actions to promote change then one would expect respondents to demonstrate a sense of depth to the question "We engage in learning" (Q3). This also corresponded with the previous questions with only 33% indicating a positive response. Questions about innovation should overlap with questions related to knowledge acquisition and sharing. In relation to knowledge acquisition (Q 15) only 22 % felt their organisations worked hard at the development and creation of new ideas. Reasons reported for the failure to develop new ideas were mainly related to **lack of resources** and **lack of expertise.** Similarly, with knowledge acquisition, the figure was even lower with only 14% % stating that their organisations worked hard at the dissemination of ideas (Q16). Problems reported indicated issues related to the **lack of empowerment:** *"people at the lower end of the organisation don't get any involvement until it is too late" and "Ideas are normally imposed".*

Ideology, Philosophy and Mental Models

By investigating respondents "mental models" we were able to gain some idea of their views to the corporate ideology and their commitment to it. In our sample 72% of the respondents expressed a negative view about these connections in their organisations. Their views stated that "There is not too much to be gained by sticking with this organization"; "the company contains many internal groups and sub-cultures that conflict with the company's strategy" *and* "I am now attempting to gain as much knowledge/expertise as possible out of frustration, which will make me more marketable outside of it".

Organisational Defence Routines

A useful definition of organisational defence routines is provided by Appelbaum & Goransson (1997) who state that "Whenever human beings are faced with any issue that contains significant embarrassment or threat, they act in ways that bypass, as best they can, the embarrassment or threat. In order for the bypass to work, it must be covered up." (Appelbaum & Goransson, 1997: 116). Defence routines can be regarded as strategic actions designed to cover-up mistakes. Motives vary but those reported include **avoidance of embarrassment** or **avoidance of threat**. The strategic actions include: (1) the crafting of messages that contain inconsistencies which are designed to appear as if (2) the messages are not inconsistent often (3) vocalised through a particular type of speech act that does not invite enquiry and (4) leads to a range of unintended and counterproductive consequences (Appelbaum & Goransson, 1997). Because most individuals use these actions, the actions become part of the fabric of everyday life. Furthermore, because so many individuals frequently employ strategies to avoid embarrassment or threat, the actions become routines that are counterproductive to the organisation. Nevertheless, the actions come to be viewed as rational, sensible, and realistic from the point of view of those participants who employ them since they become mechanisms for psychological survival.

Organisational defence routines are therefore the antithesis of a learning culture. In the survey we wanted to know whether people perceived this to be a problem in their organisations. The response to the question "Mixed messages lead to a range of unintended and counterproductive consequences" (Q5) indicated that 89% felt this to be a problem. The main reasons included the **lack of knowledge, skills or sensitivity to change issues:** *"poor change management"* and **self interest**: *"People acting on their own agenda confuse the messages"*. When asked if "people were defensive about their motives", 75% said yes. The same number 75% stated that "people hid mistakes" (Q8) and gave reasons indicating that they were sometimes subjected to a *"blame culture"* or that *"senior management used bullying tactics"*.

Systems Thinking

Respondents were asked to identify the statement that most accurately reflected their organisation (Q9) and the extent to which they could relate to a shared vision and mission (Q10). Respondents were given two choices: one positive (indicating that they were in control) and the other negative (indicating that the system was in control). Responses were divided evenly. The 50% who answered "It's the system-we have no control" (Q9) gave their reasons for not engaging in systems thinking as (1) **fear** - *"of threat/ discipline/grievance"; "the need to obey"*; (2) **organisational structure** – *"This is a hierarchical organisation"; "compliance with the system is required"* and *"directed by government policy and local politics"*; (3) **outdated control systems** – *"Dated administrative system"*. The number who gave a negative answer to the following question "Generally people work to a shared vision and mission" was, as expected, almost the same (53%). Reasons were due to the (1) **vision/ mission not being communicated;** (2) **vision/ mission not believed;** (3) **top down enforcement by senior managers.**

Respondents had already indicated that people in their organisations often worked to different mental models. For example, one response to the previous question (10) was "People/ senior managers work to their own agendas". For Senge (1990) taking advantage of market conditions or challenging outdated managerial practices requires the development of new insights. Whilst we would agree with Senge that the ability to change shared mental models through introspection is an important skill of the learning organization it is difficult to see how reflection, surfacing, and public examination of mental models can be achieved without first challenging the political processes that create the barriers to change. When many of these are caused by managers then innovative "leaps of abstraction" are unlikely to be practiced by those further down the organisation. It was not surprising then that the images people offered as symptomatic of divergent mental models were: (1) **favouritism** *"Power is centred around a few people - only people with their ear get on"* and (2) **lack of time**: *"Hectic. People rushing in all directions. No time to stand and stare"*.

Learning Environment

According to Mumford (1996), human resource professionals who recognize the value of organizational learning should focus on continuous development by identifying how people can work for the long term success of the organisation, know how to develop incremental improvements and ensure that successes and best practices are embedded in our work routines. We therefore constructed a number of questions (22-29) designed to identify the objectives of the learning environment. Those who stated that people were not clearly focussed on making incremental improvements (Q23) (61%) gave their reasons as (1) **failure to communicate** *"to all levels"*; (2) **cost** – *"Provided we can afford it"*. Reasons why creativity, innovation and adaptability might me stifled (63%) were not clearly defined. However, negative reasons for not developing the learning environment effectively included **authoritarian practices** (Q26); **politics** – *"it suits the old boys network"* (Q26); **inconsistency** – *"We don't always get to carry out staff development due to the whims of business and capacity issues"* (Q26); and **inaction** – *"We talk about it a lot but rarely practice it"* (Q26). Ensuring that people are equipped to meet the current and future needs of the organization (Q27) can be let down by (1) **untimely training initiatives** – *"Often trained after the event"* and (2) **lack of encouragement** – *"Development is available but rarely encouraged"*.

Role Behaviours of Managers

For Honey and Mumford (1992), diagnosing the interactions that occur in the "learning environment" requires an examination of four managerial roles. First is the need to demonstrate enthusiasm for learning through *role behaviours.* Second, is the *provider role* which seeks to develop opportunities for new learning. Third the system *builder role* seeks the integration of learning with other systemic processes. Finally, the *champion role* seeks to identify change agents who take initiative throughout the organisation.

Questions 30 to 32 illustrate these. Firstly, the frequency by which managers demonstrate positive role behaviours was very limited in our survey with only 14% stating that it was a regular feature. Thus the demonstration of role behaviours is limited by (1) **inconsistency** - *"Depends on the person"* or *"Some do, some don't"* and *"Depends from one to another; no consistency"* and (2) **opportunism** – *"If it suits the organisation"*. Whilst 28% were positive and stated that their management team had developed systematic learning and integrated it with the vision, mission and strategy of the organisation only 0.08% said that it was championed by change agents. Overall **Distrust of management** was indicated by the question "management are trusted by the employees". 72% of respondents disagreed with this statement. Management were said to *"say one thing and do another"*. In one respondent's organisation, *"65% of employees didn't return an employee attitude survey"* illustrating that commitment *"differs at different levels in the organisation"*.

Culture

Whilst there is general consensus amongst writers of HRD/HRM that employees should be involved with workplace decisions that affect them, when we asked to what extent "management adequately prepares employees for change", 69% indicated that it was ineffective as it never occurred (31%) or happened only occasionally (39%). The suggestion then that employees are being "trained to challenge our assumptions and views of the current reality" resulted in

39% stating that they were either unsure or in disagreement with this statement. As one respondent stated *"challenge, no way; obey orders at all costs"*. To this extent then, when asked to what extent does the organisational "culture prevents learning taking place", 36% of respondents replied very often and 44% occasionally. The inference then is, that **bureaucracy and policy often put barriers in the way of learning processes.** Such barriers occur, according to Hartmann and Patrickson (2003), when people frame concepts such as organisational commitment and psychological contract but come to understand them within an insecure employment context. In our survey, 47% stated that their organisation culture was autocratic? (Q55) and 53% stated that *"the existing culture is a significant barrier to organisational change"*. In relation to the interrelationship between culture and core values one respondent commented that *"it is the organisation's core values rather than the employees beliefs that are considered"*.

Communication

Ineffective communication and information difficulties cause barriers which inhibit learning in various ways. Our findings illustrate the high levels of dissatisfaction with respect to information and communication. 75% of respondents gave a negative answer to the question *"to what extent are staff involved, communicated with, trained and receive follow-up with regard to change processes"* (Q49). Management appear to be reluctant to discuss major initiatives with the workforce. This is reinforced by question 37 with 56% stating that *"everything was on a need to know basis"* and that the *"mushroom model"* of management was still prevalent. Change was also *"forced on employees"* and *"done without warning or staff involvement"* (Q41). Inevitably *"people acting on their own agenda confuse the messages"* that result in *"a range of unintended and counterproductive consequences"*.

Discussion

Barriers to learning can be classified by referring to the three levels by which learning is operationalised: individual, group or team and organizational. The barriers to learning fall within three main categories. These are: a) ***structural barriers*** such as communication systems, organisation structure and the logistics of operational design; b) ***cognitive barriers*** such as defensive reasoning; c) ***social barriers*** such as the methods of working or the relationships between people – although this mainly appeared to be between levels of management and the workforce.

In order to enhance performance participants need to address the problems identified and tackle them through action research. In other words, structural problems must be transformed, cognitive problems must be challenged and social problems must be dealt with through team dynamics.

In relation to organizational learning, when it is focused on efficiency and related positively to organizational performance respondents were clear that bureaucratic procedures are the main barrier to innovation. Whilst organisations innovate through the development of new systems or new technology it is the failure to think more carefully about the social system that is used to implement technology and systems. This finding, of course corresponds with a long history of similar research into socio-technical systems. What is surprising is that so few organisations in the sample appear to be addressing this. Related to this were the reasons reported for the failure to develop new ideas. These were mainly related to lack of resources, lack of expertise and an unempowerered workforce.

Respondents views indicate that corporate ideology and their commitment to it appear to be problematic. This does appear to support the literature on defensive reasoning in that avoidance of threat seems to be the main reason for lack of commitment on the one hand and the need to preserve dignity on the other. Respondents did indicate that there were often inconsistencies in communication which lead to counterproductive consequences.

Whilst Organisational defence routines are the antithesis of a learning culture many indicated that dysfunctional actions resulting from defensive reasoning often appears to represent the practice of the workplace with individuals frequently employing strategies for psychological survival. Therefore it is paradoxical that whilst such actions are rational, sensible, and realistic from participants viewpoints, they represent dysfunctional or negative learning from the organisation's viewpoint.

Respondents were equally divided in their views about the degree of participation they experienced. Although we did not seek to identify the extent to which people may have felt alienated in their work there is a good deal of research over the past century to suggest that alienation results from the application of technology, organisational structure, work design and outdated human resource systems. Nor did we identify performance management systems as an issue. However, because of the nature of the responses to the questions related to systems thinking we suggest that any future research should take theses factors into consideration. Therefore of those who felt they had little or no control over the system the reasons given related to perception of fear or threat, the dominance of compliance to the system, outdated control systems and top down enforcement of views from senior managers.

Whilst we would agree with Senge that the ability to change shared mental models through introspection is an important skill of the learning organization it is difficult to see how reflection, surfacing, and public examination of mental models can be achieved without first challenging the political processes that create the barriers to change. This seems to us to be the heart of the matter in that discussions of the learning organisation, in their reliance on descriptive characteristics, often fail to recognise the importance of the political process in large organisations. In this case we reported that the main reasons cited were favouritism and lack of time.

Responses to questions about the nature of the learning environment suggest that the people who were not clearly focussed on making incremental improvements indicated communication throughout the system to be one of the main reasons. This was sometimes reinforced by untimely training initiatives and lack of encouragement. Honey and Mumford suggestion to examine role behaviours is therefore apparent. Thus, the frequency by which managers demonstrate positive role behaviours was very limited in our survey. This appeared mainly due to inconsistency between different managers, opportunism whether learning was championed by people with skills, knowledge and sensitivity.

The literature on learning culture indicated that barriers to learning can occur through two interrelated areas: organisational culture and communication. The questions related to innovation and performance together with those focusing on relationships indicates that feedback is central to this. However, it is apparent that focusing on single negative feedback is insufficient since as we have already indicated it can lead to defensive reasoning. It is equally clear that double loop learning is also critical in order to maintain high reliability cultures. Thus, to discover that a large proportion of the sample felt that management inadequately prepared them for change was worrying.

It was also disappointing to discover that people were

not being trained to challenge assumptions and views of the current reality. To this extent then a significant proportion of the sample saw their existing culture as a main obstacle to development. As previously indicated, the main reasons for this appear to be related to management attitudes and bureaucratic practices. Communication was also significant to the extent that many reported that management appear to be reluctant to discuss major initiatives with the workforce.

The final suggestion is that managers should consider interventions related to ***structural barriers, cognitive barriers and social barriers.*** Structural barriers include an investigation into the effectiveness of systems (managerial systems, control systems, technical systems, political systems, communication systems, human resource systems). Cognitive barriers should be investigated for attitudes, knowledge skill and sensitivity to managing systems and people. Finally social barriers should be investigated for their potential to enhance performance through relationships, motivation and leadership. However, identifying organisational barriers is one thing. Having the ability to make successful interventions is quite another and requires a greater effort to learn how to establish performance through the skilful deployment of intangible resources.

Figure 1: List of Themes and questions for Survey

Organizational learning focused on efficiency is related positively to organizational performance.

1. *In this organisation innovation comes from* people promoting *their ideas individually and in teams*
2. We are efficient and effective
3. We engage in learning

Defence routines

4. I feel that the culture prevents learning taking place
5. Mixed messages lead to a range of unintended and counterproductive consequences

6. People are defensive about their motives:
7. People hide mistakes:
8. Generally people work with a high degree of commitment

Systems thinking

9. Which statement is the most accurate in your organisation?
10. Generally people work to a shared vision and mission
    See also, Q50, 54, 55,56,57, 63

Mental Models

11. What images come to mind when you think of your organisation?
12. We engage in reflective thinking
13. We engage in public examination of our work routines
14. We review strategic thinking

Overlaps with Organizational learning questions 1,2,3 related to knowledge acquisition, sharing and utilization

15. We work hard at the development and creation of new ideas
16. We work hard at the dissemination of ideas
17. Which comment do you think is the most accurate
18. Overall I would agree that people generally attempt to develop personal mastery in their jobs. .
19. We have been trained to challenge our assumptions and views of the "current reality".
20. We engage in team learning by exploring new ideas
21. We monitor and improve performance through team learning

Learning Environment

22. We are concerned to work for the long-term success of the organisation
23. We are clearly focussed on making incremental improvements
24. We ensuring that successes and best practices are embedded in our work routines
25. We work at increasing creativity, innovation and adaptability
26. We deliberately recruit people who want to succeed and learn
27. We view staff development as very important
28. We always attempt to retain staff
29. We ensure that people are equipped to meet the current and future needs of the organization.

Managers Role Behaviours

30. Managers demonstrate enthusiasm for learning and development.
31. The management team have developed systematic learning, which is integrated with the Vision, mission and strategy of the organisation.
32. We have change agents who champion opportunities for learning

Communication

33. Management regularly develops and communicates the need for change
34. Management are trusted by the employees
35. Management encourages and implements improvement ideas from the workforce
36. Employees receive relevant and timely feedback on their job performance
37. There is reluctance by management to discuss major initiatives with the workforce
38. Effective communication strategies exist at all levels within the organisation
39. Effective communication strategies are in place in order to ensure a full transfer of meaning
40. Effective two-way communication channels with management exist
41. Everyone is clear about why change is needed
42. Employees receive management support for their ideas
43. To what extent do you agree that change is always effectively managed?
44. The organisation has strategies in place in order to manage individual resistance
45. Appropriate consideration is given to employee needs when implementing change
46. Appropriate follow-up is provided in order to ensure that change is effectively implemented

Organisational culture

47. Appropriate systems, processes and relationships exist in order that learning can be shared
48. The organisation encourages risk taking

49. To what extent are staff involved, communicated with, trained and receive follow-up with regard to change processes
50. Consideration is always given to the core beliefs that employees hold
51. Resistance to change is seen as normal rather than as a sign of difficult employees
52. Job roles are designed to remove monotony and isolation
53. Employees have significant levels of autonomy in respect to their jobs
54. The organisations reliance on productivity, short-termism and bottom line results severely limits the potential gains from learning initiatives (**Relate to systems thinking**)
55. Our organisation culture is autocratic (**Relate to systems thinking**)
56. The existing culture is a significant barrier to organisational change (**Relate to systems thinking**)
57. All employee groups share the values of the organisation (**Relate to systems thinking**)
58. In this organisation, the future employment requirements are satisfied from existing employees
59. Management adequately prepares employees or change
60. The work environment is conducive to change
61. The nature of my industry/sector imposes barriers to organisational learning
62. The need to achieve professional standards of competence, for example accountancy, law, registered status etc imposes barriers to organisational learning
63. The structure of the organisation impedes organisational learning (**Relate to systems thinking**)
64. Information flows (within and between organisations) impedes organisational learning
65. Decisions within this organisation are always referred upwards
66. What industry/sector are you employed in?
67. What level are you employed at within your current organisation?

REFERENCES

Appelbaum, S.H. and Goransson, L. (1997) 'Transformational and adaptive learning within the learning organization: a framework for research and application', *The Learning Organization*, 4(3):115 –128.

Argyris, C. (1993), *Knowledge for Action - A Guide to Overcoming Barriers to Organizational Change*, Jossey Bass, San Francisco, CA.

Argyris, C. and Schon, D. A. (1978) *Organisational Learning: a theory of action perspective*, Addison-Wesley.

Argyris, C. and Schon, D. A. (1996) *Organisational Learning II*, Addison-Wesley.

Argyris, C., Schön, D. (1978) *Organizational Learning II - Theory, Method, and Practice*, Addison-Wesley, Reading.

Arnopoulos, P. (1991) 'Ideological analytics: a study of evolving world values', *World Futures*, 30, 1, 19-34.

Ashley, D. (1984) 'Historical materialism and ideological practice: how do ideologies dominate people?', *Current Perspectives in Social Theory*, 5 (2): 1-20.

Ashok, J. (2003) 'Cognition, culture and competition: an empirical test of the learning organization', *The Learning Organization*,10(1): 31-50.

Buckler, B. (1996) 'A learning process model to achieve continuous improvement and innovation', *The Learning Organization*, 3(3): 31-9.

Burgelman, R.A. and Sayles, L.R. (1986) *Inside Corporate Innovation*, The Free Press, New York, NY.

Chapman, J.A, Ferfolja, T. (2001) 'Fatal flaws: The acquisition of imperfect mental models and their use in hazardous situations', *Journal of Intellectual Capital*, 2 (4): 398–409.

Day, G.S. (1990) *Mental Driven Strategy: Processes for Creating Value*, The Free Press, New York, NY.

Elliott, D., Smith, D. and McGuinness, M. (2000) 'Exploring The Failure To Learn: Crises And The Barriers To Learning', *Review of Business*, Fall/Winter, 21,3/4.

Garavan. T. (1997) 'The learning organization: a review and evaluation', *The Learning Organization* 4(1):18-29.

Garvin, D.A. (1993) 'Building a learning organisation', *Harvard Business Review*, 71, 78-91.

Garvin, D.A., (1993) 'Building a learning organisation', *Harvard Business Review*, 71, 78-91.

Gopalakrishnan, S. and Damanpour, F. (1992) 'Innovation research in economics, sociology, and technology management: a review and synthesis', *Proceedings of the Academy of Management*, 52, 488.

Gupta, A.K. and Govindarajan, V., 1991, "*Knowledge flows and the structure of control within multinational corporations*", Academy of Management Review, 16.

Hart, S.L. (1992) 'An integrative framework for strategy-making processes', *Academy of Management Review*, 17: 327-51.

Hirschhorn, I. (1990) *The Workplace Within*, MIT Press, Boston, MA.

Honey, P. and Mumford, A. (1992), *The Manual of Learning Styles*, Peter Honey, Maidenhead.

Jaques, E. (1953) 'On the dynamics of social structure', *Human Relations*, 6(1): 3-24.

Jarrett, M. and Kellner, K. (1996) 'Coping with uncertainty: a psychodynamic perspective on the work of top teams', *The Journal of Management Development*, 15(2): 54-68.

Kanter, R.M., (1989) *When Giants Learn to Dance*, Unwin, London.

Klein, M. (1975) *Envy and Gratitude and Other Works 1945-1963*, Virago, London.

Larrain, J. (1994) 'The postmodern critique of ideology', *The Sociological Review*, 42 (2), 289-315.

MA.Steiner, L. (1998) 'Organizational dilemmas as barriers to learning', *The Learning Organization*, 5 (4): 193 – 201.

McGill, M E., Slocum, J.W., Sei, D., (1992), 'Management practices in learning organizations', Organizational Dynamics, 21, 5-17.

Meen, D.E., Keough, M. (1992) 'Creating a learning organization', *The McKinsey Quarterly*, 1: 58-81.

Menzies, L. (1960) 'A case in the functioning of social system as a defence against anxiety', *Human Relations*, 13(2): 95-121.

Mintzberg, H., 1994, *The Rise and Fall of Strategic Planning*, The Free Press, New York, NY.

Mitroff, I., Pauchant, T., Finney M. and Pearson, C.(1989) 'Do (Some) Organizations Cause Their Own Crises? Culture Profiles of Crisis Prone versus Crisis Prepared Organizations', *Industrial Crisis Quarterly*, 3: 269-283.

Mumford, A. (1996) *Creating a learning environment, Journal of Professional Human Resource Management*, 4, 26-30.

Naman, J.L., and Slevin, D.P. (1993) Entrepreneurship and the concept of fit: a model and empirical test', *Strategic Management Journal*, 14(2): 135-52.

Ouchi, W.G. (1981) *Theory Z. How American Business Can Meet the Japanese Challenge*, Addison-Wesley, Reading.

Pascale, R. (1990) *Managing On The Edge*, Harmondsworth: Penguin.

Pauchant, T.C. and Douville, R, (1993) 'Recent Research in Crisis Management: A Study of 24 Authors' Publications from 1986-1991', *Industrial and Environmental Crisis Quarterly*, 7 (1), 43-66.

Pauchant, T.C. and Mitroff, I (1992) Transforming the Crisis-Prone Organization. Preventing Individual Organizational and Environmental Tragedies, San Francisco: Jossey-Bass Publishers, 1992.

Peters, T. J., & Waterman, R. H., Jr. (1982, 1986), *In search of excellence: Lessons from America's Best-Run Companies*, Harper & Row: New York; reprint, Warner Books: New York, 1986,

Rosser, J.B. Jr, (1993) 'Belief: its role in economic thought and action', *The American Journal of Economics and Sociology*, 52(3): 355-69.

Schwartz, J. (1993) 'The paradox of ideology', *Canadian Journal of Philosophy*, 23(4): 543-75.

Senge, P. (1990), *The Fifth Discipline - The Art & Practice of the Learning Organization*, Sage, New York.

Slater, S.F. and Narver, J.C. (1995), Market orientation and the learning organization, *Journal of Marketing*, 59: 63-74.

Sun, P. and Scott, J.L. (2003) 'Exploring the divide - organizational learning and learning organization', *The Learning Organization*, 10(4):202-215.

Sykes, H.B., and Block, Z. (1989), 'Corporate venturing obstacles: sources and solutions', *Journal of Business Venturing*, 4(3): 159-67.

Watson, G., (1993) 'The fuss about ideology', *The Wilson Quarterly*, 16(1): 130-36.

Woodman, R.W., Sawyer, J.L., Griffin, R.W. (1993), 'Towards a theory of organizational creativity', *Academy of Management Review*, 18(2): 293-321.

15

MASS CUSTOMIZATION AND PERSONALIZATION IN EDUCATION AND TRAINING

*Robert J. Freund**

1. Mass Customization

The idea of mass customization is based on the observation that there is a customer interest in products that are adapted to his/her individual needs and preferences, since the adaptation will increase perceived performance. As the standard of living has increased in the last 50 years, individualization has received increased focus, since customization has come within reach of the average consumer. At the same time there has been a massive development of technologies taking place.

In this environment customers have the power to demand individually tailored products that are specifically designed and manufactured to suit their needs. Recognising the customer as a major factor in the successful exploitation of mass customization is the basis of this paper. Moreover, the increasing competition also puts pressure on other important variables such as costs and services.

* Independent expert on class customization and Personalization, Germany.

An organisational strategy to meet these customers needs, and therefore gain competitive advantages, is known as mass customization. The concept of mass customization was first identified in "Future shock" by Toffler (1971) and was later described in "Future perfect" by Davis (1987).

Stan Davis, who coined the phrase in 1987, refers to mass customization when "the same large number of customers can be reached as in mass markets of the industrial economy, and simultaneously they can be treated individually as in the customized markets of pre-industrial economies" (Davis 1987). In order to address the implementation issues of mass customization, Tseng and Jiao (2001) provide a working definition of mass customization that is very useful. *The objective of mass customization is "to deliver goods and services that meet individual customers' needs with near mass production efficiency"* (Tseng/Piller 2003).

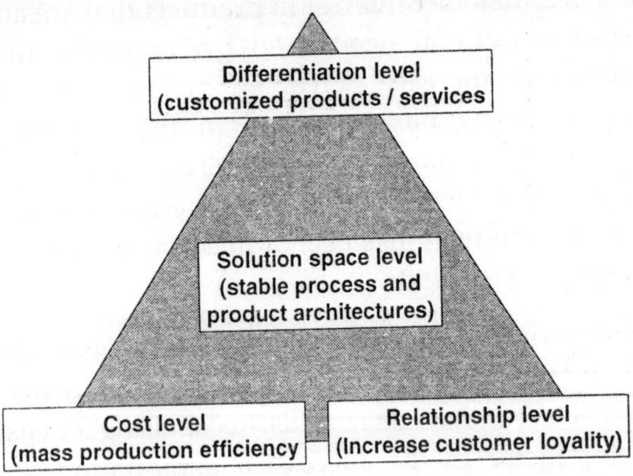

Figure 1: The four levels of mass customization (Piller 2003)

Doing so, mass customization is performed on four levels (Figure 1). While the differentiation level of mass customization is based on the additional utility (value) customers gain from a product or service that corresponds better to their needs, the cost level demands that this can be done at total costs that will not lead to such a price increase that the customization process implies a switch of market segments (Piller 2003).

The information collected in the course of individualization serves to build up a lasting individual relationship with each customer and, thus, to increase customer loyalty (relationship level). While the first three levels have a customer centric perspective, a fourth level takes an internal view and relates to the fulfilment system of a mass customizing firm: Mass customization operations are performed in a fixed solution space that represents "the pre-existing capability and degrees of freedom built into a given manufacturer's production system" (von Hippel 2001).

Every industry is undergoing a fundamental shift. No longer do they focus on producing standardized products or services for homogeneous markets. These firms have thrown away the old paradigm of Mass Production, whose focus was efficiency through stability and control. Their world is no longer stable, cannot be controlled, and therefore their operations cannot be kept efficient in the old way. Through the application of technology and new management methods, they have found their flexibility and quick responsiveness. This is the controlling focus of the new paradigm, mass customization (Pine 1993).

Education and Training

The educational model in use today in high schools was actually designed in 1892. To put this another way, while the real world has changed a lot in that last hundred years, the subject matter has not changed at all. Education should be about preparation for living in today's world. That should mean gaining job skills, personal skills, and mental skills. [...] The question is less a matter of subject matter than it is one of method (Shank 2002).

" ... we transformed education into mass production at around the time we invented mass production of industrial goods. Perhaps at the time, it was sufficient to learn the three "Rs" in order to lead a useful life, perhaps it was just the mass number of people that had to pass through the educational mill. In any case, when we democratized learning, we lost something as well as gained quite a lot. ... The problem is that we now require more than basics in order to function in society. The jobs are more intellectually challenging, and the terrain is shifting too rapidly. You won't work in the same job for a lifetime almost no matter what you do. ... We have the technologies to expedite individuality again. The real question is whether we can transform the teaching environment from factory work to tutoring. That is a complicated social and personal issue." (Lippman 2002)

In the new paradigm, learning should be individualized, localized, and globalized with aims to create unlimited opportunities for students' life long learning and for development of their contextualized *multiple intelligence* (CMI). *Student is the centre of education*. Students' learning should be facilitated to meet their needs and personal characteristics, and develop their potentials particularly CMI in an optimal way. Students can be self- motivated and self- learning with appropriate guidance and facilitation, and learning is a self-actualizing, discovering, experiencing, and reflecting process (Cheng 2002).

Customization is one of the means by which suppliers of learning products strive to differentiate their products in a world of similarity. Customization is intended to add increased customer perceived value to a product, since the customized learning product – compared with a standard product – fulfils the need of a customer more perfectly.

Technology can humanize the education environment

...bring mass customization to learning ...fine-tune the product to allow students to follow somewhat divergent paths and learn at their own rates. (Gates 1995)

Historically, companies have made strategic decision on "crafted education" or "mass education". Within these traditional paradigms, a customer may be between a customized product with a high cost or standardised product with a low cost.

"From one size fits all to customized education" (Tapscott 1998).There is a demand for customized education products in a mass market.

As the author (2001), Piller (2002) and Schickedanz (2002) pointed out, Mass Customization and Personalization can help to overcome the efficiency-paradox of developing and delivering (management) education.

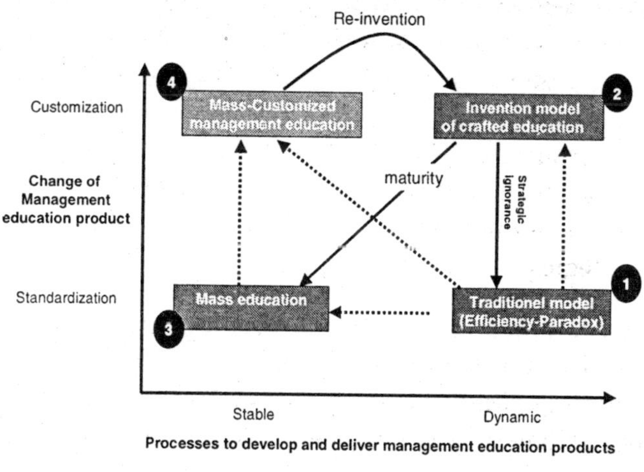

Figure 2: Product-process matrix of supplying management education (Piller 2002)

With the emerge of mass customization, the added value of customization of education products may now be manufactured with no or only little extra cost. The differentiation is, however, only effective, if the customer considers the customization to be of value. Recognising the customer as a major factor in the successful exploitation of mass customization in education market is the basis of this paper.

Education products can either be (Piller 2002)

- standardized products with slow, evolutionary, predictable changes (Field 3 – mass education: Today's "E-Learning" and virtual education providers are moving towards this model)
- or customized solutions fitting the needs and desires of each single customer resulting in a different product every time one is produced (Field 2 – invention model of crafted education)
- Mass customized management education (Field 4): The concept of mass customization may provide a solution to overcome the efficiencies of the described models and shows an alternative escape from the paradox. It moves one's thinking beyond costly customization on the one hand and pure standardisation of education on the other towards the concept of hybrid competitive strategies

However Piller (2002) did not give an answer to the question, *how* the education market can benefit from this hybrid strategy. Many solutions are technology driven, but from the customers´ point of view, education looks different.

Is "technology first" the solution for the education market?

The American Society for Training and Development conducts an annual survey and in 1998, the survey included eight hundred and one organisations, both profit and non-profit. Among interesting results: firms are spending as much as ten times per employee on information technologies as they are on training (Kwiatkowski 2001) .

- Missing still however is a whole-person understanding of how individuals learn online (more than just how they process, build, and store knowledge). Primarily cognitive solutions originally designed for the classroom solutions (and facilitated by instructors) are often not enough to meet the individual, sophisticated needs of Web learners (Roao 2001).
- Mueller (2001) headlined that "E-Learning initiatives fail in the employees' point of view"
- One important reason mentioned by Mueller (2001) is the lack of personalization
- Further aspects in which E-Learning initiatives fail are collaboration and interactivity (Hutzschenreuter 2002)
- According to a study by the Initiative D21, E-Learning is not learner oriented so far (Initiative D21 2002)

In other words, does it make sense to design a learning experience one way for John and a different for Mary ? Not really. Contrary to common belief, people do not have different learning styles. They do, however, hâve different personalities. The distinction is important, since we need to be clear that everyone learns the same way [...]. *It makes sense to take personality differences into account when designing a system* (Schank 2002) .

Personalization should be clearly distinguished from customization. Both customization and personalization are based on the assumption that a homogeneous offering is not sufficient in meeting the customers' needs. As defined by the Webster dictionary, *personalize means "to make something personal or individual; specifically: to mark as the property of a particular person"* (Webster dictionary 2003). The definitions of "mass customization" and of "personalization" implies that the goal is to detect customers needs first and then to fulfil these needs with an efficiency that almost equals that of mass production.

The major implication of individualization in education is to maximize motivation, initiative, and creativity of students and teachers in learning, teaching, and research through such measures as implementing individualized educational programs; designing and using individualized learning targets, methods, and progress schedules; encouraging students to be self learning, self actualizing, and self initiating; meeting individual special needs; and developing students' contextualized *multiple intelligences* (Cheng 2003)

It is possible to take personality differences into account by using Gardner's multiple intelligence theory.

Howard Gardner's Multiple Intelligence Theory

Intelligence is the biological potential to process information in certain ways that can be activated in a cultural setting to solve problems or make products that are valuable in a culture (Harvard Project Zero 2000). As human beings we have many different ways of representing meaning, many kinds of intelligence. Since the beginning of the last century, psychologists have spoken about a single intelligence that can be measured by an IQ test; Howard Gardners' research however has defined 8 human intelligences: verbal/linguistic, logical/mathematical, musical/rhythmic, bodily/kinestetic, visual/spatial, intrapersonal, interpersonal and naturalistic.

We all possess these several intelligences, but no two of us - not even identical twins - possess the same profile of intelligences at the same moment. In most countries throughout history, school has focused almost exclusively on language and logic.

Formal education has virtually ignored other forms of mental representation - artistic forms (musical), athletic (bodily), personal (knowledge of others and self), knowledge of natural world, knowledge of big questions. All of these "Frames of Mind" are there to be mobilized; if they are not, one could well call education "half-brained" (Gardner 2001).

Howard Gardner's work in multiple intelligence theory has powerful implications for the workplace. Evaluating Jobs from the MI-Point-of-View is really exciting, because many traditional job-profiles do not characterise the "real" job. The use of multiple intelligence in the workplace will increase creativity and productivity by enabling workers to use their strengths.

The new strategic focus in human-resources management is return-on-employee investment. That goes along with the attitude shift of employers, who now view their workforce as *intellectual capital* – a complex body of individual talents and backgrounds that should be analysed carefully and developed for maximum benefit (Kwiatkowski 2001)

Martin (2001) turned Howard Gardner's theory of multiple intelligence into user-friendly tools. Her work provides a complete system for examining staff needs, matching applicants to jobs, and supervising and training effectively. The results allow the identification of individual skills and uncovering the mosaic of skills needed for multi-skilling, multi-tasking and efficient teamwork.

Mass Customization and Personalization in Education and Training

The author's proposed approach to mass customization in education and training is based on the organisational strategy of Mass Customerization and Personalization and howard gardner's multiple intelligence theory (Figure 3)

If we take personal differences into account first (Personalization) we can use the tools from Martin (2001) to show the individual biological potential (intelligence) and the multiple intelligence job profile. Achieving economies of scale is partly possible by incorporating reusable learning objects (E-Learning and Mass Customization). Information collected during Personalization serves to built up a learning relationship for Lifelong Learning.

(1) Personal Multiple Intelligence Profile

(2) Multiple intelligence Job Profile

(3) E-Learning and Mass Customization and/or adapting Job Profile

(4) Learning Relationship and Lifelong Learning

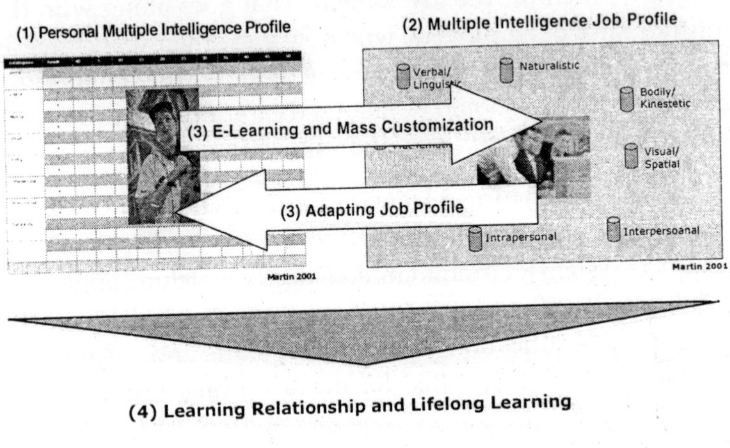

Figure 3: Personalization (Multiple intelligence profiles), E-Learning and Mass Customization, Learning Relationship and Lifelong Learning (Freund 2001)

Personal Multiple Intelligence Profile (Personalization)

The individual must do a self-assessment to identify their personal "intellectual capital". This is more than merely writing a work history or resume. It is putting on paper one's personal likes and dislikes, life style choices, what they actually learned from their experiences at work, school, family, church or any other organised activities. It involves taking a fully inventory of knowledge and technical skills either gained through experience, academic courses, reading, and travel. It involves documentation of one's personal network of friends, associates, and acquaintances. At the individual level, intellectual capital is more than knowledge--it is a reflection of the individual's personality, ability to solve problems and life style choices. From this self-assessment, an individual learns not only who they are but what they do not know and what they do not like (Kwiatkowski 2001).

People are very interested in studying their own multiple intelligence profile, however it is necessary to know much about multiple intelligence to make the right interpretation of these results. The most popular tool is MIDAS (Shearer 1995, Moon 2001).

The Multiple Intelligence Development Assessment Scales (MIDAS) was designed to provide an objective measure of the multiple intelligences as reported by the person or by a knowledgeable informant. There are a number of practical reasons why an individual, a parent, a teacher, a counsellor, or a psychologist might desire such an assessment. First, the MIDAS provides information regarding intellectual development, activities, and propensities not generally available from standardized intelligence quotient (IQ) and most aptitude tests. Second, the MIDAS provides information directly from the person's (and/or significant other's) experience that can be used to inform educators to personalize learning, curriculum design and to enhance the counselling process (Morris 2002).

The author prefers tools developed by Martin (2001) because she turned howard gardner's theory of multiple intelligences into user-friendly tools to provide an objective measure of the multiple intelligences as reported by the person *and* her work provides a complete system for examining staff needs, matching applicants to jobs, and supervising and training effectively.

Multiple-Intelligence-Job-Profile

Educators across the United States, in Europe, Australia, South America, Asia, and Africa have repeatedly demonstrated the beneft of using Gardner's theory to identify and mobilise knowledge. However, industry and the professions have been slower to apply the theory and realise similar benefits. One reason for this has been the lack of demonstrated correlation between the general intelligences identified by Gardner and the specific practices in professions.

Throughout most of his writings, Gardner refers to a series of typical cultural occupations associated with each of his eight intelligences as 'end states.' While such end states serve as instructive examples of ordinary career paths, it is important to realize that all of us represent a blend of each of his eight (8) theorized intelligences [...] and that most occupations in life necessitate a blend of many of his intelligences [...] Almost every occupation [...] consists of a variety of responsibilities that touch on several of Howard Gardner's eight (8) intelligences. In other words, many different talents, skills, or to cite Gardner, intelligences are required for each occupation. What this means is that it is important to develop and nurture all of your various intelligences. Please note that these list only scratch the tip of the much larger MI occupational iceberg (Morris 2000-2002).

E-Learning and Mass Customization

Bridging the gap, we can educate the people or adapt the job profile.

TABLE 1

Lists of just some general occupations that need Gardner's eight Intelligences (Morris 2000-2002)

Intelligence	*Occupation*
Verbal / Linguistic	Archivist, attorney, author, call centre operator, comedian , copywriter...
Logical / Mathematical	Accountant, actuary, analyst, astronomer, auditor, banker, biologist, bookkeeper ...
Musical / Rhythmic	audio-video technician, band member, choir or choral director, choreographer, conductor ...
Bodily / Kinestetic	Acrobat, actor, actress, aerobics instructor, architect, artistic painter, assembler ...
Visual / Spatial	Advertiser, architect, artist, builder, carpenter, cartographer, chess player ...
Interpersonal	Administrator, anthropologist, bartender, businessperson, chess player ...
Intrapersonal	Politician, psychiatrist, receptionist, salesperson, self employed person ...
Naturalistic	Agricultural engineer/worker, astronomer, beachcomber, biologist, botanist ...

Customization of Learning Products

The customization of learning products is possible throughout the different steps of the value chain of an education vendor and can address all distinguished dimensions in which learning processes differ (Hutzschenreuter 2002).

E-Learning and Mass Customization:

Achieving economies of scale is partly possible by incorporating reusable learning objects. The IEEE (Institute of Electrical and Electronics Engineers), a non profit, technical professional association of more than 350,000 individual

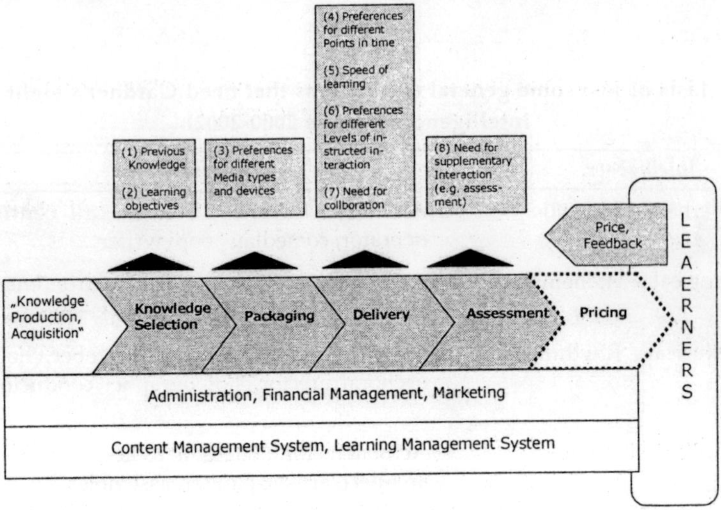

Figure 4: Customization along the "education value chain" (Hutzschenreuter 2002)

members in 150 countries, has a Learning Technology Standards Committee which has defined learning objects as "any entity, digital or non-digital, which can be used, re-used or referenced during technology supported learning."

These learning objects are self-contained items or may be combined or sequenced to form longer educational interactions. In order to use learning objects, they must be tagged or labelled so that the contents are properly known to all potential users.

Learning objects are reusable. For example, a learning object that defines the basic principles of hydraulics could be used by courses for auto mechanics, construction workers and millwrights. Many countries are researching the use of learning objects, especially in the use in distance education. It is clear to see, how curriculum designed through an outcomes-based process will be able to make use of learning objects (The Commonwealth of Learning 2002, Bannan-Ritland 2000).

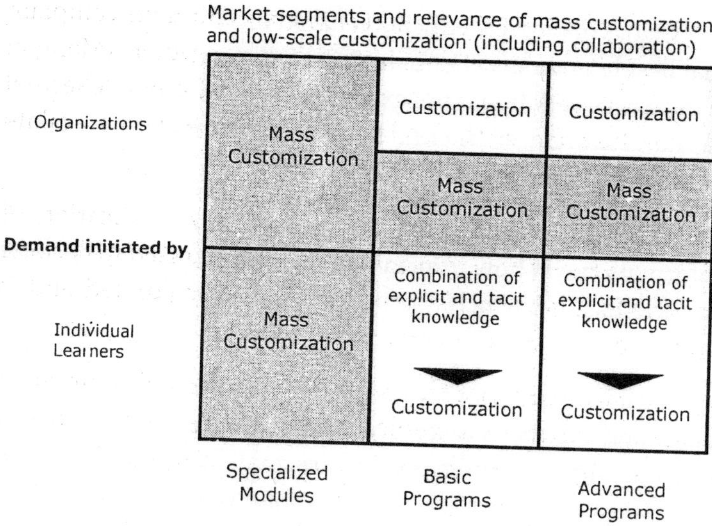

Figure 5: Market segments and relevance of mass customization and low-scale customization (including collaboration) of management education (Hutzschenreuter 2002)

Learning objects can be arranged in a fixed order – like at static web page where the place where certain information appears is already predefined. However mass customized learning products will require that the learning objects like text, graphic, diagrams, audio/video, interactive tools, etc. will be put together in real time in order which will depend on the person needs and preferences. Human being would not be able to do this on a large scale, therefore a software (configurator) must be used. The recent progress of information technology makes it possible, however a strong attention must be drawn on methodologies used.

Moreover one problem can not be solved by technology (Figure 5): Learning products can not be mass customized in regard to collaboration. A decreased level of social interaction and therefore limited flow of tacit knowledge may result. This problem cannot be tackled, because real-life social interaction is unique in its nature (Hutzschenreuter 2002)

Critics of medical education based on computers complain that beside manners are not learned from computers (Mangan 2000). Social isolation is not exactly the way to foster intellectual capital if human interaction helps to associate and assimilate new information (Stowe 2001).

Learning is dependent on the use and application of information – in how information is contextualised to become knowledge. That such a process is socially mediated and is dependent on social interaction is evident.

Learning programmes are broken into smaller component parts and can be reassembled for individuals or groups of learners. The learning objects are materials, together with assessment exercises for each component part. *It seems trite to point out that objects themselves cannot learn. But this lies at the heart of the pedagogic issue. Subject and object are inverted. What are called learning objects are in fact the subject of learning.* So what should be – or could be – a learning object? In our view, this is the outcomes of learning, the knowledge created, at all its different stages and in all its different forms. Learning objects are not created by course or materials developers, or even by learning facilitators but by the learner themselves. The primary role of the computer based learning platform is not in the delivery of the materials but in facilitating the transformation and communication of ideas as knowledge. The reusability of learning objects is in recording and storing that knowledge and in recommunicating and retransforming the experience and practice of learners and participants in both an individual and group context. In other words, the computer or ICT based learning environment is a process tool to support the creation and transformation of knowledge through learning objects (Attwell and Malloch 2002).

Martin Owen, a UK expert, points out [...] ICT becomes a new learning object, on top of other disciplines. This is a failure. There should be a transformation in the way we approach ICT. We should think in terms of "learning processes" and no longer in terms of "learning objects" (European Commission 2002b).

Learning Relationship and Lifelong Learning

Information collected during Personalization serves to build up a learning relationship for Lifelong Learning.

you can't lick customers, so join them : Enlist their power on your behalf. That means a shift of focus from selling to learning. Customer Relationship Management as it's usually practices doesn't do that as C. H. Prahlad observes: "Most CRM strategies view customers as outside, static entities; The goal is to obtain a 360-degree view of each customer – hence, the need to automate and integrate various customer interface touchpoints.... It's a company-centric view of the customer, with a focus on efficiency gains." [...] A fully developed customer-learning process will have four traits

- First it will emphasize communication over information mining. Without a process of mutual learning – which permits smarter buying and selling-there's little basis for customer loyalty in a low-friction knowledge economy.
- Second, customer learning needs to be integrated across functions – that is, not just confined to marketing, sales, and service but reaching into new-product development and even human resource and finance
- Third, the process should create a kind of relationship capital that is as valuable to the buyer as it is to the seller: Indeed, both sides should be able to quantify the value of relationship. There are a number of well-tested ways for sellers to measure the value of their customers. Flipped around, those tools become measurements of

the value of customer capital to the buyer: Switching costs [...] are one token of what loyalty to a seller is worth; [...]

- Finally, the customer learning process should be so visible day to day that you can't imagine running the company without it (Stewart 2001).

Lifelong learning, however, is not just a simple summing-up or integration of traditional education programmes and modern learning opportunities. Instead, the approach to lifelong learning includes fundamental differences in educational content and perspectives: While traditional educational institutions have been (and still are) primarily concerned with transmitting knowledge, modern learning opportunities and the lifelong learning approach put the emphasis on the development of individual capabilities and personal learning competencies. *At the heart of the lifelong learning concept is the idea of enabling and encouraging people "to learn how to learn"* (European Commission 2002a, National Board of Education Finland (2002).

Further Work

Project's goal is to answer the question: How to overcome the efficiency-paradox of developing and delivering education. The answer may be the use of Mass Customization supplemented with multiple intelligences theory by Howard Gardner. The project will be carried out in a few stages by a consortium of partners spread across Europe.

The initial stage of the project is scheduled on the second half of 2003. At this stage following actions are planned:

- Carry out several questionnaires and data processing works in order to create a personal MI-Profile database. Different groups of people will be encouraged to make a self-assessment to identify their personal "intellectual capital". Already developed and published tools and methodologies will be used for the research (Martin 2001).

- Evaluate jobs from the multiple intelligences point of view. This research will be carried out in the twofold form. Firstly the data obtained from the research mentioned above will be sorted out according to the occupation of participants and analysed accordingly. Secondly people representing management level could be surveyed as for their perception of people personal profiles that are fit for given jobs.
- Compare personal MI-Profiles with Job-Profiles. It will be very interesting to research and analyse the gap between personal profiles (arranged according to the jobs occupied) to the perceptions of management level of what kind of people would be fit for certain positions.

The results obtained from these actions taken in the first stage will be a foundation for further research scheduled on 2004. Its goal is to research the validity of the methodologies and tools already published for such kind of research. If the data obtained from the research was incomplete or incoherent it would be necessary to develop new tools needed to accomplish the main goal of the project.

So far a pilot research, which goal was to collect personal MI-profiles, has been already carried out in Germany. As a result 150 questionnaires were collected. The initial analysis of the data seems promising, however it is necessary to continue this research to draw credible conclusions. Currently because of the highly diverse studied population as for occupied jobs it is impossible to draw final conclusions as for jobs-profile.

In the next months further researches are planned which would concentrate on the following target groups:

- Shopping malls staff – In cooperation with HR managers in such centres a research of staff's personal MI-Profiles is planned. Certain sub-groups like cashiers, physical workers, cleaners, guest service staff, security staff, etc. can be isolated here if we consider job position as a criterion. Since this studied population could be considered as heterogeneous, where certain homogeneous similar sub-groups (stratums) can be isolated, the use of stratified sampling technique will be legitimate. In this sampling technique, the whole population is initially divided into homogenous, exclusive sub-groups and then units are selected from each stratum for study. The research is planned to be carried out in the form of paper questionnaires.
- Students – In cooperation with some polish universities a similar study is planned. It may be interesting to study students' population, because the majority of them is already employed or is going to take up work in the nearest future. Thus not only the scientific aspect, but also a practical application of the results would be interesting (especially for HR managers). Since all students at the chosen university have an access to the Internet at the headquarters or at home electronic format of the questionnaire will be used.

After the data from this research is collected and analysed the prospective stages of the project will be connected with efforts to set up and validate the set of quantitative metrics to assess personal MI-Profiles and job-profiles. Comparing the metrics values will allow assessing the gap between these two dimensions. With the use of e-learning and mass customization concept this will help to make a given person fit for a given job or a given job fit for a given person and to overcome the efficiency paradox in developing and delivering education.

REFERENCES

Attwell, G., Malloch, M. (2002): Approaching an electronic community from the perspective of mutual learning. Available online at http://www.uu.nl/content/2002%20ECER.pdf

Bannan-Ritland, B. , Dabbagh, N. , Murphy, K. (2000): Learning Object Systems as Constructivist Learning Environments: Related Assumptions, Theories and Applications, in: Wiley, D. H.: The Instructional Use of Learning Objects. Available online at http://reusability.org/read/

Chen, S. (2001): A Personal View: What Multiple Intelligence Theory is and how to use it, Newsletter of the Center of Teaching and Learning. Available online at http://web.jccc.net/academic/ctl/PDF/CTLMarch01.pdf

Cheng, Y.C. (2002): Linkage between Innovative Management and Student-Centred Approach: Platform Theory for Effective Learning Invited Plenary Speech presented at the Second International Forum on Education Reform: Key Factors in Effective Implementation organized by Office of National Education Commission in collaboration with UNESCO and SEAMEO, Bangkok, Thailand, 2-5 September 2002. Available online at http://www.ied.edu.hk/apcelsq/new/files/cheng2-5sep02.pdf

Cheng, Y.C (2003): Local Knowledge and Human Development in Globalization of Education. Keynote Speech Presented at The International Conference on Globalization and Challenges for Education organized by National Institute of Educational Policy and Administration (NIEPA) from 19-21 February 2003, New Delhi, India. Available online at http://www.ied.edu.hk/apcelsq/new/files/cheng19-21feb03.pdf

Davis, P. (2001): TRANSFINE Transfer Between Formal Non-Formal and

Informal Learning. Available online at http://www.transfine.net/Documentation/Project-01-02_en.pdf

Davis, S. M. (1987): Future perfect, MA, Addison-Wesley publishing company, INC.

European Commission (2002a): European Report On Quality Indicators Of Life Long Learning. Available online at http://europa.eu.int/comm/education/policies/lll/life/report/quality/report_en.pdf

Europea online at http://europa.eu.int/comm/education/programmes/elearning/wn2002_03/what2_en.html

Fernandez, P., McCarthy, I.P., Mena,C., Viesca, C. (2001): Mass Customization in the Digital Age. Presented at the 1. Worldcongress on Mass Customization and Personalization, Hong Kong, China

Freund, R. (1998): Was kann das Bildungsmanagement von der Automobilindustrie lernen ? Vortrag auf dem Europäischen Kongress Kompetenz 1998, Qualitätsmanagement in der beruflichen Weiterbildung, Stuttgart, Germany

Freund, R. (2001): Welche Auswirkungen hat Mass Customization auf das Management der beruflichen Weiterbildung. Vortrag an der Pädagogischen Hochschule, Freiburg, Germany

Gardner, H. (1993): Frames of Mind. The Theory of Multiple Intelligences

Gardner, H. (2001): An Education for the Future. Available online at http://www.pz.harvard.edu/WhatsNew/Amsterdam.htm

Gates, Bill (1995): The Road Ahead, Newsweek, November 27, 1995

Harvard Project Zero (2000): Adult Multiple Intelligences MI Basics. Available online at http://www.pz.harvard.edu/ami/mibasics.htm

Hutzschenreuter, T. (2002): E-Learning and Mass-Customization, Research Paper No. 92

Initiative D21 (2002): E-Learning: Wahrnehmung und Themenbewertung der Internetweiterbildung, Bonn, Germany

Kwiatkowski, S., Stowem C. (Editor) (2001) : Knowledge cafe; Intellectual Product and Intellectual Capital, Warszawa, Poland

Lippman, A. (2002): Interview Lippman on Learning: Fundamental Changes. Available online at http://www.syllabus.com/article.asp?id=6073

Mangan, K. S. (2000): Medical-School Group Proposes Huge online Library for Students, Chronicle of Higher Education, November 17, p. A65

Martin, J. (2001): Profiting from Multiple Intelligence in Workplace, Burlington USA

Martin, J. (2002): Multiple Intelligences And the Practice of Law: A New Framework. Available online at http://www.abanet.org/lpm/newsletters/articles/newsarticle12305_front.shtml

Mena, J. (1999): Mining E-Customer Behavior, DB2 Magazine, Winter. Available online at http://www.db2mag.com/db_area/archives/1999/q4/mena.shtml

Moon, Yong-Lin (2001): Measuring Multiple Intelligences in Korea.

Available online at http://aped.snu.ac.kr/cyberedu/cyberedu1/eng/eng21-01.html

Morris, C. (2000-2002): Occupations needing Multiple Intelligences. Available online at http://www.igs.net/~cmorris/smo_comments.html, 2003-06-24

Morris, C. (2002): Howard Gardner's Multiple Intelligences, the MIDAS and Career Development Possibilities. Available online at http://www.igs.net/~cmorris/ocetf.html

Mueller, G. (2001): E-Learning-Konzepte fallen bei Mitarbeitern durch, in: Computerwoche Online, 06.12.2001

National Board of Education Finland (2002): Assessing Learning-to-Learn, Helsinki, Finland

Piller, F. (1998): Kundenindividuelle Massenproduktion, München, Germany

Piller, F. (2000): Mass Customization, Wiesbaden, Germany

Piller, F. (2002): Are we practicing what we preach ? – Strategic Perspectives of the Management Education Industry. Available online at http://www.mass-customization.de/download/pil2002-7.pdf

Piller, F. (2003). Mass Customization, 3rd edition, Wiesbaden, Germany

Pine, J. P.(1993): Mass Customization, Harvard Business School Press, Boston, MA.

Rao, A.J. (2001): Recognition of Conative and Affective Behaviour in Web

Learning using Digital Gestures. Presented at 1. Worldcongress on Mass Customization and Personalization, Hong Kong, China

Schickedanz, C. (2002): Mass Customization und E-Learning: eine lernende Beziehung. Available online at http://ddi.cs.uni-potsdam.de/GML2003/Workshops/schickentanz/ThesisGesamt.pdf

Shank, R. C. (2002): Designing World-Class E-Learning, McGraw Hill

Shearer, B. (1995): The MIDAS: A Guide to Assessment and Education for the Multiple Intelligences. Columbus, Ohio: Greydon Press, USA

Stewart, T. A. (2001): The wealth of intellectual capital, Brealey Publishing London, United Kingdom

Stowe, C. R. B. (2001): Foundains for intellectual capital – challenges and opportunities for institutions of higher education in Kwiatkowski, S., Stowe, C. (Editor) (2001) : Knowledge cafe; Intellectual Product and Intellectual Capital, Warszawa, Poland

Svensson, C (2001): The customer at the final frontier of mass customisation. Presented at the 1. Worldcongress on Mass Customization, Hong Kong, China

Tapscott, D. (1998): Growing up digital: the rise of the net generation. New York: McGraw-Hill, USA

Toffler, A. (1971): Future shock, Bantam, New York

The Commonwealth of Learning (2002): Skills Development through Distance Education, Vancouver, Canada

Tseng, M.M. and Jiao, J. (2001): Mass Customization, in G. Salvendy (Ed.) Handbook of Industrial Engineering, 3rd edition, New York: Wiley, 2001, pp. 684-709.

Tseng, M. M., Piller, F. (2003): Upcoming book "The customer centric enterprise: Advances in mass customization and personalization" (to be published at Springer in June 2003).

Von Hippel, E. (2001): Perspective: User Toolkits for Innovation, The Journal of Product Innovation Management, 18 , pp. 247-257.

Webster Online (2003): http://www.webster.com/cgi-bin/dictionary?book=Dictionary&va=personalize

16

STRUCTURAL AND PROFESSIONAL PREREQUISITES FOR THE DEVELOPMENT OF FUTURE VOCATIONAL IDENTITIES OF NURSES - IN ESTONIA, GERMANY AND FRANCE

*Gabriele Laske**

(Contributors: M'Hamed Dif, Softa Jons, Krista Loogma and Raivo Vilu)

Introduction

The process of creation and formation of identities is determined both by societal conditions affecting the individual and by individual talents, inclinations and activities. Developing an identity is an achievement of the individual. It is an internal process where societal influences and individual capacities and dispositions meet and generate an internal process that can lead to the formation of identities. But an individual's work or occupational identity also is determined by external, societal influences that are adjusted, responded to or rejected based on the individual's personal talents and inclinations.

The project "Vocational Identity, Flexibility and Mobility

* Gabriele Laske is Manager and Senior Researcher at ICCR: www.Iccresearch.com.

in the European Labour Market" (FAME), funded under the Fifth Framework Programme of the European Commission, investigated how the individual deals with the interaction between structural, societal influences and demands and personal tendencies and inclinations. To approach these questions the project partner conducted three major research units: 1) context development through literature research; 2) investigation of employers' perspective; and 3) investigation on employees' perspective.

The aim of the research on employers' perspective was to find out from employers how according to their opinion work requirements for their employees have changed in recent years. Semi-structured interviews with employers were employed as the methodological tool to investigate their perspective on the subject of research in four contrasting sectors (metal working industry, health care, telecommunications/IT and tourism). The findings of this unit were supposed to reveal:

— Recent changes in the formation and manifestations of occupations and vocational identities based on the information available through our limited samples.

— The actual need for flexibility and mobility in the work practice of companies (case studies) as far as this was mentioned by the interviewed employers.

— Changes in the workplaces and occupations: Employers' findings were not meant to describe new/old skill requirements and profiles of workplaces or other already well-known labour market data. They focused upon the question of how employers experience and value their employees' capacity to deal with changes and how this affects the process of identity formation.

Firstly, research on employers' perspective was meant to help identify the requirements of employers with respect to their employees. On the other hand, it was expected to provide an insight into current and anticipated changes of work and occupations. Many studies of changes of the workplace design and new skills requirements in Europe have already been conducted. However, this survey on the employers' perspective was not intended to provide additional results but rather served the purpose of providing a contrast to and complementing the third research unit, that was the investigation on the employees' perspective.

This article presents findings on employer's perspective of the health care system in Estonia, France and Germany. Data mainly stem from limited samples of interviews with experts and human resource managers from health care conducted by the national partners. The findings presented are not supposed to give a general picture of the health care sector especially what concerns the nurse profession. They present findings from case studies with the aim to complement them with findings from interviews with employed nurses of the same institutions. The author made some attempts to interpret the different manifestations in the health care system of the three countries and how they may affect nurses' attitude towards their work. It must be stated that these interpretations are somewhat risky given the small size of the samples and the lack of an in depth investigating of the health care sector in France and Estonia.

Description of the Structural Context of Health Care in Three European Countries

Estonia is known as one of the countries that are still, in one way or another, undergoing a transition process shifting from a planned and state-controlled economy during Soviet times to a democratic society with open markets. Therefore the Estonian partners provide the project with the interesting context and development of a nurse profession with an occupational identity that was shaped during Soviet times and that later became adjusted to fundamental changes affecting the whole society. In so far the health sector was challenged to accommodate organisational, educational and personnel changes. Private hospitals were founded, new curricula for education and training of nurses were developed and the practice of hiring changed. Unions of nurses suddenly had a say in the negotiation of wages. Strikes already have taken place, for wages were considered as far too low.

The 1990s can be characterised as a turbulent period for the Estonia labour market. The flow of labour was high. While the plan system no longer determined the distribution of labour and employment security, hiring and firing became a new, up to now unknown mechanism of human resource policy. However, it had to be done efficiently in order to keep the right employees and dismiss those who could not keep up with the new demands. Nevertheless hospitals had to be careful to not damage their reputation as employer and by that losing loyalty of staff they wished to keep or to lose their attraction as prospective employer. Finally, the implementation of new medical technology became a challenge for hospitals and nurses that was not known before on this scale. Altogether nurses in Estonia had to face major changes in employment policy including the new thread of unemployment as well as new technological, organisational, and educational demands. Nurses who had been educated during Soviet times had to undergo exams with new curricula if they wished to raise their status and wages as employees, otherwise they remained regarded as less valuable employees. The latter also is related to the introduction of modern medical technology.

From a structural point of view the transition process fostered the political position of nurses in society through the foundation of nurse associations and the professional paths became more differentiated, amongst other reasons due to the possibility of employment in private hospitals. In addition, the process of institution building like those of nurse associations went hand in hand with the creation of new vocational nurse profiles at work and in training programmes. This did not necessarily imply a general upgrading of the status of nurses. Health care services in rehabilitation, for example, still are less valued and remunerated than services of high level surgery. Wages are uneven depending on the employment contract and the hospital. Larger hospitals offer more complex and expensive services. In some cases they turned out to be the more popular employer than the small hospitals because they could offer higher wages. The role that nurse associations play seems to be important in respect to the development of a new concept and profile of the nurse profession. Via their lobby they are gaining political influence in respect to educational directions and organisation of courses and classes. They are done in cooperation with medical schools and government in order to create new vocational standards. Associations also serve as a resource for information inside the sector through their published magazines on health care issues.

Having been trained under the old or new curricula are still important employment criteria. Nurses trained under the new curricula have a higher status than those trained under the old curricula during Soviet times. Meanwhile nursing has become an independent discipline making it even possible to enter an academic career in nursing. Only state and communal hospitals are authorised to hand out certificates. Private hospitals are excluded from this process though they are only allowed to employ certified nurses. Here one faces a contradictory element of the transition process in the Estonia health care sector. As private hospitals started from zero in the beginning of the 1990s they had the opportunity to create a new organisational culture. Therefore, new work concepts and identities of nurses that are fostered by the new curricula rather find ground in private hospitals than in state hospitals, where to a certain extend structural and habitual behaviours from the Soviet past still persist. The new occupational profile of nurses that goes along with the emergence of a new set of values also is connected to the need for commercialisation of the health care sector. These new organisational features more likely are performed in private hospitals. This includes organisational and work-related features like, for example, greater responsibility and independence of nurses, new emphasise on quality of nursing, working in small teams and last but not least higher wages. Though even in private hospitals the new partnership model regarding communication and cooperation between doctors, nurses and patients still has a long way to go before becoming a daily work reality. Also there is the contradiction concerning the training and certification of nurses. This takes place in institutions that still struggle with behavioural and organisational patterns of the Soviet period, while health care institutions that have already successfully overcome such patterns are not authorised to give out or accredit certificates. Finally, nowadays Estonian employers' perception of the essential that makes a good nurse does not seem to be very different from that of a hundred years ago. Nurses mainly should be interested and devoted to their profession as a mission. It is the image of charitable mission under the supervision of doctors. In addition to such a outdated nurse image, safety and stability in respect to work and workplace are values of growing importance.

During the last ten years **German nurses** working in the health care sector also had to face substantial structural changes. Nursing in Germany is viewed as a profession with strong historical roots. During many centuries churches (nuns, district nurses), religious and charitable groups like the red cross developed specific health care services by building and running hospitals, care institutions for the elderly and other charitable and health care institutions. Today these historical roots still influence the constitution of the German health care system insofar as it is split into a large variety of bodies of responsibility that only recently have formed one political body to stand up and negotiate with policy makers and legislature. However, it still has to be considered as a fairly incoherent and rather weak voice, while the medical profession represented by doctors relies upon a strong political voice of their associations.

During the last ten years the German government put in place a series of major structural reforms regarding the financing and organisation of the national health care system. After a period of expansion, specialisation and increased integration of latest technology a new challenge became pressing. That was how and by whom the increasing costs and improvements should be paid. Cost explosions forced politicians to take initiative pushing the German government to restrict and control health care services. Today, service providers have to document every single step and prescription of treatment and have to justify why no cheaper treatment could be chosen.

These structural changes affect all units of the health care system. For example, major restructuring and reorganising efforts in hospitals became necessary. One example is to abandon the old hospital concept by which patients received rather long term treatment and care even while already recovering. To reduce the costs for stationary treatment a concept of health care is now favoured that supports patient's ambulant pre and post treatment instead. Hospital wards organised as profit centres and the flattening of hospital hierarchies also are seen as new solution. While each physical service and medical treatment has to be documented and is reimbursed only when acknowledged by the health insurance, social interaction and communication with patients no longer form part of the required standards. The psychological and social aspects of health care suffer while at the same time today's patients even more strongly request personally satisfying services. Hospital staff often finds itself exposed to these contradicting demands of health insurance restrictions on the one hand and patients' expectations on the other hand. With increasing competition between health care providers hospitals are forced to provide patient-friendly services to become more attractive to their customers. Customer orientation, high quality of nursing and economic efficiency are the new criteria not only hospitals have to meet but also other health care institutions like residences for the elderly, ambulant services, etc..

Until about 1995 statutory health insurance used to cover the financial load of health services for the elderly who were no longer able to live without substantial help and health care provisions. During the 1990s, as a response to demographic shifts due to the ageing population, the German insurance system decided that it was no longer capable to provide all these services and to cover the costs. Therefore the government introduced an additional statuary insurance in order to cover the increasing expenses. One aim was to financially support elderly and disabled people in need of substantial help and health care provisions in a way that they could continue living as long as possible in their private homes with the support of ambulant health care providers. This special care insurance (statutory for every German employee) suddenly made additional money available and encouraged the development of a new market for private and charitable ambulant health care providers. A large number of jobs were created and this market is still growing while the need for jobs in hospitals slightly decreases. In respect to job creation one expects the ambulant health care services to flourish in the future though there is a great personnel turnover due to its stressful physical, psychological, and interpersonal demands.

Initial education and training in the German health care system is designed like other VET programmes of the German dual system, but vocational schools for health care are not under the governance of the state like most other vocational programmes. General guidelines exist regarding education and training for certified nurses, but each body of responsibility insists in introducing a specific approach and ethos to the apprentices regarding the way of how to provide health care services.

Human resource management of hospitals see nurses facing an increasing complexity at work. Information and communication technologies, management and the control of complex data processing in addition to higher demands on patient orientation redefine the traditional profile of health care services. But also in Germany society's expectations still cling to a traditional image as the always friendly woman, devoted and willing to provide low and inferior services no one else would like to perform. This prejudice is only changing slowly. Many citizens start to experience increasing costs for health care, a fact that might make people rethink their ideas and images about the health care system and health care providers.

The first research phase emphasised on how employers see changes affecting job structures and occupations in a given sector and how that influences identity formation processes related to the work context and specific occupations in different national health care systems. In this context it is interesting that the **French health care system**, rated as one of the best in the world by WHO in terms of four basic criteria: the overall level of health attained in the population; degree of health inequalities within the population; health system responsiveness to change and patient satisfaction; distribution of financial burden. The system seems to be obviously well established and equipped to satisfy most of these criteria.

Within this system, the status of nurses is well established, but is lacking social acknowledgement in comparison to the medical profession represented by doctors. This is especially true in terms of compensatory salaries due to increasing work load and responsibilities nurses have. However, a strong professional identity and attachment to the ethics of the nurse profession provide a powerful potential to continuously integrate medical innovations and the use of modern technology. Of course, organisational structures, the workplace and job design need to correspond to and support learning processes. Also, the work organisation in hospitals requires further learning. Since doctors primarily have functional (medical) responsibilities, services and the daily work in wards are mainly organised by senior nurses.

Although the organisation and hierarchical order in large institutions of the French health care system are characterised as heavy and very complex, employer acknowledge a general acceptance and engagement of employees regarding innovation and continuous learning. This indicates that employees receive some sort of incentives and encouragement to learn and evolve during their professional life.

As for job security in health, it is dependent on the nature of employees' working status and the institutional character of the sector in which they are working. Generally, in the public sector (basically hospitals), jobs security is primarily guaranteed by the status of civil servant. Unionisation is relatively high for this category of employees. By contrast, there is no life-time employment guarantee within the private sector. Although, employees are generally attached to their profession and work within the boundaries of the French system, there is an increasing inner-European and border mobility, fostered by nurses' desire (especially within the private sector) for higher salaries and better working conditions, that has created an interest for job opportunities outside of France. For example, some nurses in the Alsace region prefer to work in Switzerland where salaries are relatively higher than in France. In summary, from the employers' perspective, nursing in the French health care system is regarded as a professional group of high status protected by unions and integrated in a highly institutionalised and regulated system. Nurses generally have a good qualification and flexibly respond to the necessities for continuous learning. It is also stressed that all nurses (of both sectors: public and private) show a strong identification with quality of services provided to customers.

The results of employers' interviews conducted within the public and private segments of the French healthcare sector show that professional identities of hospital nurses and doctors are undergoing important structural changes. This is basically due to the following recent reforms and developments:

Health care related technological advances has increasingly allowed home-use of disposable medical equipment by patients. This has effectively contributed to a decrease of short-stays in hospitals. The tendency has been further reinforced by the emergence of the ambulatory medicine, auto-diagnostics and social-security-organised home care. At the same time, there is an increased need for long-stay beds in hospitals, coming up basically from partially or fully dependent patients. Therefore, the reform launched in these hospitals takes into consideration these structural changes by optimally combining an increased efficiency (through quality insurance control) with reduced cost of the universal health care coverage.

Within the new structure of health care management, 24 regional hospital authorities have been established for planning health care needs and setting hospital annual budgets. These authorities have to contract with individual hospitals to define objectives and requirements with the aim of creating pools of excellence by merging hospitals and closing down, if necessary, those hospitals whose occupancy rate is lower than 60%. The budgeted funding is allocated according to a system of accreditation used to identify efficient hospitals.

In order to track down health care spending and to improve the functioning of the sector through computer-based technologies, each social security affiliate is given a smart card called "VITALE" linking him or her through a secured computer network with all kinds of health care providers: public hospitals, private clinics, general practitioners, specialised doctors, nurses, etc. As this card enables a direct electronic transfer of the patient's medical records and prescriptions to health care reimbursing funds, it is also used as an instrument of controlling health care spending, and ultimately to be able to take appropriate sanctions against hospitals and doctors in controlling expenditure.

The introduction and implementation of 35-hour-regime within the hospitals. Given that, this regime has increased the work burden and involuntary time-flexibility, especially for nurses, it is at present under reconsideration to be further readapted to the nature of work within the health care sector in general and hospitals in particular.

Under discussion with social partners in the hospitals

is the project of increasing and making more fluid the internal mobility of nurses between different departments of the hospitals (not subject to the usual formal constraint of job-transfer). Outside the "pool for compensation and replacement", the other nurses' internal mobility is still limited to the units of the same department.

It may be necessary to state that the complexity of hospitals in France is linked to their respective size. Usually small clinics are private. Within the French health care system there exists an inter-professional exchange of proximity and high quality service provisions for all affiliates of the social system without any kind of discrimination. Therefore, private and public employers in the sector and their customers are highly attached to the specificity of the French social security system.

As already stated, the questions the project raises have little to do with whether a health care system is perceived as good or bad. The question guiding the first research phase was how employers perceive changes in the sector and whether these changes affect work profiles and occupations in a way that identities at work are being adjusted or not. In this respect no major dynamics or shifts seem to occur in France. The French health care system is so well established and financially well equipped that it evokes a high level of satisfaction for the customers. From a structural point of view no specific demands or changes seem to currently affect the nurse profession.

Reflections

The first observation that is striking by looking at the three national employer perspectives of health care systems in Estonia, Germany and France is how much the recognised problems differ. Each national set of problems is of a very different nature. But one also has to take into consideration that the perceived problems or tensions are subject to national political discussions and the awareness of the necessities for change or resistance towards change. A German researcher investigating the French health care system may come to very different observations and conclusions simply because of the national bias when looking at problems and problem solving strategies in another country. But the results of the employers' perspective are very valuable exactly because of this national bias. They reflect the different national discussions and perceptions of the health care systems nurses also are aware of and exposed to. For example, major developments and experiences of nurses in Estonia are either influenced by broken occupational paths due to the transition process, or they are linked to having a superior status when already being trained under the new curriculum. In general, nurses in all three countries have no difficulties in finding work, but the thread of unemployment and the possibility of being fired has become a new element of uncertainty in the working life of Estonian nurses.

In Germany, the dominating factor pushing for change is the economic aspect; that is the growing financial load of health care expenses. Major legislative and financial interventions have caused changes throughout the system at different levels. This affects organisational structures, nurses' work profiles, concepts of care and also one of the fundamental elements of nursing, the interaction between the nurse and the patient.

In France, in spite the fact the health care system is highly regulated by the ethics of the professional core and the public authorities, it seems that there is enough potential for learning and innovation promotion on the employers and employees' side and that the health care system still satisfies the overall national needs with free choice and equal access to same quality of services to all. This is secured through an inter-professional interactivity and complementarity between and within its two segments, guaranteed by the universal coverage of the social security system.

Regarding current changes of the health care systems, which affect the occupational or professional identity of nurses, Estonia's health care system is in the process of developing democratic social bodies. In the case of nurses in Estonia this means the development of a professional profile that fits a free market economy and democratic processes. Associations and unions as nurses' public voice push the transition process from old nursing concepts from Soviet times towards a new nursing concept. A major tool for this transition process was the development and implementation of a new curriculum. Estonia's nurse associations and unions right now mainly act on the macro political and economical level in order to foster the development of a new sectoral structure. Here one has to consider the size of the country with a health care sector that is fairly manageable in terms of its quantity.

Germany and France face a different social and economic situation. Both countries have to deal with an ageing society and its financial implications. But their health care systems react differently. In Germany, there exists a strong political demand on the national health care system to reduce costs by finding ways to rationalise health care or to financially outsource certain care supplies for the recovery period or for the elderly. But the elderly are not the only source creating economic problems. In the future, the German health care system cannot be financed the same way it has been financed during the last fifty years. Health care insurances are confronted with a kind of cost explosion that has reached its limits. And reforms already undertaken have not yet solved these financial problems. Nursing in Germany is embedded in a system that is under strong financial restrictions and that undergoes one reform after another while not giving much attention to the institutions and professionals who are providing care.

In France, the consequences of an ageing population are also dealt with on an economic level, but predominantly in social-technical terms. There seems to be a strong tendency to cope with and compensate these demands by implementing new technological equipment that can support home-based care. In general, seems that the German health care system almost exclusively focuses upon cost reduction combined with documentation and reorganisation of services, while the French system's efforts go into rationalisation through latest technological developments combined with providing very professional health care services. The strong technological approach especially becomes obvious through the introduction of the French smart card. This card serves as a tool to collect and steer all medical and health care treatment data from each social security member and to mediate the reimbursement of the services received.

Insofar, health care and nursing undergo changes of very different nature and degrees in each of the three countries. These changes challenge structures and the workforce while employers and HRD strategies try to respond by adjusting the workforce's capabilities to changing structural demands. Estonia's health care system is in the process of creating new democratic bodies and structures, while also being responsive to economic demands. This has the effect that all nurses are required to retrain according to the new curricula which provide qualification for the new democratic, organisational and economic demands. If a nurse who has been educated during Soviet times does not undergo such training she will ultimately remain in a disadvantaged position professionally. This means that nurses, who were trained and who worked during Soviet times have to develop a new professional identity that fits the new society and a new occupational profile respectively.

As mentioned before, in Germany the main emphasise is placed upon cost reduction while still demanding high quality standards of care. But to a certain extent the pressure for cost reduction and rationalisation while at the same time providing high quality health care services is contradictory. Nurses face a situation where the time for providing direct care is increasingly reduced and extremely restricted. But they are required to provide better quality of care and services. This raises the question of how individual nurses deal with the increasing pressure and if this affects their occupational identity and work ethos. The French health care system meets new demands by implementing latest medical technology and data processing. This also shapes and influences the professional identity and work experience of nurses as does the complex structure of the system. French nurses have an educational level close to university degrees and reliable work place security as civil servants. These facts combined with strict hierarchical structures and the implementation of advanced medical equipments certainly affect their professional identity in a different way. So far it could be shown that the structural demands that affect nurses in all three countries is of a quite different nature.

Three Evaluation Criteria of Employers' Perspectives and Their Manifestations in the Three Countries

In order to compare or better to understand the different manifestations of important structural features that help develop professional and occupational identities various evaluation criteria have been combined to three criteria: the process of learning, organisational conditions and individual inclinations.

1) *Learning:*

This element emphasises how employers' perspectives perceive initial and further education of employees. Do they agree with the qualifications accomplished through initial education and training? How do they assess initial and further education in respect to job and work requirements and their effect on occupational identity formation? What insights or information was given regarding a rich or poor learning environment employees are exposed to at work? Are there any implicit or explicit statements on how poor or rich learning possibilities at work affect the nature and change of identity formation?

2) *Organisation:*

This criterion concerns the conditions of work organisation which are closely related to the dimensions of a poor or rich learning environment at work. Are job profiles flexible and open or are they restrictive and sealed? Closely related is the question of hierarchical structures like, for example, whether certain management levels require a specific certification or not. Is the organisational and institutional structure open and flexible or rather sealed so that it does not allow for sharing power and responsibilities with colleagues?

3) *Individual:*

In respect to the different processes of identity formation the question of how much autonomy is allowed when performing ones job or profession seem to be essential. It was also investigated how companies' specific occupational or professional conditions give employees options for taking on a wider range of responsibilities. Another important factor seem to be the specific elements the individual employee identifies within his or her work or occupation: For example, is good work performance connected with occupational and professional pride? What role does the product, the service, the team one works with and the company's reputation play in this context? Or, to rephrase this question: where lies the pride in performing a specific job or occupation?

In order to understand how the nurse profession is shaped by structural requirements and human resource management intentions in the three countries of investigation the findings and patterns of the above defined criteria and their manifestations in the three countries shall first be presented.

Learning and the Learning Environment

Considering how structural conditions of the Estonia health care system affect learning in nurses' occupations, one outstanding element obviously are the new curricula for initial education and training. These curricula not only serve the new occupational demands and are of better quality than the old ones because they are more linked to practice, but being trained under the new curriculum also give nurses the image of being a professional that has adjusted to the new Estonia society and even to European labour market standards. In order to prove oneself as a useful professional member of the society after the transition from the Soviet regime one has to be certified according to the new curricula. Otherwise one is stigmatised with a certification that was valid in a society that no longer exists and is not appreciated today. The second structural factor affecting learning of nurses and giving new perspectives for educational mobility, is the introduction of curricula for the nursing professions at an academic level.

Certainly, there are new necessities and demands as are the implementation of new medical technologies and new legislative requirements, which have asked for creating new curricula. The way they are incorporated into negotiations between occupational associations and the government show that education and learning right now also strongly are perceived as an instrument to establish the nursing profession in the newly emerging societal and political context. This goes in line with the new requirements for continuous education. If one does not meet these demands one loses ones reputation as qualified nurse. But the emphasis on Estonia's personnel management in health care does not seem to be very much laid on a new paradigm for the workforce as it is discussed in Western European countries. There the ideologically loaded arguments are that organisational, technological or economical changes ask for life long learning, employability, mobility and flexibility. Obviously in Estonia it is much more important that employees show the willingness to let go of old Soviet working habits and are interested in adjusting to the new labour market demands and corresponding work attitudes than to be shaped due to a new workforce "paradigm", that has become fashionable in the western countries.

Initial education and training of German nurses is estimated to no longer meet the needs of a complex and fast changing environment qualified personnel has to face. But given the non-unified, strongly heterogeneous group of interests of German health care providers who all run their own schools for educating nurses, no change towards more adequate concepts of vocational education and training for nurses can be expected in the nearer future. Learning through further and continuous educational programmes while at the same time working is the major tool to meet the new demands nurses are confronted with as well as to step up the career ladder. In order to become a qualified nurse initial education and training are obligatory. But to establish oneself as a professional and successful nurse one needs to take on initiative while learning on the job and taking advantage of in-house offerings for further and continuous education and training.

In each case study with personnel management of German health care institutions the need for continuous learning for health care professionals was stated. Within the process of the ongoing restructuring of the German health care system a redefinition and redesign of nurses' work profile and skill requirements continues. To keep up with the demands of such fundamental changes that take place at a very fast speed, qualified personnel must participate in continuous learning. In addition, the multi-disciplinary aspects of the profession that include complex social interactions and the need to cooperate in a ward team and with different organisational units in the hospital as well as with other professions have made nurses' workplace a highly challenging learning environment. Qualified personnel are asked to participate in a complex programme for further education and training. Each hospital of the conducted case studies had its own in-house training programme and also tried to take advantage of other training providers in order to qualify their staff. Further education for career development is also fostered but not mandatory.

In France initial education for nurses appears like participating in an initiation that allows to enter a well established status group capable of giving strong work place security and professional pride. In order to become a nurse one has to attend a nurse school on average for three years. Successful completion of vocational education and training as nurse is certified with a "Nurse State Diploma" which is regarded equivalent to a university degree. Hospitals recruit nurses on the basis of their diploma. There they have to work another year as a nurse trainee before becoming a registered nurse with the status of a civic servant in public hospitals. There exist several well defined tracks to step up the career ladder like, for example, state registered anaesthetist nurse, surgery nurse, child nurse or senior nurse. These specialisations only can be achieved through further education in specialised schools for the duration of one to three years after one already has gained work experience as a general nurse for at least two years. After successful completion one is certified with a State Diploma. Besides the professional track as civic servants in public hospitals, French nurses have the option to move into the private sector. This however also requires regulated further education, either one needs to get an Inter University Diploma for health care in order to work in companies, or one has to prove successful practice as registered nurse in the public sector for three years. After this period it is possible to practice as free-lance nurse and establish ones own health institution.

Overall, after having passed formal initial and further education and training, continuous vocational training only serves as an instrument to update and adapt to new technological or medical requirements and changes. Training courses seem to be well attended and obviously accepted as professional requirements nurses in France are willing to respond to even though their attendance does not provide any accreditation or promotion. Insofar, the main basis for learning as a nurse is strongly bound to the attendance of nurse schools. While in Germany one acquires, for example, a diploma as surgery nurse by attending classes besides working full day as nurse, the French system requires stepping out of ones professional life in order to study for the specialisation one strives for. In France, learning to become a nurse is very much school oriented. This has the advantage of freeing the trainee from the daily workload while at the same time there is little orientation towards practice.

In the three countries one finds different forms of formal vocational education. From the project's perspective the differences identified are not related to the nature of the curricula (which may also differ tremendously), but they address the societal and structural aspects. Since a decade Estonia has started to negotiate and create new curricula that will shape the concept of being a nurse very differently from what is considered as old curricula from the Soviet period. In Germany, the multitude of different bodies of responsibility keep the ways of initial education and training German nurses receive heterogeneous though there is a general requirement guidance given by legislation. In France, one can observe highly regulated and advanced education programmes for nurses. It would be interesting to look more deeply into the processes of self-directed and informal leaning that evolves under those different conditions, as well as how the different ways of initial education foster the formation of vocational identities.

Regarding Organisation and Workplace Organisation

Again the main emphasis of organisational changes in the Estonia health care system right now does not seem to be laid so much on reorganising workplaces and reengineering hospitals' organisational structures. More important seems the creation of a new character and structure of the health care system and therefore the emphasise is laid on the establishment and functioning of occupational and professional associations that politically can recruit and represent health care professionals. Large public hospitals still have rigid hierarchical structures as job management of nurses works from top down. At the same time the sector becomes more differentiated due to the development of private hospitals and health care providers. Major developmental shifts in organisation rather seem to take place on an overall sectoral level than on the micro-level of hospital or ward organisations. Financial matters are more and more taken into consideration. The system has shifted from a general financing of institutions like hospitals towards a system of funding services by demand. Therefore, medical institutions often have to face the problem to not providing services for all those who are in need as "nobody can be served only out of good will any more". A social mechanism to take care of those who cannot afford to pay for health care services is not yet in place. The new financing system obviously supports a process of decentralisation and marketing of large hospitals. Also a continually rising level of medical technology causes reorganisation of technical qualifications which is seen to become more and more important.

The situation in small and local hospitals is different. Not being technologically very advanced makes them prefer to emphasise on the human aspect of health care service. Also, a new model of cooperation between nurses, doctors and patients has been introduced, which is more satisfying for all actors and asks for more responsibility, at least from nurses. But up to now in practice this team model is rather an exception though, in accordance with the new understanding of the role of nurses, associations try to propel it forward.

To summarize, the main emphasis of changes in Estonia's health care system is laid upon the reorganisation and establishment of political bodies and their societal efficiency. To make organisational structures of hospitals more efficient is very important and a question of economical survival. For nurses who on a daily basis have to deal with ward and hospital structures this situation may in some cases expose them to a certain flexibility as the transition process in the long run does not allow organisational structures to be too rigid and hierarchical. This slight uncertainty of who is empowered, what structures will remain, what changes may next be required, etc. could serve as an element that fosters a rather open organisational structure and the option for nurses to take on initiative of being responsible and to work more independently.

Fundamental organisational changes are taking place in all fields of the German health system. These changes are propelled forward by the new statutory quality requirements and a new financing system for health care services. But the reorganisation of hospitals is linked to the question of how to provide high quality services on the basis of lower budgets. In order to be competitive hospitals' management and staff have to become inventive and creative to speed up a process of reorganisation which reduces costs while nevertheless providing high standards of health care and medical services. The same principles apply for ambulant services and resident care institutions for the elderly. Health care provisions for residents and patients have become more labour intensive due to the increasing age average of the residents that requires more intensive care. The statutory requirement to document every step of treatment and service provided has not yet been fully integrated into all work processes. Personnel still struggle to find ways to integrate this additional demand into their work. In summary, reorganisation processes and new tasks that need to become integrated into nurses' work are highly challenging and often seem to reach the edge of putting the demands on personnel too high.

Organisational challenges may exist for the French health care system but are not seen as revolutionary factors but rather as a normal incremental process of necessary changes. Changes occur, for example, due to advanced technology that facilitates an increased use of home-disposal equipment and products to better take care of patients at their private homes. This has the effect that the number of short term patients in hospitals has decreased. This tendency was reinforced by the development of ambulatory medicine, auto-diagnosis and home care services. Hospitals therefore are now facing an increase of long-term patients, mainly because of partially or fully dependent patients including elderly people who require long-term care that cannot be provided at home any longer. Hospitals try to face these structural changes with increased efficiency to reduce costs, pushed by the control of quality insurance. Regional authorities are responsible to oversee the hospitals of the region, define objectives and requirements with the aim of creating pools of excellence by merging hospitals. The smart cart for social security affiliates, which enables a direct electronic transfer of the patient's medical records and prescriptions to the health care reimbursement funds, is also used as an instrument to track down health care spending. The electronic networking of the French health care sector obviously is highly elaborated and dominates processing and structures of medical and health care supply.

The public and the private sector are complementary to each other within the national health programmes. The private as well as the public sector is embedded in an overall health care framework by the social security system. Both, public and private hospitals are subject to government approval for their location, development and major investments for medical equipment. For each medical specialisation a bed-population ratio is given which directly affects the development of hospitals. Therefore, the private sector rather appears to be a mechanism for allowing a certain amount of non-public institutions in order to give the population a sense of having multiple choices. There obviously is no approach to create another overall organisational or health care paradigm as an alternative to what can be found in the public sector. Private hospitals in Estonia on the contrary obviously function as spearhead for new organisational and professional developments.

In Estonia associations and unions as nurses' public voice push the transition process from old nursing concepts during Soviet times towards a new nursing concept. A major tool for this transition process was the development and implementation of a new curriculum. The need for restructuring hospitals' organisations is recognised but seems to only move on at a slow pace. Smaller and private hospitals are the institutions where new organisational approaches most likely can be developed for they do not have to struggle with the resistance of old organisational structures from Soviet times.

In Germany, there exists a strong political demand on the national health care system to reduce costs by finding ways to rationalise health care or to financially outsource certain care supplies for the recovery period or for the elderly. The rationalisation processes affect the organisation of hospitals as well as the work organisation of nurses. Another new element is the necessity to document all steps of treatment and care which up to now mainly is seen as an additional workload and not as a tool to make work processes more transparent. It seems that young nurses have fewer difficulties to adjust to these new requirements and even to appreciate the element of reflection that the documentary work requires. The pressure for stronger economically oriented health care services and the different tools implemented to reach this aim most likely will change the work profile of nurses in Germany.

In France the process of rationalisation within the health care system seems to have a longer tradition than in Germany. Also one has to consider that it is a fairly homogenous system with two major pillars; that is the public and the private sector. This may have helped to keep the French health system more efficient. The mechanisms for rationalisation could be even more strict than in Germany, but also more powerful. The structure of the system itself obviously is not questioned or challenged because of new structural demands. Making reference to it as being complex and heavy points to a structure that has been built up by strong interest groups over many years. Nurses therefore may feel on the one hand very secure, on the other hand they seem to request more flexibility and independence at work.

Individuals' Relation to the Nurse Profession

Personnel management in Estonia stated that nurses should most of all be interested in their vocation as a mission. But it has been admitted that wages are too low and are contradicting the high responsibility nurses have. Given the lack of acknowledgement and social status it is very difficult for nurses to develop professional pride. Their professional associations however are striving for raising the social status of nurses and for providing them with a new self esteem. Nurses shall no longer consider themselves as being just 'helping hands' for doctors, but see themselves as belonging to an independent profession. Also the new curricula can be understood as an instrument to raise the professional status given that by the new standards one also becomes certified to work in other European countries. But the strongest source of identifying with the profession is seen as being rooted in having a mission. Only smaller hospitals seem to offer additional identification with the institution, maybe because of a more family like work environment.

Qualified nurses of the German health care sector are considered as having a strong professional identity. Many of the case studies have pointed out that one does not enter this profession if one does not really wish to work as a nurse. Yet the image of the nursing profession as a merely helping mission is changing. At the same time personnel managers nowadays are looking for different personality profiles when interviewing prospective employees than several years ago. The motivation of having a helping mission is no longer seen as sufficient, on the contrary, to a certain extend it rather seems to be a hindrance to become involved in the profession's administrative and economic aspects.

From employers' perspectives the type of work required from nurses as well as organisational changes had a strong effect on the nurse profession during the last years. Individuals who decided to work as a nurse are exposed to many different economic and organisational interests and tensions. They have to meet patients' growing expectations regarding services including those of patient's relatives. They have to keep up with the developments in medicine and health care, need to manage their work and work environment economically, be motivated to continuously learning and attend further educational activities. Nevertheless, health care managers perceive the profession as very interesting and manifold while at the same time it provides a high potential for pressure and strain. In general, personnel management considers the nurse profession as very challenging and rewarding.

Although in France the nursing profession is socially less esteemed than the medical professions, nurses in general have a strong professional identity and attachment to the ethics of their profession including a high capacity to continuously integrate any kind of work-related changes into the socio-economic and technological environment. Indeed, the strong professional identity serves as an engine for continuous improvements through continuing learning during ones individual working life. But the lack of social recognition that manifests itself in low salaries that do not compensate for the increasing work load and the high responsibility towards patients, rather results in a shortage of nurses. Another aspect that makes the profession not very attractive is the lack of professional independence. How much autonomy is allowed in performing the work tasks is dependent upon doctors and internal assignments. Such restrictions make French nurses, who have the possibility, prefer to work in neighbouring European countries where working situations are more attractive and salaries are higher than in France.

Reflections:

In all three countries employers say that the professional or vocational identity of nurses is very strong. However, Germany and Estonia show an existing ideal of a nurse that is dominated by a healing mission, whereas in France nursing is regarded as both, a mission (of "nursing" and "medical" care) and profession. Each system also makes employees struggle with structural restrains. In Estonia especially low wages seem to be a big factor, in Germany, the economical requirements one has to meet, and in France, like in the two other countries as well, it is the lack of social recognition and specifically for France the lack of independence at work.

Demands on Flexibility and Mobility

In Estonia, employers mentioned the need for functional and organisational flexibility of nurses. Demand and practice of functional flexibility are widely spread. There are nurses who can work as a non-specialised nurse as well as senior nurse and also be responsible for training of other nurses. Organisational flexibility often means that nurses have to be able to be relocated every day to other hospital wards because of their specialisations. Again one has to consider the size of Estonia which makes a career path of high specialisation for nurses useless for such specialisation may only be needed of one to five persons in the whole country. Therefore, high versatility is the dominant feature nurses in Estonia have to develop.

As the findings show, there also is a high demand on flexibility nurses have to face in Germany. This applies especially to psychological responses towards the social environment at work, patients, colleagues, or physicians. This is also true regarding the reorganisation and other organisational processes and keeping up with new developments in medicine and health care. However, the demand (though of the same character) looks differently in the case of ambulant health care services and qualified care in residential institutions for the elderly although the tensions and strain they have to deal with are similar. Mobility is required especially when working for ambulant health care providers. To visit 12 patients in different homes often two, sometimes three times a day requires a great capacity to adapt to different environments and people during a short period of time. Also a need for more organisational mobility regarding nurses' employment in hospitals was mentioned.

In respect to career mobility nurses generally step up one, sometimes two career steps. Horizontal mobility is much more common than the interest for moving into a leading position of some sort of management. This also would require additional university studies, mainly while working for employees in health care seldom are financially that well equipped that they could study without earning a living at the same time. Finally, nurses feel they abandon their profession when moving into management which they perceive as a very different type of work.

Horizontal mobility in the French health care system is mainly limited to internal mobility within public hospitals. The mechanism to assign a nurse to another ward generally is functionally determined and voluntary. It also is formally organised on the basis of new permanent work contracts between different wards or units of the same hospital. But French employers expect changes regarding the range of internal mobility of nurses. The idea is to open the exclusively limited functional mobility within hospital units or wards towards a wider in-house mobility between wards and departments.

In the large hospitals of France, only a small percentage of nurses exists whose work is more challenging in respect to spatial mobility. As far as functional flexibility is concerned, all nurses have to adapt continuously their work profile to requirement of change in their domain through continuous vocational training. A pool called "pool for compensation and replacement" is dominantly made up of general nurses, assistant nurses and a few specialised nurses who are on a permanent work contract as civil servants. The members of this pool are functionally and horizontally mobile within different departments of a given hospital. The pool is meant to solve the problem of peak work loads by optimally combining labour flexibility with reduced health care costs through increased efficiency. Insofar, the pool works as an internal hospital 'temporary employment agency' whose employees are permanent workers, but are assigned to different wards on a temporary basis. Being a member of this pool allows for developing the skill of being functional flexible through the daily demand of polyvalence and adaptability to different medical or care situations and working conditions. Nurses belonging to this pool are highly attached to their profession, much more than to a specific ward or hospital.

Conclusions

Obviously nurses in Estonia are asked to be much more flexible than their colleagues in France or Germany given an often daily adjustment to different work environments. These nurses definitely also have acquired the polyvalence of the highly flexible compensatory pool of nurses in French hospitals. German employees emphasise more on the demand of psychological flexibility: to be customer oriented regarding the different demands from different customers as are patients, doctors, other hospital units or patients' relatives. A very rough conclusion could be that the structural conditions in Estonia may be most favourable for moulding a future flexible profile of the nurse occupation. Though there is a strong pressure for change in the German health care system, it mainly emphasises on economical and rationalisation aspects which not necessarily lead to more flexibility at the workplace, but certainly to more pressure. Also in France, there is an increasing move towards rationalisation that is confronted with the patients' free choice and equal access to same quality of health care services (within the private and public sector) to all citizens with minimum costs to the social security system. Nurses as well as doctors are increasingly required to be more interactive with their work and patients, and at same time be highly flexible in their adjustment to new technological and medical demands.

From the structural aspect of the different health care systems one can see that Estonia is in the process of basically reorganise its system fundamentally while the German system struggles with seeking solutions for the uncontrollable increase of costs. There can be some serious doubts about whether the instruments implemented may fully work. Therefore, the German system right now is in an unstable situation while the French system, on the contrary, has been successfully established.

Also, the image nurses themselves have about their profession differ in the three countries, a fact that reflects in their initial education and training. Nurses in Germany and especially in Estonia are seen or expected to be basically driven by a caring mission. As for nurses' mission in France, nurses are strongly attached to the ethics of their mission which is twofold: "acte propre" as a nurse nursing and caring with, autonomy, responsibility and a relatively high level of psychological and relational interactivity with the patients, and the purely medical mission (acte prescrit) which characterises their daily work-related relational interactivity with doctors within hospitals or clinics . Moreover, they are able to exercise (with a high level of flexibility, mobility and relational interactivity with the clients) their profession as free-lance nurses (as it is the case with free-lance doctors.

It has become clear that nurses in all three countries already working in this profession for several years have developed strong vocational or professional identities, though the three health care systems offer different contextual conditions. To which extent the structural influences and demands affect and shape the occupational or professional identity differently may be seen with the findings of the project's investigation on employees' perspective.

REFERENCES

M'Hamed Dif, Forms and implications of work related identity transformation: Preliminary findings of "FAME" project investigation in the French case (presentation at ECER 2001(EERA/VETNET) Lille, France, 5-8 September 2001

M'Hamed Dif, Summary of employer-interviews' findings in France. In: 2nd annual scientific FAME-report

Gabriele Laske, Employer perspective health care sector in Germany - Context information regarding the German health care sector with focus on nurses' work, German contribution for FAME-Warwick meeting 18-20 July, 2001

Gabriele Laske, Summary of German findings of employers' perspective in health care, metal industry and telecommunication. In: 2nd annual scientific FAME-report

Krista Loogma, Initial conclusions on employers interviews – Nurses (Presentation on 24th Jan. 2001 Athens; Fame – Project meeting)

Krista Loogma, Raivo Vilu, Estonian contribution for FAME-Warwick meeting 18-20 July, 2001 "The evaluation and findings on Employer interviews"

Krista Loogma, Raivo Vilu, Estonia Health Care. In: 2nd annual scientific FAME-report

17

LEARNING FROM A POSITION OF POWER: FEMALE ENTREPRENEURS IN MALE-DOMINATED BUSINESS CONTEXTS

*Daniele D. Flannery**
*Elizabeth Coyle***

Introduction

Research into gender and learning in the workplace is ongoing. Emerging themes include the influence of power on women's formal and informal learning within work organizations (Munroe, Holly, & Rainbird, 2000), learning leadership (Wajcman, 1998) and networking styles (Ibarra, 1993), and the types of work knowledge women produce and value (MacKeracher & McFarland, 1993/1994). Additionally, women's workplace learning researchers have investigated the influence of women's acts of accommodation and resistance to power (Fenwick, 1998; Bierema, 1999), the development of alternative forms of knowledge in response to power issues (Fenwick, 1998, Fletcher, 1999), and the influences of social location or positionality on women's learning (Bierema, 1999; Fletcher, 1999).

* Associate Professor, The Pennsylvania State University-Harrsiburg.
** Assistant Professor, Elizabeth Town College, Elizabeth Town, PA.

While issues of power, position, agency, and women's learning in relation to oppression within the patriarchal structures of organizations have been examined, little attention has been paid to the interaction between women's workplace learning and positionality when women operate from a position of privilege.

Two studies have explored women's learning in relation to issues of power and privilege in work organizations, but did not fully explain how this occurred during their learning. Bierema's (1999), study of women in Fortune 500 companies noted that the change agents in her study believed that they were in a unique position of power to lobby for social change within their organizations. However, she did not explicitly link how their perceived privilege within the organization influenced the use of that privilege.

Fletcher (1999) investigated how female design engineers responded to the power structures of male-dominated work organizations during their learning. She found that the women continued to use and highly valued relational learning approaches in the workplace even though the larger work organization did not recognize or reward the types of relational knowledge that the women employed. However, how they learned to wield enough power to continue to use their preferred ways of learning without jeopardizing their careers is not clear.

A workplace setting where women operate from a position of privilege is within businesses that they themselves own. Globally, women-owned firms comprise between one-quarter and one-third of all businesses (Center for Women's Business Research, 1999). While women remain underrepresented among entrepreneurs, their numbers are expanding rapidly (Clothier, 2001). However, little is known about this burgeoning population (Clothier, 2001). Thus, it is within this literature on the female entrepreneur that further insights were sought on the interaction between women's workplace learning and positionality when women operate from a position of privilege.

Literature on female entrepreneurs has focused on the psychological (Fenwick & Hutton, 2000; Nelson, 1987; Rozier, 1995; Wells, 1998) and relational aspects (Chaganti, 1986; Kamau, McLean, & Ardishvilli, 1999; Wells, 1998; Fenwick & Hutton, 2000) of women's learning. While these studies identified that the female entrepreneurs were agents of their own learning, recognized that the women's positions of power as heads of their organizations influenced their ability to choose what, when, and how they learned, they did not fully delineate how this occurs. Furthermore, they largely ignored the larger context of the historical, cultural, economic, and positional social structures in which the female entrepreneurs were operating their business and its influence on their learning. This is significant given the fact that previous studies of female and male entrepreneurs indicated that environmental factors (Kolvereid, Shane, & Westhead, 1993) and position in society (Birley, 1989; Spinder, 2000) play a role in entrepreneurs' perceptions and business activities.

Additionally, these researchers (Fenwick & Hutton, 2000; Nelson, 1987; Rozier, 1995; Wells, 1998) drew conclusions about female entrepreneurs' learning based on sample populations that combined women who operated their businesses in both female and male dominated business arenas. These studies did not take into consideration the structures of power within the varying contexts of male- and female-dominated industries and their possible influence on the women's learning.

This study endeavored to fill those gaps. As such the goals of the study were: (a) to explore the influence of both context and power on the learning of female entrepreneurs operating their companies specifically in male-dominated business contexts, (b) to investigate the notion that positionality influences women's creation of knowledge, and (c) to explore how women are both shaped by and shape their learning experiences through their acts of agency.

Research Question

Does, and if so how does, positionality and agency within shifting contexts influence the learning of female entrepreneurs in male-dominated business arenas?

Theoretical/Conceptualization Approach

Poststructural feminist theory (Collins, 2000; Mayberry & Rose, 1999; Tisdell, 1998) provided the theoretical framework for this research. Poststructural feminist theory maintains that women's position within gender, race, class, and other structures of privilege and oppression influences how they make meaning of their experiences (Collins, 2000; Flax, 1989). It also believes that women do not always accept their particular position within society's power structures when they experience oppression in their lives. Instead, women can choose to accommodate (accept) or resist the oppression by engaging in acts of agency (Collins, 2000; Flax, 1989; Mayberry & Rose, 1999). The relationship between women's position, which can change from one context to the next, their subjective experience of their position, and their agency determine how women define who they are, how they create knowledge, the kinds of knowledge they create, and the knowledgc they believe to be true (Tisdell, 1998).

Design

This study employed a phenomenological methodology to investigate the learning experiences of a purposeful sample of female entrepreneurs in Central Pennsylvania who operate their businesses within traditionally male-dominated business contexts. Participants were identified through published listings of women-owned and minority-owned businesses, through economic and small business development organizations, and through a snowball sampling strategy.

Data Collection

Primary data collection procedures included open-ended, semi-structured interviews and the critical incident technique. The women were interviewed twice on-site at their respective businesses for approximately three hours. The interviews focused on descriptions of the varying contexts in which the women learned, their subjective experiences of power in these contexts, and how issues of power and context combined to influence their learning.

Demographics

A purposeful sampling of twelve female entrepreneurs operating their businesses in the arenas of agriculture, communication/technology, construction, finance, manufacturing, geophysical scanning, recycled products and sales, auto glass repair, and patent law served as participants in this study. All of the women played a primary role in the start-up and daily management of their businesses and held at least majority equity in their business. All but one of the women operated their businesses either as a sole proprietorship, a limited liability company, or as a privately-held corporation. This woman headed a non-profit philanthropic foundation. The number of individuals employed by the women ranged from two to eighty. The length of years in business ranged from three to twenty two years and all of the women had experienced gross revenue increases over the past two years.

The women in this study ranged in age from thirty two to fifty five years. Eleven of the women in this study were Caucasian and two were African American. All but two of the women continued their education beyond high school. Three of the women held graduate degrees.

Data Analysis

Transcripts were analyzed in tandem with the tape recordings of the interviews, field notes and a reflective journal kept by the researcher. An indexing and categorization system was developed from the events, ways of thinking and feeling, and patterns of behavior described by the women. This system of analysis was used for each sample unit along with an analysis of emerging similar themes, patterns, and relationships that existed across the participants' narratives. Each new sample unit was analyzed in relation to the previous data collected. Expanded versions of the invariant themes that revealed the deeper meaning of the women's learning experiences were then developed.

Results

The women's main focus was on conducting business. However, in order to do so, they needed to develop a body of knowledge to deal swiftly with the issues that arose from their gendered positions in order to get to the business at hand. What was unique for these women was that they perceived themselves to be in a position of privilege and power rather than oppression during gender-related encounters, resisted attempts to place them in a position of oppression, and were acutely aware of how the contexts of their gendered positions shifted from one setting to the next. The women's perceptions of themselves as being in gendered positions of power, their acts of resistance rather than accommodation, and the variable gendered contexts in which they learned resulted in the development of an extensive knowledge base on how to garner and wield their power.

The women generated these lessons of power on their own through a process of trial and error, and by integrating the knowledge they learned from their gendered positions in previous work settings and during their childhoods. All but one of the women believed that these were lessons that they more than likely would not have learned otherwise had they not been faced with gender-related issues in the course of conducting business. Furthermore, they felt the repertoire of skills they developed in response to their gendered positions was more extensive today compared to when they first started their business ventures, and they expected that their knowledge would continue to expand in the future as they continued to build their skills.

Learning to Garner Power

Over the years the women learned a number of ways to secure power as female entrepreneurs during gender-related encounters. The women garnered their power by (a) creating a powerful presence when they were the only woman or one of a handful of women in a group of men, (b) reading and manipulating power dynamics associated with gender to establish a power base, and (c) learning to use the old boy network to their advantage.

Creating a powerful presence. Many of the women learned the importance of making their presence known in a roomful of men, of responding quickly when their expertise was challenged by business colleagues, and of using dress to secure power and credibility.

> It [having my credibility challenged] makes me more determined to be more aggressive. If I really believe in moving from one point to the other, then I say [to myself] okay, just do it, go for it, you'll do it. Just that little self-talk, saying you are not going to hold me back. I worked too hard. I've come too far and I'm going to move past you. That little self-talk does it.... (OD)

The women also learned to garner power through dress. The women used dress as a very specific technique to establish power and credibility with customers, clients, and business associates. In some cases dress was used as an anticipatory tactic prior to a proposal presentation to offset potential assumptions that a woman could not possibly know what she is talking about in a male-dominated industry.

> Well you will automatically get far more attention and there is instant credibility that goes along with it [power dressing]. Don't ask me why but there is. And when I do a pitch I wear, I have three or four $500 suits but they look great and I wear all my best jewelry. I make sure I have my diamond and, you know, it's part of it. (LD)

In other cases, dress was used to establish credibility with colleagues and employees at construction work sites. For the two women in the construction industry, "dressing the part" with work boots and hard hat played an important role in fitting in with the guys in the trenches and for establishing credibility as leaders of their organization with employees. LO recounted,

> For the most part I just wear the logo sweater like the rest of them [employees]. I don't really need to be above them. I'd rather dress regular with them.... When I go to corporate meetings when buyers are there, they're in suits. So you definitely have to come up to their level....

Reading body language to secure power. The majority of the women described the heightened awareness of gendered power dynamics they developed over the years. Their observations skills often yielded valuable information in the moment to decide what their next move would be.

When the women felt that a group of male associates or potential clients doubted their expertise, they first silently read body language to get a sense of the power dynamics in the room. Based on the information they ascertained from reading the body language, they then chose appropriate strategies to shift the power base in the room to their advantage.

> Well I turn red and that is something I really don't like to do when I feel it [my credibility being challenged because I am a woman] happening to me. I just have to get my mind somewhere else. I take a few deep breaths and I sort of just wait until that goes away. I'll think about the beach or I'll think about being in a pool or about gardening. They don't know it, but that's what I do. And then I come back with well I'm sorry you feel that way, that you can't take what I say as credible and then go forth with whatever comes back. I've been doing this for 20 years... (OD)
>
> What I am experiencing is, I walk in and their attitude is sort of like who is this person. And then I quickly get into my presentation and they realize I know what I'm talking about, I can answer their questions...But then I will read them. If somebody looks confused, I'll make no qualms about stopping and saying, 'you look confused. Am I answering, are you following what I'm saying?' And they'll either say, 'yeah' or 'no not at all' and it well help me revise. I'm reading their body language. Again, one of the tactics at that point is to get them to talk so I have a minute to think, okay, where to regroup. (GC)
>
> When I want to be taken seriously.... You know, lots of direct eye contact, lots of lowered voices, not quiet but just not shrill.... I smile a lot, but then it's quickly juxtaposed with alright back to business, almost catching people off guard. I

> look at a lot of people in the eye. I pick people out and talk to them, then I pick another person out and talk to them. Speaking loudly, clearly, and picking the right pace. You can't talk too fast and you can't talk too slowly. And I guess I personally try to strike a balance between being really professional and friendly at the same time.... (GC)

One woman in the construction industry offered a particularly detailed example of how intensely she observed gendered power dynamics and then used the information learned to her advantage.

> I think the males have a way of doing these things [reading people} just in a different manner. They use it in a group setting, an association or business meeting. They have a way of reading whether they have your support or not. They can read you. Whether it's good or bad they can usually think, I can change her mind or I can change that persons mind. ...They usually have more of their gender than the female gender. So they don't have to work on so many people as a woman has to work on. They might just have to pick out one and that is the woman. As the woman you have five or six of them that you have to deal with. And he might say well I can change her. Just let me talk to her. I'll get her to change her mind. One of them would be designated to approach the woman. You can see that. Like I said just pay attention.... But then I say I know what I'm talking about and I know why I'm here and this is the way it's going to be. Do you get that gentlemen? This is the way it's going to be. And he'll say I don't agree with

> that. And he can say that, by just doing that, they [the men] will come with help. And that is how they handle that reading. (OD)

One woman went on to describe how she, as did many of the other women in the study, then used the information she gained through observation to establish a power base and "work" the room to win support for her viewpoints and business decisions.

> ...and if I feel so intimidated by being with too many [men], I'll single out one, one or two and I'll work on them instead of all of them...you might see his reaction when things are said and you watch for reactions of people and when you say something whether they are paying attention to you or not. And the ones that pay attention to you are the ones that usually you can deal with.... You pick the ones that either had a reaction against one of the men or one that genuinely listened while the rest of them were just not caring. You learn to judge people... (OD)

Learning to use the old boy network to their advantage. The largest body of knowledge produced by the women was related to the old boy network. This is not surprising in light of the fact that this was the most commonly cited gender-related issue encountered by the women in the course of doing business. The women learned that they didn't have to go to the "top dog" to make an initial contact with a prospective company and to make contacts with potential clients in unconventional ways. They also learned how to send in an intermediary to establish a foothold into the old boy network, and to "name drop" to establish a linkage with the old boy network.

One women was in a restroom at a professional conference when another conference attendee, Karen, commented on the suit she was wearing. She later called Karen and eventually landed a $800,000 consulting contract in the pharmaceutical firm where the woman worked.

> Karen obviously, just by the way she was dressed right down to her shoes, was somebody who shared the passion for fashion. The fact that she could make that comment [about my suit] gave me an opportunity. I saw that as an opportunity to kind of say hey here is who I am. Here is what I do and then for me to follow up three weeks later and just....it gave me a help to get kind of [say] remember I'm the girl with the suit in the bathroom. It doesn't make your deal, but it gives you an opportunity to kind of network in a different way. Women network differently than men. I know I wouldn't have called Karen if we hadn't had that discussion in the bathroom. I mean it is just weird... There are just certain things that woman do better and are more creative in just like the story I told you. I mean women are more creative in figuring out maybe I don't have to go to the top dog company. Maybe I can go to the people underneath who feed information up to that person. Men don't think about that stuff because they don't want to be bothered with anybody who they rule not important enough. Whereas you know that's not the same mindset that women have. Women will do whatever it takes to get the job done. I mean men will do that too, but their approach is very different. (LD)

One woman, whose husband is a field manager in her heating and air conditioning company, learned to use him as an intermediary to link to the old boy networks that she could not initially enter.

> I can fit in with some of the boys' clubs, but there are some boys' clubs that will not let you in. First it was like you are going to do this with me and I don't care if I am a woman. You are going to have to deal with it. But now it's like I'm not even going to fight these people. These are people that are third generation companies that do not understand it, don't want to understand it. I'm in a club called Associates. It used to be an all men's club. I'm president now. But there are some clubs that I am not going to get into.... I just happen to have my husband as my manager. He is the person I trust who is [already] in the old boys' club.... Sometimes I alternately get in anyway because now they love my husband so much they will tolerate me. My husband is so likeable.... First it made me really upset. Now it's like it can't be all that awful. Everybody can't like me so you just have to take it in stride that you sent the best man in. It's like a war. Send the best man in that can do the job, woman, man, whatever. ...you have to use that kind of self-confidence. (FG)

Another woman learned to use "name dropping" to establish connections to the decision makers in the old boy network. She also learned that it was necessary to do extensive research prior to presenting a business proposal to an all male group to get a better feel of the power dynamics of her audience prior to going into the meeting.

> I have not once gotten into a room, and it can be all men, and started into a presentation, had any difficulty. I think, you know, if you can get into

> the room. The power has to be in your security in terms of doing the presentation and the value you have to offer. And I think knowing your audience is key to that. You know, what are they looking for, what are their therapeutic areas. If I happen to mention that we're working with the Jim M., you know, maybe drop some of those names so that they know you're connected to the people they want to be connected to. That there's more of that that you have to do [because you are a woman], I think, to kind of solidify and validate who you are in making this presentation. (LD)

Learning to Wield Power

The women also shared the numerous lessons they learned on wielding their power when gender-related issues arose. They included: (a) commanding respect by setting limits and boundaries and by being better than the rest; (b) choosing to do business elsewhere when they encountered gender-related issues with clients, customers and business associates; and (c) deciding to use their power judiciously to maintain their client and customer bases.

Commanding respect by setting limits and boundaries and by being better than the rest. The women learned early on in their businesses that they had to set firm standards on how they were to be dealt with in order to establish respect in their industries. One woman recalled how she learned to take a firm stance when men at construction sites used foul language in her presence.

> Our people and the people that dealt with me learned real fast that I meant business. I was serious about it. I gained tremendous respect. For example, the language barrier ... I would go into a meeting in a conference room in a job trailer and I

> would be the only woman there. It was necessary for me to be there because I was the decision maker. But they could not talk without using profanity every other word. ... Whenever it happened repeatedly and they were talking to me I would just say excuse me. I'm not talking to you that way so I really don't expect you to talk to me that way. Now if that is the way you want to talk, I'm not going to talk to you. And that's the part I just established right up front that you do not use the language. You do not have to talk that way. You can communicate even if you have to do it on paper, but that is how you communicate with me. To this day they slip but they apologize.... Even in the construction industry you do not have to subject yourself to stuff that you do not like. I did a lot of jobs I didn't like, but I have no choice. I had to do it. But I did have a choice in how to communicate and how I was to be taken and how I was to be addressed and dealt with. (OD)

The women also set clear boundaries in relation to sexual comments made to them in the course of doing business that commanded respect as well.

> I've had some guys ask me out. They have no idea what I look like. So that type of thing [sexual comments] can happen even on the phone. And there's a way of telling them, I thought of you as a gentleman. I'd like to continue to view you in that way.... Lot's of times I refer to myself as 'we' if the conversations get too personal. I always say 'we' even before Jim [my boyfriend] was in the picture. I always referred to myself as 'we'. Oh we are going to Italy or we are going back to Germany, you know. And so it sends the message without being so overt. (LM)

The women also learned that one way to command respect was to keep meticulous records of telephone conversations and prior business transactions in case someone tried to challenge a decision they had made or the quality of their work. They found out there was power to be had in documentation.

> I just had one call and he said you know you are behind on this job. I said well I was just out there and I don't think we are behind on this job and you are trying to tell me I'm going to have to work my people Saturday and Sunday when you are still there. I' can't do anything until you put it in [the heating system in first] type of thing. They still try to use that man thing with well I got control here and if you don't do this and do that I'm going to have you thrown off this job. Well I beg to differ with you. I've got documentation here... I called your office five times. When did you call? Is it possible? I don't think it's possible that I didn't get your message. Well I know I've called and I say well let me go get my phone log. What phone log? I said well we keep a phone log of every call that comes into this office and what time and what day. I said if you've done that [called me] and I haven't gotten your message then I've got a problem with my organization and I appreciate your input and it just turns all around. So that kind of thing and the teaming up that they [men] do ....then it changes. (OD)

The women also learned that they could gain respect and power by tapping into their past history of success. Excelling at their work and producing the highest quality products undercut the beliefs on the part of some individuals that women didn't know what they were doing in male industries.

> When all this men networking is going on that is how they make their decisions from what other people tell them. It isn't necessarily what is on paper. It's what do you know about this one, or how did that job go, or ...so I have to make sure that every job we have is a smooth run job, a safe job and a job that did not cost anybody any extra money or any extra time. Being right on top of it because when they do this little networking thing it benefits me because they could say oh yeah they did a great job. They got in there and got out of our way so we could get our job done and we actually made profit on that job. That networking that they [the men] do on that level is very, very good as long as you have that respect, do your job right. You do what you are supposed to do; you do it right and efficiently and move forward without repeated phone calls. (OD)

Choosing to do business elsewhere. The women felt that as heads of their organizations they had the power to simply not renew a contract with a customer or client or refuse to deal with a business associate who presented gender related issues during the course of doing business. While they didn't always choose this option, the longer they were in business the more freedom they had to be selective.

> At first, I would say the first nine years was quite a challenge of being accepted, of being dealt with, you know, on a one-on-one basis instead of more or less, you know, the situation. But after that you're sort of established and people sort of know that you're here to stay and that you're capable of doing your stuff. And then occasionally, this just happened to me last week and I was standing with a business associate at a conference looking at a

> book display. He said, 'you might want to look at this because it's got a lot of recipes and you know you have to do the cooking, you have to take care of your family and all that and this might be more interesting to you than to look at this book on supplies and materials.' Yeah, it was like; you would like this publication better because it's got homey things, woman things in it. (laugh) On the other hand this one has business stuff, pretty detailed business oriented. And I'm thinking what do you think I've been doing for 30 years? I wear more than one hat, but my primary hat is running this business. I just said, 'sure.' I rolled my eyes and I just said, 'sure.' [I thought] that's it; you're not getting business from me. You won't get business from me. You don't respect me going in, you won't respect me after getting my business. (OD)

Deciding to use power judiciously. The women wielded their power wisely when dealing with clients and customers. Even though the felt they had more power to simply not deal with someone who was particularly challenging to them as woman once they were established more firmly in their business ventures, they realized they still needed to use discretion in order to grow their businesses.

The women who ran the organic vegetable farm with her husband described how she learned to be more cautious when dealing with customers who challenged her expertise as a woman in the agriculture business. She realized that she could lose business if she spoke what was really on her mind.

> Well I had that background where I'd been in business and I didn't have to deal with it [expectations that women didn't speak up]. I'm

> coming from Jersey and big business where I didn't have that problem. And I'm coming into Podunk land and I'm like no, you don't understand. I don't play by your rules. I'm just that way. I've always had a big mouth and I've always said what I thought. And I did learn that, you know, probably I didn't need to say as much of what I thought. I did have to do business with some of these people. (DC)

Another woman described the balancing act she performs while consulting in the pharmaceutical industry when she has to tell a male client that he is headed in the wrong direction.

> I think my biggest challenge is that um, when you are a consultant and you get asked by a client to do something and you need to push back at them. I think that there's a huge distinction made between how a woman does that effectively and how men do it and what the perception is from the other end. I think it's kind of like the old, you know, women are perceived as being bitchy and men are perceived as being assertive, you know. You have to be very careful about that. That is something that we as a firm talk a lot about. And we have figured out collectively as women [in the firm] how to articulate or how to say no to a client and do it effectively. And I think we've become pretty adept at doing that, but it's a challenge. (LD)

This woman also described how she consciously cushioned her responses when she had to confront a male client.

> Oh, I think men are much more direct. I don't think they would think about anything, I just think it is just out there. I've been on conference calls

> with other consultants; there is usually a fair mix in our field. I would not say this is a predominantly male field at all. I would say that the clients I have are predominantly male. But when I am on the phone with clients I am very thoughtful about how I say no in a positive way. Whereas my male counterparts, not all of them but some of them, will just say you know what this is a good way to do that and let me tell you why. Where I would say something like you know some other options you might want to consider would be... So there are just huge decisions... (LD)

Conclusions

The findings from this investigation indicated that the women's position of power as heads of their own organizations, their personal power, and their use of power within shifting gendered contexts resulted in the creation of an extensive and context-specific body of knowledge on garnering and wielding their power. The women were comfortable with and accustomed to wielding their power as leaders and decision makers in their organizations. When confronted with gender-related issues in the course of doing business, the women drew upon this baseline of knowledge.

However, there were other elements at work as well. The women were acutely aware of the power dynamics surrounding these gender-related encounters and perceived themselves to be on the offense rather than the defense during these experiences. Because of their awareness and perceptions, they moved quickly to resist attempts to diminish their power. Their practiced use of power as leaders of their organization, their perceptions of power and privilege rather than oppression, and their acts of resistance rather than accommodation intertwined to produce a deep and focused reservoir of skills when confronted with gender-related issues in varying contexts.

Implications for HRD Research and Practice

This study suggests the need to further explore the learning of women who perceive themselves in positions of power in varying gendered work contexts in order to more fully understand the nuanced relationship between power and women's workplace learning. Additionally, these results indicate the need to more fully attend to the larger societal structures of power that exist within the workplace and the ways in which women and men work and learn. Finally, human resource development practitioners should centrally locate notions of power and context into the content of the educational programs they offer to increase awareness of gendered issues of power and how these issues might impact workplace learning.

REFERENCES

Bierema, L. L. (1999). A model of executive women's learning and development. *Adult Education Quarterly, 49*(2), 107-121.

Birley, S. (1989). Female entrepreneurs: Are they really different? *Journal of Small Business Management,* 27(2), 32-37.

Catalyst. (2000). *Cracking the glass ceiling.* NY: Catalyst.

Center for Women's Business Research. (1999, March 4) *Characteristics of women entrepreneurs worldwide.* Retrieved April 6, 2002, from http://www.nfwbo.org

Chaganti, R. (1986). Management in women-owned enterprises. *Journal of Small Business Management, 24*(4), 19-29.

Clothier, S. (2001). Cracking the glass ceiling in Europe. *The British Journal of Administrative Management, 24*(2), 21-29.

Collins, P.H. (2000). *Black feminist thought* (2nd ed.). NY: Routledge.

Fenwick, T. (1998). Women composing selves, seeking authenticity: A study of women's development in the workplace. *International Journal of Lifelong Education,* 17(3), 199-217.

Fenwick, T., & Hutton, S. (2000). Women crafting new work: The learning of women entrepreneurs. *Proceedings of the Adult Education Research Conference* (pp. 112- 120). Vancouver, BC: University of British Columbia.

Flax, J. (1989). Postmodernism and gender relations in feminist theory. In M. Malson, J. F. O' Barr, S. Westphal-Wihl, & M. Wyer (Eds.), *Feminist theory in practice and Process* (pp. 51-69). Chicago, IL: The University of Chicago Press.

Fletcher, J. K. (1999). *Disappearing acts: Gender, power, and relational practice at work.* Cambridge, MA: The MIT Press.

Ibarra, H. (1993). Personal networks of women and minorities in management: A conceptual framework. *Academy of Management Review, 18*(1), 56-87.

Kamau, D., McLean, G., & Ardishvilli, A. (1999). Women entrepreneurs: Maintaining business success through human resource development. *Human Resource Development Quarterly, 18*(2), 753-761.

Kerka, S. (1993). *Women and entrepreneurship*. ERIC Clearinghouse on Adult, Career, and Vocational Education. Columbus, OH: Ohio State University.

Kolvereid, L., Shane, S., & Westhead, P. (1993). Is it equally difficult for female entrepreneurs to start businesses in all countries? *Journal of Small Business Management, 31*(4), 42-53.

MacKeracher, D., & McFarland, J. (1993/1994). Learning working knowledge: Implications for training. *Women's Education des Femmes, 10*(3/4), 54-58.

Mayberry, M., & Rose, E.C. (Eds.). (1999). *Innovative feminist pedagogies in action.* NY: Routledge.

Moore, D. (2000). *Careerpreneurs.* Palo Alto, CA: Davies-Black Publishing.

Moore, D., & Buttner, H. (1997). *Moving beyond the glass ceiling*. Thousand Oaks, CA: Sage.

Munro, A., Holly, L., & Rainbird, H. (2000). My ladies aren't interested in learning: Managers, supervisors and the social context of learning. *International Review of Education, 46*(6), 515-528.

Nelson, G. W. (1987). Information needs of female entrepreneurs. *Journal of Small Business Management, 25*(3), 38-44.

Rozier, C. (1995). Female entrepreneurs in a female-dominated health profession: An exploratory study. *Journal of Developmental Entrepreneurship, 3*(2), 149-163.

Spinder, D. (2000). Entrepreneurship-a learning process: The experiences of Asian female entrepreneurs and women in business. *Education and Training, 42*(8/9), 445-452.

Tisdell, E. J. (1998). Poststructural feminist pedagogies: The possibilities and limitations of a feminist emancipatory adult learning theory and practice. *Adult Education Quarterly, 48*(3), 139-156.

Wajcman, J. (1998). *Managing like a man: Women and men in corporate management.* University Park, PA: The Pennsylvania State University Press.

Wells, S. J. (1998). *Women entrepreneurs: Developing leadership for success.* NY: Garland.

18

GLOBALISATION AND ETHICAL QUESTIONS IN BUSINESS EDUCATION: A CASE STUDY FROM SLOVENIA

*Dr. Irena Marinko**

Introduction

Joining the European Union and the developing globalization processes have been among the most discussed questions in Slovenia. In May 2004 this small transition country became a part of the European Union and has thus faced the questions of globalization and loss of its recently gained independence. Since Slovenia was independent only a couple of years and is very small, Slovenians were proud when they obtained independence and feared that their small country and few big enterprises might quickly be sold out to foreigners with a different culture who could destroy Slovenian national identity. Slovenian economists stress economic benefits of the European Union and of the globalization processes while writers and other pro-national people ask how to protect the national identity. Economic interests in countries that joined the European Union and have been undergoing the process of globalization are to develop people who speak the same language, are thus able to communicate, have similar habits and behavior and can, because of similarities, accept adherents

* Director of College for Business Secretaries, Slovenia

of foreign nations. National interests in the opposite require that students know and appreciate their mother tongue, that they maintain their national characteristics which make them different from other nations, that they try to preserve land and enterprises in the country's ownership, that poverty and unemployment do not increase etc.

This paper quotes opinions of several Slovenian politicians, economists, directors, writers and scientists and it is obvious that they have different ideas about joining the European Union and about globalization. To make suggestions about the future human resources development under the conditions of globalization, we sent questionnaires to a number of Slovenian business teachers who are directly responsible for development of the next-coming generation. The analysis shows that the educators understand both the economic and national interests, benefits but also dangers of the globalization and that they have been trying to make both ends meet. It would be very easy to say that economy is the only factor that counts but we know that globalization brings about also poverty, increase of unemployment and important ethical problems concerning competition, ecology etc. All the countries that lived in unions can also prove that such liaisons are not only a benefit but also a source of problems. Therefore it is important to find a positive approach to the problems, and consider especially people who are going to teach the generation that will have to cope with the problems of globalization in their full capacity, and in a very short time.

Slovenian Joining the European Union and Globalization Processes

Slovenia has been a part of Europe since 6th century when Slovenians settled in the place between the Alps and the northern part of the Adriatic. Till 822 Slovenia was an independent state, then it became a part of the Frankish empire, Slovenians were christianized and thus entered the

West-European cultural area. In the Middle Ages Slovenians followed South-German law and regulations, and established towns, monasteries, castles and university. In the Renaissance Slovenia had some famous architects, diplomats, and university professors. Slovenia helped to defend Europe against the Turks. During the Reformation period Slovenia produced about 50 books in Slovene language. King Josef I proclaimed Slovenian citizens free among the first in Europe. In 1848 Slovenians required that Slovenia should become an independent state again but did not reach this status. After 1918 Slovenia started a new connection with the South-Slavic nations and remained a part of it till 1991 when it separated from Yugoslavia and again became independent.

Members of the European Union proclaimed Slovenia an independent country on 15th January 1992. Already in those years and even stronger in the following ones was the idea that Slovenia should join the European Union. All Slovenian most important political documents have supported this idea up to the very moment when Slovenia really joined Europe. The president of Slovenia, Dr.Drnovsek, always emphasized the importance of joining the European Union. Also other important Slovenians expressed positive opinions about joining the European Union, among them especially directors of some big firms, some scientists, president of the Slovenian Academy of Sciences and Arts etc.

Martin Kopac, director of a large Slovene company, Alpina, stressed that economic benefits of joining the European Union were much more important than the possible dangers. And if something is good for economy, it will serve also education, health and cultural area (Kopac, 2004).

Another director of a large Slovenian enterprise Iskratel, Andrej Polenec, also hoped that joining the European Union would increase business development of his firm, and develop especially the quality of business behavior and business ethics, which had not been stressed enough in Slovenia (Polenec, 2004).

Bostjan Zeks, president of the Slovenian Academy of Sciences and Arts, said that our joining the European Union would enable a quality and flexible university educational system which would include much more students and much more university professors from all parts of life. In accordance with the Bologna process our education should get shorter, more effective and the dropout rate should become considerably smaller (Zeks, 2004).

However, there have been negative opinions as well.

Alojz Rebula, a contemporary Slovenian writer, thought that our decision to join the European Union was unavoidable if we didn't want to become impossibly isolated amidst the increasingly globalized world. But this should not mean that Slovenians could have any illusions about the political and social sphere because Europe did not include Christian values in their statute (Rebula, 2004).

Joze Mencinger, one of the most important Slovenian economists and rector of the University of Ljubljana, expressed his ideas and doubts in the economic field, although the latter is by the majority of others supposed to be one of the benefits. According to Dr.Mencinger, the European Union is no more what it was at its beginning or at least 10 years ago. Those who founded the European Union actually wanted to provide peace and coexistence among the states that had been fighting for centuries. This could be reached by economic liaisons within the then social-economic model. But this model has in the last years almost disappeared and was substituted for by the model of American capitalism with the interests of shareholders as the only force of economy. Dr.Mencinger thinks that the idea of Europe becoming the most effective, knowledge-based society, is not only utopian, because Europe has been moving in quite another direction; it is also wrong, for economic cannibalism does not lead much further than a short-sighted placing the production there where it is possible to get the worker for a dollar per day. By including new members, the European Union has been changing into a non-homogeneous association that produces anxieties. Although some less developed economies can count with a kind of a natural convergence because of the free acquisition of knowledge and modern technology, the up to now results of economic development in the new members of the European Union do not ensure this. It seems that joining the European Union will bring more benefit, but the European Union is a kind of a big Yugoslavia with objectively similar problems and people should better take them into account than speak about European values which disappear especially if never existed (Mencinger, 2004).

Another university professor, Cirila Toplak, thinks that European values have not been only democracy, law, personal freedom, equal rights, work, religious freedom, belief in ratio and critical thinking, solidarity, etc. but also arrogance, intolerance of different social groups, exclusion, competition, tradition of military fights, and the feeling of superiority (Toplak, 2003).

Suggestions for Education of the Future Business People in the EU and in the Globalized World

Slovenian business teachers will be among those who will carry out the human resources development in Slovenia therefore we tried to find out what they thought about joining the European Union and globalization and how they would try to prepare business students for these processes.

Colleges in Slovenia are institutions of the tertiary level of education and enroll students who first finished 9 years of elementary school and then 4 years of the secondary school with leaving examination (five subjects). College teachers must have at least a university diploma (but MA or MSc are preferred), pedagogical qualifications, and several years of working experience in the field of economy, e.g. in enterprises and other firms.

Eighty questionnaires were sent to 4 Slovenian business colleges (Academia Maribor, Leila Ljubljana, Visja strokovna sola Novo Mesto and Visja strokovna sola Brezice). We received answers from 30 college teachers leading the following courses:

Business English and German: 7

Economics: 5

Information Science and Computing: 4

Accounting and Finances: 3

Work Organization: 3

Slovenian Business Language: 2

Public Administration and Company Law: 2

Fieldwork Placement: 2

Psychology of Work: 1

Management: 1

The main hesitations that Slovenian college teachers have regarding our joining the European Union and globalization are as follows: some of them are afraid that Slovenian land and firms could be sold out among foreign people, that foreign brands will prevail over the Slovenian ones, while Slovenian firms will have difficulties to reach foreign markets, that there will be more unemployment, that the rich will become even richer and that there will be much more poverty. Since Slovenia is a small country, there are fears that we will not be able to get on in such a big union and that foreign culture will prevail, that our national identity might be lost, and that there will be an enormous increase of administrative work. While our college teachers think that joining the European Union is a fact that should be accepted, they are strongly against the American economic system and against competition. Only one of the teachers is convinced that joining Europe and globalization processes are thoroughly positive.

To prepare their business students for their future work, Slovenian college teachers would include in their courses especially the following subjects:

1. Team work (22)
2. Communication skills (19)
3. Better knowledge of life in foreign countries (17)
4. Listening skills: how to listen, be ready to listen (16)
5. Developing tolerance t of foreigners in the cases of cultural differences (16)
6. Considering foreign ideas (15)
7. Increasing trust in a common future of all nations (15)
8. Being more open and accessible towards people and especially foreigners (14)
9. Flexibility in contacts with foreigners (13)
10. Better knowledge of foreign languages which should be easy to understand, e.g. slow and clear speaking, not using dialects, not too many professional expressions etc. (13)

Our college teachers suggest that the following themes should be included in the courses taught at business colleges:

Economy in the European Union (21)

Culture of foreign countries (14)

States and people (13)

Ways of everyday life in other countries (13)

Life and work philosophy in foreign countries (13)

Stereotypes concerning addressing, greetings, titles (12)

Enterprises in different countries: working time, health protection, work values, behavior, dress, smoking, libraries etc. (11)

National identity (10)

Managerial knowledge (10)

Telephone skills (10)

Business meetings (9)

Technical knowledge (8)

Holidays in foreign countries (8)

Environmental problems (7),

etc.

Teaching methods that the college teachers would use:

Discussion (26)

Group work (20)

Case studies (19)

Individual seminar work (18)

Role-playing (16)

Contacts with foreigners (16)

Seminar works (15)

Simulation (14)

Some suggested also a quiz, video-conference, contacts by Internet, lectures of foreign teachers, native speakers, inviting directors of successful firms, work in pairs etc.

To provide for the national identity and to develop Slovenian self-confidence there are suggestions that teachers should acquaint students the tradition of the economy and trade in Slovenia, show examples of successful Slovenian entrepreneurs, introduce a special subject on Slovenian language in specific areas (e.g. technical, commerce, business Slovene), require shorter papers about Slovenia, its inhabitants and the way of life, emphasize our positive view on culture, language, ethnology, and arts.

Only a few teachers mentioned that they had already participated in seminars on intercultural relations. Three of them were in Germany after the fall of the wall and the seminars were about conflict solving because of the differences between the West and East Germany. One was in Great Britain comparing the school systems and two participated in two Slovenian seminars organized by Faculty of Economics. So the suggested subjects and themes are mainly original ideas.

The sample is rather small (only 30 teachers) and their suggestions refer only to educational contents and methods. However, the opinions of teachers reflect a good knowledge of the situation, and a tolerant, neither strictly economical nor quite national point of view on the future human resources development in the processes of globalization. Their suggestions of new subjects show a tolerant, modern approach, which acquaints students not only with subjects that are already taught at other European universities, like teamwork, communication skills, foreign languages, but also quite new subjects like listening skills, foreign countries, tolerance towards foreigners, trust in a common future, being more open etc. Also the new themes that they mention show that the teachers already try to acquaint students with economy, culture, states and people, life and work philosophy, enterprises etc. in foreign countries.

Subjects, suggesting development of the national identity, are ethical and non-discriminative and can in no way cause national hatred or similar problems.

Further Perspectives of human resources development under globalization

Politicians, directors, and scientists who have a positive opinion about Slovenian joining the European Union mentioned that Slovenia would have to improve its education, make it more effective, and decrease the dropout rate. Colleges and universities and other schools will have to improve basic elements, especially include much more students and recruit new university professors from different spheres of life. We should think about new courses like business behavior, business ethics, problem-solving, conflict management, knowledge management etc.

Our college teachers, and similarly the rector of the University, Dr.Mencinger, think that globalization leads into the model of capitalism which is rather short-sighted by its considering only the interests of shareholders. This will soon bring about problems because of the social injustice and conflicts. However, our joining the European Union is a fact and we should try to do the best out of it. We will have to renew the contents of courses and use contemporary teaching methods. The new learning contents include especially team-work, tolerance, foreign languages, culture of foreign countries, foreign enterprises, environmental problems and so on. We should also emphasize Slovenian language.

Since the main subjects at our Business Colleges are foreign languages (English and German), Slovenian Language, Communication Skills, Work Organization, Office Procedures, Management, Economics, Public Administration, Company Law, Information Science, Computing, Psychology of Work and Fieldwork Placement, we can say that our program already now acquaints students with knowledge that they are expected to have in a globalized world. It is possible to improve the courses by including more conversation, more lessons and projects which develop team-work, work in groups, by developing listening skills (reports on viewpoints of other students, role playing, analyses and comments on foreign articles, watching foreign TV programs), by developing flexibility in contacts with foreigners so that we include native speakers, by comparison of differences and common characteristics between nations, by development of positive thinking, by emphasizing interests of all people and similarities among them, by personal development to make students more open and accessible, conflict-solving, shorter texts about foreign countries and their inhabitants and similar.

Although our curriculum seems to be good and we have a number of new ideas to renew the courses, we should still be aware of the fact that globalization moves forward and that we should do something to fight for a more just world. Many progressive-minded people think (New Socialisms, 2004) that there is no alternative to current neo-liberalism and corporate globalization and that all future-directed thinking about human society and social change must necessarily unfold within the narrow lines of what the market renders possible or rational, we should resist these opinions. Our business studies should include also subjects and themes that will acquaint students how to shift away from such overly economistic orientations.

Globalization is failing in so many ways: we see the dangers of imperialism and war, environmental destruction, inequality, in short globalization neglects all needs but those of profits and the market. Therefore we must start to introduce also themes and subjects on building an economically viable, redistributive, eco-sensitive and democratic future. This will require much more new courses on values, social justice, new business ethics that will not be limited by needs of the market and profits but will introduce new forms of socialisms.

REFERENCES

Bossel, H. (1998). Earth at a Crossroads. Cambridge: University Press.

Devetak, S. (2001) Obrobje v primezu globalizacije-problemi in dileme politike EU do jugovzhodne Evrope. Anthropos, 4/6, 68-76.

Globalisierung: Von der Vision zur Praxis. (1997) Zurich: Versus.

Jancar, D. (2004). Ura evropske resnice za Slovenijo. Delo, 3/1/2004, 13.

Kopac, M. (2004). Izgovori ne bodo pomagali. Delo, 3/1/2004, 16.

Kornhauser, A. (2004). Odprta vrata niso za zapeckarje. Delo, 3/1/2004, 14.

Martin H.P., Schumann H. (1997). Pasti globalizacije. Ljubljana: Co Libri.

Mencinger, J. (2004). Unija-zdruzba za cas sedmih debelih krav. Delo, 30/4/2004, 12.

New socialisms. (2004). London: Routledge.

Polenec, A. (2004). Navajeni smo na konkurenco. Delo, 3/1/2004, 15.

Rebula, A. (2004). Predvsem vprasanje samozavesti. Delo, 3/1/2004, 13-14.

Stabej, M. (2002). Slovenscina v evropski jezikovni mavrici. Druzboslovne razprave, XVIII, 40, 157-168.

Toplak, C. (2003). Zdruzene drzave Evrope. Ljubljana: Fakulteta za druzbene vede.

Vreg, F. Globalizacija in elektronska demokracija. Teorija in praksa, 38, 1.

Zeks, B. (2004). Veè ambicije, prosim. Delo, 3/1/2004, 17.

INDEX

❑❑❑